Entrepreneur
of
Life

HUGO VALDERRAMA

Title page TK

ENTREPRENEUR
OF

Para el pastor Rafael
con gran cariño y afecto.
Mi libro #10

Valderrama
Sep 2023

HUGO VALDERRAMA

Printed in the United States of America

First Printing, 2022

ISBN 978-1-66785-490-8

Hugo Valderrama

hfvalderrama@yahoo.com

Contents

Dedication

*This book is dedicated to all my readers, who have supported and
delighted me whenever they comment on or remember any
of my writings, phrases, or teachings.
A big virtual hug to everyone!*

—

Hugo F Valderrama S

Preface

Over the years, I have gathered life experiences managing organizations, leading companies, advising leaders, and resolving numerous critical and challenging situations.

When I review my past, to my surprise, I find teachings in my writings that allow me to learn.

I have managed to accumulate numerous reflections based on many real episodes and, as such, I present in this book a compilation of the thoughts and practical conclusions of common knowledge built going through the manifold challenges of each day in this business called life.

I hope that my readers find one or several chapters that make them think and cause their neurons to move to complement my reflections, criticize them, disagree with them, confirm that they seem to be correct, or indicate that I forgot something important or made a mistake. I will be pleased with that because it means I will have managed to create value and contribute to their lives and minds or ideas, even by contrast. If they get to act or execute or change something in their lives, then I will have served my purpose.

Enjoy the book! I suggest that you go to the table of contents, find a chapter whose title draws your attention, read and reflect on it, or note what comes to mind, and conclude the matter. You may repeat the process with another chapter and so on. The choice to read everything is entirely yours.

Choose only what captivates you. If there is anything that does not interest you, discard it. However, do not argue with me. I learned from a great friend, with respect to the content of his lectures, how to approach "arguable" topics. When you are going through my writings, pretend that you are in a supermarket. Put whatever you like in the cart, and if you do not like something or do not share the same view, do not put it in the cart—issue resolved!

Hugo F Valderrama S

You have to let go to improve, grow, move forward, or rest

A ttachments are burdens that cling to us, and one day, they accumulate to weigh so much that they overpower us.

A ship can sail off once the anchor is released.

A friend told me the difficult story of when he became a widower with three children, the oldest being five years old. He could have given himself over to grief and taken life the hard way without a partner. However, he was extremely practical, and it allowed him to rebuild his life. He decided, "either I bury myself with her, or I let her leave my mind and remember her with gratitude." This decision later allowed him to open his heart to find a new partner, who helped him raise the young children and made him happy.

This reflection is about letting go, and the sooner, the better. A person who does not let go drowns and does not evolve.

In business, people keep believing that they are the same admirable bosses they once were, although they are no longer the same.

Some people continue to believe that they are the husband or wife of an amazing, wonderful human being who no longer exists or who has left and is with someone else.

Further, some individuals act as if their late parents still exist, and everything remains static and indefinite out of respect for those who are no longer around.

This is not an invitation to stop having feelings or being human. We have feelings, and we are humans, but there is a reasonable mourning period. Some of us need more and others less, but the duel cannot last a lifetime and, much less, turn one into a statue, paralyzed for the rest of their lives.

You have to let go. It is important to let go of both the bad and the good.

In life, everything is transitory. All changes hurt, but the faster we evolve to accept our new condition, the faster the wounds will heal.

Letting go is accepting the facts and starting over again.

If we miss a unique opportunity or lose money, a property, a friend, a job, a sibling, or anything valuable to us, we must accept the loss as soon as possible. That is the only way to begin the path to reconstruction, healing, and a new life.

I have gone bankrupt three times, a matter that induces pain and shame. However, after such difficult situations, you have to accept what happened, learn from the experience, and get up with courage to keep fighting and start over in other settings, with different points, ideas, and people. As the saying goes, "what's done is done." It is best not to cry over spilled milk.

Accepting that one is born with a physical disability is a difficult process to the extent that the disability is notorious. The process involves experiencing mockery, pity, repudiation, or rejection. The most difficult thing is to accept ourselves as we are, after which we let go of the feeling that represses us or ties us to negative, inferior, repressive, vindictive, guilty, or resentful behavior. We begin to change and grow toward a new attitude and a new life full of strength, power, confidence, and courage that leads us to seek achievement, stability, fulfillment, and happiness on our new life path.

Everything around us looks different when we accept and detach ourselves from what once was and is no longer, and we perceive our reality neutrally, with hope and as a new opportunity—a clean slate. I detach, I accept, I let go of my past, and I learn to build my present, and consequently, my future.

If I do not let go, I cannot release myself from suffering and pain, and I will not have opportunities. Do I want to be a masochist and remain in the worst pain? Or do I decide to live and find again the happiness waiting for me just around the corner or when I turn the page to write a new chapter of my existence?

Choose to live your life.

Without problems,
life loses its flavor

Long live the problems and difficulties.

A day without problems is one without meaning. Even on vacation, we are not free from them. For example, we can forget something, fall, get sunburned, get bitten by mosquitoes, become sick, find the person we wanted to meet, run out of money, get drunk and create a mess, almost drown, get robbed, or forget our toothbrush, pajamas, tennis shoes, or sunscreen. The list goes on.

My son, who studied in the United States, says that his dream is to have a "carefree life." Hopefully, he will achieve it.

Several years ago, I realized that we need to enjoy life, which is full of daily challenges. Bad or good surprises come almost every day. We have two options: let our problems depress and overwhelm us or see each problem as an opportunity to improve ourselves and enjoy overcoming the challenges and difficulties. Life is not different from the games that children have on their computers or game consoles, where they encounter challenges or traps and have to evade, jump over, or face them to accumulate points or lives. If they are careless for a moment, they can die or be killed (well, life is not so drastic for some).

Difficulties and challenges define our everyday life.

Most of my days are a race against time. I do not know if you have the same situation. I wake up with a plan of the vital tasks that I must conduct, and during the day, I receive calls, messages, emails, letters, or unexpected visits. Several of them alter the order of the tasks that I had proposed to complete on that day. For example, when a friend passes away, you have to go to pay respects to their family. Other examples include my wife's car accident, my daughter getting sick and being taken to the emergency room, an unexpected charge on the cell phone bill, slow internet at the office, heavy rains for three hours, and strikes and marches in the city, all day.

What do we do with the changing priorities in our daily schedules? Adaptation is the key word. We reorganize ourselves and devise a new plan for what we can accomplish under the new circumstances. Some issues will be addressed, and others will be postponed. There is no other remedy. You accomplish what you can with the resources at your disposal.

Similar to what we described above, certain distractions happen in the office too. Systems fail, appointments are early or late, bosses change priorities, clients go into crisis mode, and competition moves and outpaces us. Further, the government dictates rules that change the course of our plans and the business, and an event in the global economy affects the company and becomes the top priority overnight. Moreover, a key person in the organization falls ill, and we realize how vulnerable we are because they were handling something that no one else grasps or understands in the same manner. Additionally, the payment from a large business or important client is delayed, and there is not sufficient money to pay the staff. Therefore, you have to rush to get the rest of the money. You have to save the company and everyone at that time while ensuring that no one notices or is affected. In certain cases, the client's equipment fails, and we cannot resolve the problem because there is no replacement for the defective part—total emergency! We detect a vital consideration that had been overlooked in a project that was progressing well, and the project is now in danger of being 90 days behind schedule. Someone who is faithful to the organization resigns because they have received a scholarship to study in Germany. The key collaborator for a client meeting calls in to report that they are sick. An important order arrives, requiring me to work late to deal with it because it is the end of the month or the quarter. An important visitor arrives, and I am required to stay with them until late.

Real life does not look anything like our plans, even if we make them the previous day, because real life comprises challenges and opportunities.

In conclusion, we came to the world to be firefighters and engineers: either we put out fires, or we solve problems with ingenuity. That is life. How good it is to be a firefighter or an engineer!

—3—

Learn to take risks and improvise
for success

Success in a profession, business, or trade is often linked to one's commitment, dedication, and intelligent efforts. Other times, it is linked to the "intelligent ignorance" of someone who naively thinks an idea is achievable and, without measuring the risks or disadvantages, jumps into the void and achieves their dream, like in a fairy tale.

Many successful businesspersons lack training but have the nose, vision, intuition, and a tremendous conviction that they can reach their goal. I have met extremely successful businesspersons who did not finish high school, famous artists who did not study music, and landowners who only had a love for agriculture and instinct. Many professionals are never good in their careers, but they are extraordinary in other areas.

Only a few things are given away in life.

When one closely examines each successful person's story about how they achieved their exceptional goals, one finds five constants: risks taken with courage and ingenuity, excellent achievements in unknown fields, discipline/quality in performance, years of dedication/commitment, and finally, someone believed in them and either bought, hired, promoted, or recommended them. In the world, we have many success stories in most disciplines.

Undoubtedly, successful people have shown to be innovative in fields that were not necessarily their specialties. Their common trait is that they risked everything for their goal. They strived to do better than the best, differently from others, and knew how to overcome challenges and difficulties skillfully and intelligently. Despite blunders, rejections, and failures on their way to success, their persistence and tenacity, along with their conviction and self-confidence, enabled them to accomplish admirable results.

Several extraordinary cases provide concrete examples. Bill Gates and Steve Jobs never finished college. Einstein was bad at math. Madonna was fired from her waitressing job for her poor performance. The Beatles had been rejected by famous recording companies and had to work with a nearly bankrupt company. Ronald Reagan was a bad actor, but he was elected president of the United States for two terms. Shakira was disqualified by her singing teacher at school and told to devote her efforts to something else because of her disastrous voice. Silvester Stallone was a football player and a porn film actor. Jean Claude Van Damme was a ballet dancer, taxi driver, and pizza delivery man. You will be thinking about similar, albeit not so famous, cases around you. These may include your neighbors or classmates who never finished their courses, doctors who either never practiced or practiced little medicine and are excellent salespeople today, lawyers who either never practiced or practiced little law and are exceptional landowners and ranchers today.

Life is full of examples like the ones mentioned above. Many people have made their careers in scenarios different from those of their original profession or trade. They have achieved success after long years of struggle and tenacity along a path that many had either never planned on or dreamed of but were years away from achieving.

We must reflect on the abovementioned cases and draw lessons from them. Fear of the unknown is normal, and we all feel it. It paralyzes many, while it motivates others to risk discovering what is beyond and accept the challenge of measuring themselves against something for which they are not properly prepared but believe they can achieve and do well. In other words, they fear the unknown but do not inhibit themselves from trying. They are eager for an opportunity to explore things and do not refuse the trial or the attempt.

A guiding principle is also found in each person's conviction about what they can and will achieve. They assume themselves to be already what they envision for them and act accordingly until realizing one day that they are already what they had dreamed of becoming.

It is as if they had fallen blindly in love with an idea that turns out to be the engine of their existence. They only see the goal and the way to achieve it and act as if they are hypnotized and following subliminal orders without feeling fear or fatigue.

The road to success is a kind of trance that successful people go through in the first days, months, and years before becoming famous for being the best in a certain discipline. Successful people subsequently wake up from that trance and realize everything they could endure, do, create, and transcend.

I invite you to enter your trance of success.

Deception abounds, and people fall for it all around

Not everyone around us who call themselves our allies, partners, or friends are what they say they are.

In today's world, people have learned to lie and convince others that their behavior is authentic. They are champions of lies and deception—tools they use to achieve their purposes. It is becoming increasingly difficult to detect deception. It is like a counterfeit money factory that uses increasingly better technologies and quality paper to imitate real bills—ordinary people can hardly tell the difference between a real bill and a fake one. They are professional imitators and comedians who are highly skilled in playing their victims to attain their goals.

In my early days, when I was learning to take my first steps as a manager, a colleague of mine was already an expert in handling the pressures and urgencies of his boss, an excellent manager.

He would always tell his boss that the task requested of him was ready and that he would present it in a couple of days when they could set a meeting. However, he would immediately run off to complete the task that he had assured his boss was ready but that he had inadvertently not completed. He succeeded most of the time, and his boss did not discover the deception. When he failed, he invented another convincing tale to escape the situation.

It is extremely common to get involved or be invited to a meeting where one is shown an idea in seemingly great detail and the arguments to support a cause or a project. However, when one earnestly delves into the details and investigates and verifies them, the project turns out to be a pipedream or a hoax to gain followers. In reality, nothing or little of what was presented is true, as it occurs with certain news that appear in the newspapers, where a highly reliable source might not be that reliable.

Some people use deception to pretend to be someone else or convince us that they have a particular intention. However, they approach us because they are interested in our help for an issue that they do not mention. They present it as a surprise when we have become involved and can no longer escape the situation.

Some other people tell us fictitious or supposed stories and ask us for our opinion, position, or experience in this regard to extract privileged information or trick us into believing certain events or incidents that have not taken place in real life. Many people have been robbed with this method. Examples include con artists making them surrender goods to save relatives in supposed distress or emergencies or investigators making them confess when they are caught in a trap—a method used in homicide or robbery cases.

Deceptions can reach a level of ingenuity that makes a parent give their child to strangers, convinced that the child would be safe and have a better life with them, based only on promises and dreams that are sold to them and later turn out to be intricate lies to scam people. Thus, many young women have been taken to other countries and forced into prostitution, and if they resist, they are killed. It is an infamous tale.

Deception also happens in investments, where money easily grows 10 or 100 times in a short period (the notorious pyramid schemes). People fall for this scheme every day because they allow themselves to be carried away by the illusion of a dream and false testimonies given by people who assure them that they have made excess money. They listen to some important figures who have been used to be living testimonies and inadvertently help other desperate people to get into the pyramid scheme.

Every day, we see the sale of supposedly wonderful inventions that cure baldness, reduce body weight, or remove wrinkles in a few days. Those who buy these products realize that the dream they were sold was a lie. The advertisement is one thing, and the small print another. The actual product they receive provides everything except the advertised effectiveness. Instead, it is described as a vitamin or supplement or natural therapy for well-being.

How many young women and ladies have been deceived by a man who made them dream that they would live a rosy life together? These men are then allowed advances but then quickly leave the picture, leaving the women mired in the sadness of having been used and cheated.

How many men have been deceived by women who made them believe that they are unique? A woman might tell a man that he cannot love her as much as she loves him. In the end, he is tremendously surprised to discover that he was being manipulated by making him feel small and through constant monitoring. She demands for visits and calls but only after gaining control of his calendar or planner so that she can continue seeing other men. It is extremely difficult to discover the deception, depending on the skill of the manipulator.

You must already be noting some factors common to all deceptions: dreams, promises, illusions, performances, tricks, lies, traps, etc. People continue to fall for economic, personal, business, religious, political, amorous, friendly, and family deception.

What antidotes do we have?

There are several antidotes: verify facts and references from other people, share with wise people any proposals we receive and listen to their advice before making a decision, measure the risk, stop being naive, and be aware that "if it sounds too good to be true, it probably is."

Continuity in staying in shape

S taying in shape is a continuous challenge. We can stay in shape for several years but not forever.

Let us look at the case of an athlete as the most obvious and simplest example. What happens to a champion of marathons or athletic races, a swimmer, a cyclist, or a football or tennis player relative to their competitors after they cross the age threshold of 35–38 years? Can they stay in shape to remain the champion, number one, or the star? It is not sufficient to train every day, have a good coach to guide, correct, or challenge them, or have the spirit and the will. There is a moment when the body says that the time has come to withdraw or change. The evidence becomes clear as the performance begins to decline, and previous records are no longer achievable.

As for beauty or attractiveness, what happens when you are over 40 or 50 years old, and the new generations begin to outpace you, all new and better? Roles change, and you become the parent, uncle, teacher, professor, researcher, or boss. However, you will leave the pool of young promising stars and move on to the set of experts who are recognized for their great trajectory. As time passes, you will assume the role of a grandparent, philosopher, intellectual, or simply veteran.

Intellectually speaking, something considerably similar to what has been mentioned occurs in both sports and acting, in movies, or on TV, although the trajectory tends to be longer. If a study is conducted with people aged between 55 and 65 years, the evidence would show that the majority suffer an intellectual decline, without this being a problem or a limitation. The moments of lucidity are continuous for a long period, but it begins to decline with respect to the fresh, more up-to-date minds for whom the time has come. As with everything, there are notable exceptions. We know there are no fixed rules and that there are extraordinary people who break all the expected limits and are above the average of the cases I have just described, but they are only a few.

At some point, we must recognize that the passage of time demands generational change. We must open ourselves to changing our role to be the counselors, managers, or mentors of young people and let the new generations, with their new ideas, figures, and forces, lead. Of course, experience gives us the vision that young people lack. However, we no longer provide the right fit or the appropriate observation. Nevertheless, if we have been champions, we must remember that we are descending from a considerably high position—we will continue to be above many for a good period. Nonetheless, we will no longer be among the top three.

This process that I have just described is natural and normal. However, some people refuse to recognize that time inexorably passes, and the changes become evident to everyone except the one who does not want to recognize the variation.

Of course, an athlete, an actor, or a famous intellectual may have achieved high or outstanding levels in their specialties. They will always surprise us, despite the years, but undoubtedly, at some point, they will no longer be what they once were.

Something similar happens in companies. There are no eternal organizations or enterprises with infinitely continuous success. Neither are there employees in positions that enable continuous, perpetual success. Companies have their moments of weakness, products that are no longer popular, and services that are no longer in demand. In the case of employees and processes, technologies change, the required skills evolve with the times, and, consequently, we reinvent ourselves and launch new products or services, or we are killed by the competition— in the case of businesses—or incompetence—in the case of individuals.

When one accepts the change that I have just described, there is immediately immense joy in the activities performed, the opportunities to transform oneself, and the new paths that life opens. They are new experiences and conditions worth choosing, trying out, and, of course, enjoying.

I would add that the key is to **maintain both balance and adaptability in "good shape."** Thus, we will be sufficiently flexible in dealing with any change in life successfully.

Cultural differences and key motivations for success or failure

How many times have we seen a strict, threatening, intimidating, impolite management style, capable of damaging one's image and self-esteem, that compels people to work under the pressure of apprehension, fear, or panic?

Who has not had a boss with the abovementioned profile? This is a boss who causes everyone to work quietly while they are present, and when they leave, everyone feels free to become themselves and chat and relax.

Fortunately for me, I was born when management methods underwent major changes, in the era of participation and open-mindedness, where "you" are important to the company. During this period, "you" were included in the dialogue, team, company building, and sharing of ideas. "You" had the company's ear, and your thoughts were considered.

People respond to different stimuli.

I am particularly proactive and produce results in advance that generally exceed what is expected of me without requiring supervision or special guidance. I am creative by nature. Consequently, having a boss who breathes down my neck and inquires every two minutes whether I have performed a task or considered this or that has never worked for me. They only managed to make me feel uncomfortable as if I were under hyper-surveillance and my abilities or experience could not be trusted. Such a situation led me to change organizations or my attitude or caused me to become aggressive and argumentative, apart from being rebellious.

At the other extreme, some people only function under pressure and orders—without one or the other, they remain static or devote themselves to having a good time and procrastinate. These people need their boss to tell them what to do, supervise them frequently, correct them, and push them. This type tends to be more accustomed to having demanding, authoritative bosses, without whom they do not perform adequately.

There is a great variety of people and bosses, just as there is are various plants. Some plants grow in the desert with minimal water and extreme heat and cold. Other plants need excessive light and water, while some other plants grow in the dark with little water. If you were a plant, what would be your characteristics and favorable environment? Would you need extensive care, or would you grow in the wild? Would you be very resilient, or would you dry easily? How fragile are you in the company? Are you like a cactus or a rose? Are you a fern or a palm tree?

Cultural differences can lead to huge mistakes that resemble the examples and reflections that I have mentioned thus far. A Chinese boss managing people in a Latin American country like Mexico must learn the ways through which they can obtain the best results from the type of personnel they are managing. Of course, the personnel of a manufacturing plant are not the same as the professionals of an engineering consulting company. Further, the Chinese work in an environment and conditions considerably different from those in which Mexicans work, whose motivations may be completely different from those of Chinese personnel. There may be coincidences in some respects, as we are all human beings, but misconstrued or mishandled differences can produce effects contrary to the intended outcomes.

A foreign friend started his company in Colombia, and within six months, he had lost 40% of the staff he had so carefully hired. Today's youth are not willing to endure poor treatment with so many options available. The era of insensitive bosses and people spending 35 years at the same organization has possibly ended. Nowadays, people prefer modern work environments with pleasant colleagues and participative, respectful bosses (which does not imply that the boss is not demanding).

The same thing happens at home. Nowadays, children demand their independence. Teachers can no longer beat pupils at school. Parents must respect their children in their process of development. If the children do not perform their tasks well, the authorities could end up being involved, and the parents would be warned to improve their treatment and let their children live with certain discretion and freedom. Parents, similar to the teachers and bosses of this era, have to learn to listen and manage their authority in a way that earns the respect of their children, as with students or employees, in a participative manner and by respecting their opinions and differences. They should motivate the children to perform tasks so that results are accomplished by conviction and not by force.

Today's actions and tasks are accomplished through conversations, where clear and concrete agreements are reached between the parties involved. Of course, someone has the authority, but it is different from the past when there were parents, teachers, or bosses whom you could not talk to or look in the eye and had to obey blindly. Previously, respect was earned by force and threats as well as other motivations, such as religion. There were hierarchies and rankings that had to be respected without protest and thinking. Currently, although we are not necessary at the opposite extreme, we enjoy a mixture of authority, camaraderie, counseling, and support that was unthinkable in the past.

Each person has a different world. Today's management must have an individualized approach to each person. There is a guiding principle that characterizes each managerial style. However, it is necessary to have a personalized touch in their management of each employee, like parents who have their style and way of being but an approach and way to handle each child according to their personalities.

In any case, regardless of the condition, we must strive for the highest individual productivity, which requires each person to be sufficiently motivated and effectively managed to give 100% of their capabilities. If these reflections are considered, the opposite effect may occur, with the group producing at 50% or less consequently.

The Godfather: Results

What can ensure the permanence of an individual in an organization? What can keep a company or an organization alive in the market? Who can ensure success in any area, whether in academia, the professional field, athletics, or artistic interpretation? The Godfather: Results.

If a person or organization shows consistently good results and maintains them over time, the person or organization will remain. Otherwise, they will be extinguished or reduced to the minimum.

However, the results must be equally quantitative and qualitative. In other words, a company can obtain extraordinary results in product sales, but it may have accomplished this by exploiting its employees and suppliers and even by destroying the environment. The quantitative results are impressive, but the qualitative results are a disaster and, consequently, the company does not deserve to stick around.

What good is a person who produces extraordinary results but also destroys people and can only work when there is no team, who has conflicts with almost everyone, creates arguments, and generates misunderstandings and a bad environment? The Godfather Results must strike a balance between its two vital components: quantitative and qualitative.

What is the use of a company where everything is commendable—a good internal environment, fair treatment of the suppliers, employees, and the environment, and excellent interpersonal relations—but does not make sales or generate the revenue and profits necessary to remain in the market or viable?

What is there to say about the colleague and collaborator who never performs the tasks assigned to them or poorly performs them and continuously fails? Qualitative results are not sufficient. The quantitative part is vital for the balance, and it is equally important in an organization.

In a soccer team, an inept goalkeeper will hinder the chances of winning. However, a star player who has a bad temper and a poor relationship with the other players creates an unpleasant atmosphere and receives yellow or red cards despite making goals. In an integral sense of the word, what he does with his right hand, he destroys with his left. That is, they add on one side and subtract from the other, and eventually, the result is ZERO. In other words, avoid adding or subtracting, or it will be too much or unnecessary.

If the Godfather Results accompany us in a balanced manner, quantitatively and qualitatively, we will be the star and will shine for as long as the Godfather is with us.

What if the Godfather Results are not present in what we do? Turn it off, and let's go!

Life changes

I have seen in the experiences of other people and my own that drastic changes are usually painful as we live through them or as the process unfolds. Nonetheless, they are refreshing in the long run. When the transformation is complete, the anguish and suffering subside, and one embarks on a new path in life.

Not all people make radical changes in their lives, but many accept such challenges, while others are forced to do so. A typical example of a radical change is when a person who works for a company is asked to move to a different city or country, generally coupled with an occupational change. Everything is new and different!

Another case is when a person suffers persecution in their country and has to leave behind their homeland, and even their identity, to protect their life. Such a situation compels them to change their established profession, customs, and, as we said at the beginning of this reflection, their life.

On a personal scale, I had the opportunity to witness an inevitable change. My mother had begun to lose sight in her left eye, and almost simultaneously, she began to lose sight in her right eye, both owing to glaucoma. Although she underwent surgery to change the internal tubing of her eyes to reduce the internal pressure, after the fifth surgery, the situation became unsustainable, and my mother was totally blind. Throughout the course of the gradual loss of her vision, my mother complained frequently and felt worried and scared. However, when the blindness was final, my mother's fears and complaints disappeared. She decided to learn to defend herself in her new condition. She began to enjoy listening to the radio and the television and liked to be read news and stories. She learned to make phone calls and move around in her room. Eventually, the subject of her eyes was no longer a topic of conversation or mortification.

People who move to a new country, who find themselves with no family, friends, or acquaintances, and who have a completely blank resume for their sudden change in occupation have to begin life as a newborn. They have to learn the new customs of the country where they reside and adapt to their new way of life. Searching for a job, trade, or endeavor is more than challenging in an unfamiliar environment if it is a forced change owing to a life-or-death matter. If the change is due to a job transfer, the challenge is still high but simplified because of the sponsorship and guaranteed work.

What about people who need to use wheelchairs after an accident? It changes their lives dramatically. What would you do if something like this happened to you? I hope it does not happen to you. Adapting to changes in life and planning a new route where everything is new comprise the right strategy to follow. The glorious past does not exist. We have to live in the present and learn to enjoy it and cherish it. Constantly thinking about what we once were and what we once had does not help us move one millimeter forward. When one accepts their new condition with dignity, whatever it may be, one can begin a new path and advance toward the construction of a new dream, which is ultimately one's new reality.

I once spoke to a senior executive who had just been laid off from a multinational company where he had been working for over 30 years. When we spoke, he still felt like he was vice president of the company. The reality was that at his age and in his condition, he was nothing more than an unemployed person with few options to regain employment. Of course, he had received a good financial settlement upon his departure, but he had not realized that he had to start a new life because the one he had for more than 30 years was now over. His work condition then was that of an unemployed person with a low probability of securing a job and without alternative plans. He was three years away from being eligible to receive a pension—a challenging situation indeed.

A typical life change occurs when one leaves college in search of a job or an income-earning opportunity based on what one studied. This is such a natural change, and in a time where one is willing to do anything, many people do not even notice it. Those who appreciate it the most are those who have a hard time establishing themselves or finding something to do. There is the frequent case of the person who studied engineering at a relatively unknown university and then having no choice but to start a business by getting a taxi and making transportation their business and their life. What about the person who becomes a widow? This is a complex life change, especially if they have small children, large debt, and deep pain in their soul. What does one do after the loss? You have to start a new life. The old one no longer exists, and you have to build a new path with enthusiasm and courage. You have to overcome the situation and start from scratch or even less, but you have to do it as soon as possible. Once the change occurs and we stop complaining and suffering, we can understand that there are other options and that life presents us with challenges from which we have to learn, sooner rather than later, to cherish and enjoy our new conditions and accomplishments.

I am sure that you have other life changes in mind that you have had to experience on a personal scale. You may know someone who lived them. You will find that the pattern is the same. It begins with fear, suffering, complaints, nostalgia, depression, insecurity, and then a stage where reflection on the new situation generates a new life plan and, with it, new challenges, flavors, illusions, fronts, alternatives, experiences, achievements, and, of course, a new life.

I have had the opportunity to live through numerous life changes, and more are awaiting me. What is my attitude toward these changes? I take on the challenge with courage. At first, I experience fear of the unknown or the loss of what I have had thus far, coupled with excessive pain, but I reflect quickly and make plans for my new situation and face it with poise. Life is a continuous cycle of "birth, life, and death" in many aspects, ultimately for which we came to the world.

The importance of not making assumptions and acting quickly; not everything is logical

I assumed you were going to do it... Suppose the dollar rises... I suppose you disagree... I suppose it will come today, as always... I suppose it will rain tomorrow... This is how we make several assumptions that many times lead to serious and even fatal mistakes.

How are you? Tomorrow, we will sit down to work out the details on how to handle this urgent matter. There is no problem if we are 10 minutes late. Let us give the matter another thought to ensure that the best decision is made. We need to have the opinion of those absent, and with their positive vote, we will be in unanimity or consensus, and we can then proceed with the execution of the task. Will they decide within the day, or are they all going to give elegant excuses for not taking action? Would they have any idea of the importance of making quick decisions and taking action?

What do you think of this? If we do not buy, they will not do it either. If the price of oil goes down, the dollar will surely go up. With this new procedure, all the steps will be streamlined. Once this standard has been published, there will be no more deviations or faults. If Ecuador beats Colombia and Colombia beats Peru in soccer, it is most likely that Ecuador will beat Peru, if they ever play. If they approved that credit for me, how will they not approve credit for you when you earn more than I do?

Not everything follows logic, and many times, there is no sequential chain of direct correspondence between events.

By now, you must be thinking about several anecdotes and experiences that you have had regarding the effect of assumptions, or you must have reflected on the consequences that inaction from a lack of decision-making brings over time (What about a delay in the treatment of a serious illness or an urgent operation?). You may also have formulated ideas about the best complement to assumptions—assume that everything has its own logic (For example: If my girlfriend loves me, surely my mother-in-law will also love me).

I have often had the opportunity to talk with collaborators when they were experiencing a period of considerable personal or professional difficulty. I have found that most of the time, in response to the problem, they assumed something that was not true and acted based on that. Other times, simply out of insecurity or fear, they did not act or make a decision, and vital time passed until the problem became irreversible. It may also have seemed logical to them that something should go in one direction, and to their surprise, it went in another.

"I left an urgent note on your desk saying that you had to call the manufacturer upon your arrival yesterday, after lunch, to confirm the dispatch, as otherwise, they would cancel the order. How was I supposed to know that you would not return to the office in the afternoon if you always go out for lunch and come back? I got busy afterward and only found out that you were on a trip the next day when there was nothing more to do. If I had known, I would have called the manufacturer directly."

"We wanted to perform well, as always—with the highest quality and professionalism—so that the client is satisfied with our work, even if we have to take a couple of extra days apart from the two months that we have already invested, to deliver the results. Two days later, we have not delivered the task, and we have just received word from the customer indicating that by virtue of our negligence to send them what they requested from us and the delay in responding to their request, they had decided to assign the business to another supplier. I do not understand what happened, as we were working for the client, developing the task with the greatest possible care and dedication. This client is ungrateful, unappreciative, and unfair. They gave their business to others because they did not want to wait for us."

"We arrived at 2:05 PM, and they no longer let us submit the envelopes with the tender and the annexes, after we had invested entire weeks of teamwork, with a group of 12 professionals, almost without rest even on weekends. It is unfair! The deadline was 2 PM on Tuesday, the 13th, and they did not wait for us. Why did they not give a 15-minute extension?"

"We won the previous game with the right strategy. I do not understand what went wrong this time, as we used a strategy similar to that in the previous game. The opponent was the same. On the field, I had the impression that we were playing against another team. How did they manage to change the way they play to shut us out 5 to 0?"

"We should have bought this medication to normalize their blood density so that the heart attack could have been prevented. Who would have thought that he would have a heart attack precisely last night when we had already thought of buying the medication today so that he could start taking it? Some things happen in life that leave one trembling with fear. Now, what do we do if they die? Can we forgive ourselves for not acting in time?"

If we practically summarize this reflection, we can phrase it like this: *Never make assumptions. Verify first, make a decision, and act now, or someone else will do it for you. Remember that logical facts are only given in school or college for the purpose of teaching. Real life does not follow logic, and if it does, it is an extreme coincidence.*

The dashboard, a practical reflection

I once had the opportunity to travel in the cockpit of a large plane on an international trip, where I fully appreciated the last half-hour of the flight and its final approach. In that experience, I learned and verified, in real time, what I had lived several times in the business world. I realized that my work was exactly the same experience as being in the cockpit preparing for landing. Therefore, I drew some extraordinary conclusions and reflections from the experience, which I now want to share.

In the half-hour before landing, the pilots engage in a series of procedures and extensive communication with what is referred to, among non-aviators, as the control tower. The tower indicates when to change course and fly over an area other than the one scheduled. It communicates with a couple of approaching planes and makes planes change height and speed. The pilot and co-pilot talk, and both move or press buttons and change numbers. The pilot pulls levers, and the plane turns and continues to descend. The truth is that above the clouds, through the pilot's window, you cannot see anything. The challenge is clear. The pilot and co-pilot must navigate through instruments, relying solely on what the devices register or indicate. They are, however, in command of the aircraft and can make it follow their instructions instantly (increase or decrease height or speed or change course).

As I witnessed the activities of the pilot and co-pilot, the number of clocks or gauges on the front of the cockpit, the conversations with the control tower, and all the verifications or exchanges going on, I thought about businesses. *I imagined that I had a company and that it was a single plane.* I wondered how close we are to that clear-cut example of managing, monitoring, and controlling the results of a process that takes us from one objective to another in record time, with variable conditions and several restrictions.

Do the modern dashboards and balanced scorecards bring us closer to what I saw in the cockpit of the plane? We have a control tower that gives us instructions. Do we have something similar to the "autopilot"? We have a flight plan that we can **verify by the minute**. What preparation do we have in case of an emergency? Have we done certified hours in a business simulator? When an order is given, is it fulfilled?

How about a pilot negotiating with the plane to decrease or increase its speed or for the plane to decrease or increase its height or turn 30 degrees to the right? How about a pilot asking for permission to face a storm or handle a mechanical failure or an emergency landing that has to be consulted with a foreign "high command" who is unavailable? What if the pilot orders the crew to do something, and they are left wondering what to do, or they do not obey the orders, or they execute them half an hour later, or they do not agree with them? What if the pilot ignores the control tower?

Issues like the ones I have mentioned present themselves every day in business, preventing it from obtaining results. The dashboard is vital and depicts the condition we find ourselves in, but it is about so much more.

The information we need to determine how the business is doing may not be obtained promptly, and in some organizations, it takes days to obtain information that may be unreliable. Often, businesses navigate without a control tower or the radio assistance that guides them through the predefined or programmed course. Obviously, there is no autopilot in business. Decreasing or increasing height or speed is not an immediate matter. Although we know when business plans begin, we are not sure when they will end. We often know how much has been spent on resources but not when it is too late to react.

What about our crew in business? Do they follow orders immediately? Are they all properly trained? Do they know what to do in an emergency? Do they have discipline? Do they help each other? Do they clearly understand their mission? Do they understand that they are the face of the company in front of the client? Do they manage the assets entrusted to them and for business purposes? Do they understand the meaning of "first things first"? Do they know that time is key and limited? Our corporate crew does not respond appropriately to the questions I have just asked.

Meanwhile, what can we say about preparing the aircraft so that it leaves on time and without failure, takes what is necessary on the flight, is clean, with a full gas tank and all the vital elements and functions verified, and the crew arrives on time to prepare for a safe trip? Do our businesses have everything running like this? Is everything planned, scheduled, verified, and executed perfectly?

We can look for explanations and say that the comparison to an airplane is not exact and that the company is not comparable. However, the reflection I have made serves to show that the aviation industry has plenty to teach us and is way ahead of us in accomplishments, results, precision, quality, processes, control, emergency management, risk minimization, training, and customer service.

Aviation is not the perfect industry. However, observing in detail a large plane that flies from one destination to another, as if that plane was a company, offers a perspective that makes it easier to analyze what we need to attain or accomplish, where we are today, and how much we can move forward.

Any dashboard should be able to answer one question relative to the objective pursued in any segment of our trajectory, which must be divided into smaller sections, if we want to achieve a successful trajectory. The question at any time is simple: **How are we doing?** Do we have the answer? If we have it, then we can make decisions based on which we can take action. Otherwise, we have to stand still or decide to act blindly. Either entails risks for the crew, the passengers, and the plane.

I think it is worth taking action in our company to answer the **key question: How are we doing?** If this question is not answered on a plane every second, landing will be extremely difficult.

Pentaval: methodology and instrument for business and personal diagnosis

In addition to several years of research, I have directly worked in more than a hundred companies of different sizes in various industries. Further, by working in and studying business and humanities, I have acquired considerable experience and knowledge. Based on these credentials, I have developed a diagnostic instrument that facilitates and streamlines tasks when a specific situation needs to be analyzed. This tool poses ten questions or functions that are worth examining and verifying and that are based on the expected response of a representative sample of those involved in the process to be studied through field diagnosis.

To develop the instrument, I used as basis traditional checklists for verification. However, instead of using "it has" or "it does not have" as answers, I used a single field with a score of 1 to 10, where 1 is low, and 10 is high. The application of the instrument yields a direct rating of the status of the function, department, person, or question that needs to be analyzed. A rating below 6 means that we have something serious or extremely bad. A rating between 6 and 9 means that we have a good situation but with an opportunity for improvement.

The power of the PENTAVAL instrument is in the combination between what I have just described above (Focused Self-Assessment) and the use of five questions that must be answered. Each question uses up to three keywords (Words with complete meaning that directly answer the question about the function, department, person, or concern, using as few articles or prepositions as possible, like in internet searches). The five questions are supported by the concept of analysis developed by scientists in cognitive psychology— Joseph Luft and Harry Ingham (Johari Window)—for studying the processes of human interaction. The PENTAVAL instrument is a practical and modern application, as well as simple and quick to perform, using the following five questions (5 assessments in one): What is the best? What is the worst? What is lacking? What is excessive? What needs to be changed? The instrument assesses the answer to each question in an open and controlled manner, with a maximum of three keywords.

Suppose we want to evaluate a project manager's work in the project they are leading, and we apply PENTAVAL as a diagnostic instrument, assuming that they are the function we want to work with (the "function" appears in the left column of the second example). Suppose that the project manager has not performed well and that their users or the most prominent people with whom they have had contact are evaluating them. The example below is a summary of the different answers we found. *The Focused Self-Assessment gives a score of 3*—they are performing poorly as a manager—and the answers to all five questions resulted in the following keywords:

The worst: disorder, lack of control, absence

The best: willingness

Lacks: experience, knowledge, method

Excessive: bad temper, threats

Needs to change: supervision, attitude

The diagnosis is quick, concrete, and concise. Simultaneously, it is extremely revealing. Would you continue with this project manager?

If we want to evaluate the function of integration in a work team and we ask them to assess themselves with PENTAVAL, assuming they are not performing well or it is not a good time, the overall classification obtained is a Focused Self-Assessment of 4. The answers to the five questions are as follows:

The worst: scattered, independent

The best: expertise, knowledge

Lacks: agreement, approaches, unity

Excessive: ideas, egos

Needs to Change: attitude, inflexibility, pontification

The proceedings do not seem ideal for the team. However, there is room to improve, and now we know what is happening and what to do.

To illustrate further a failing team, the PENTAVAL instrument shows the status of the assessment of other vital functions in an ongoing project.

PENTAVAL:
Instrument for Focused Self-Assessment (FSA) and practical application of the Johari Window (JW)

Instructions

1. In the second column, rate from 1 to 10 (1 being the lowest and 10 being the highest) the functions listed in the first column
2. Answer using **only one to a maximum of three keywords** (With their own meaning and, if possible, without articles or prepositions) what you consider is the best, the worst, the main thing(s) that is/are lacking or in excess and what you would change in each function listed in the first column on the left. If you are responding by hand, please use clear and concise print. If you do not have a keyword in mind, leave the space blank.
3. Below, in red, the first row illustrates how to answer the questions.

Concept Functions	1 to 10	The best	The worst	What's lacking?	What's excessive?	What needs to change?
Example: Assessment form	8	Simplicity		– More features – Logos	Nothing	Word
Project management	3	Willingness	Disorder Lack of control Absence	Experience Knowledge Method	Bad temper Threats	Supervision Attitude
Team integration	4	Expertise Knowledge	Scattered Independent	Agreement Approach Unity	Ideas Egos	Attitude Inflexibility Pontification
Work team's satisfaction	5	Members	Results	Definition Leadership	Ideas	Management method
Quality of customer relations	6	There is work	Credibility Trust	Results	Discussions (edit)	Responses Informality
Understanding of the customer and their requirements	7	Evidence Client Intelligent	Initial errors	Results People assigned	Politics Making time	Speed
Clarity in the methodology to be used	5	There are several	Not defined	Decision	Unproductive meetings	Leadership
Instrument complexity	4	Several simple	Some complex	Decision	Roundabout	Leadership
Customer satisfaction	5	Wants to continue	Distrust	Results	Meetings without purpose Informality	Results
Consultants' skills and experience	10	Competence Suitability	Disintegration	Unity Leadership Management	Disorder Waste	Work method
Unification of criteria and styles	4	Feasible	Leader does not decide There is no leader	Decision Leadership	Consensus	Interactive method

PENTAVAL is a considerably powerful diagnostic instrument. A single table shows the details of a function, department, person, or group, as well as the degree of difficulty or well-being. It also shows the root of the problems, a matter that immediately triggers the plans to be made and the actions to be taken to improve outcomes.

ACPM for business or
personal success

I t is curious how at the end of the investigation, I could find an acronym that facilitates mnemonics (ACPM), although it does not necessarily find the ideas in the same order in which they should be applied. The important thing is to remember the first letters of each key idea to accomplishing business or personal success.

If you want to ensure your business and professional success, you must start by establishing the goal that you want to achieve, and you must be **clear** about what you want, which is not always the case. I have asked that question many times. What do you want to achieve and when? The answer is usually scattered or not very precise, and that is generally why one does not attain the result. Some simple examples are the following questions: Do you want to have money? How much? When? Answer precisely.

Organizations aware of where they are progressing to and when they want to reach there devise plans and then take actions that enable them to achieve or exceed their objectives or at least get considerably close to them. The general problem of most people is that they do not know where they want to go. Years pass, and there is no visible progress because there are no clear objectives, or they keep changing. Thus, a person does not reach anywhere in the end.

You have to set an objective or goal and then devise a plan to achieve it. Once it is achieved, you can set a new objective in a specific field.

After you have **clearly defined the goal** you want to reach, you have to determine **how** to reach it, which requires devising a plan A and a plan B. The "how" is vital in the plans because they represent the strategy for achievement. The objective refers to "what" you want to do. The "how" refers to the tasks that we must conduct to make the "what" a reality—the goal or objective.

Once the plan is defined, we must exercise **control** over it to ensure that it is conducted properly. Following up on our progress in fulfilling the tasks necessary to achieve the objective will allow us to determine how we are doing and adjust our actions over time to minimize deviations and make improvements toward the accomplishment. If we cannot answer the question "how are we doing?," then we have no control, without which we are adrift.

In summary, the letter "C" refers to **clarity** in the objective, the **how** of planning, and the **control** to achieve it.

There are other important Cs worth mentioning. To avoid extending myself, I have summarized them as follows. The first one is **quality**

(Especially by applying the 5 Ws + H method to ensure that every project undertaken is always complete: Who, What, Where, When, Why, and How). There is a vital "c" for when one faces difficulties or aggressive competition, which is **creativity** (innovation at the right time, resourcefulness). Another crucial "C" is **commitment,** along with **conviction** and **trust,** which constitute a winning trio for a person or company to reach their goal, also considering how much work is conducted. In terms of **communication,** fluid and frequent **conversation** during any project makes all the difference in the teams or among individuals to attain **cooperation** from third parties, which is vital to meeting objectives.

In any case, on the path toward the goal, there are times when we must consider the possibility of making **concessions** that will facilitate or support us in reaching the goal. Without concessions, many times, things do not happen.

One last essential "C" is **change** because you have to either manage the change or make changes to fulfill the objective or reach the goal. Change implies adapting quickly in the event of an unplanned situation that forces a revision of the original plan or refinement in strategy (how the tasks are going to be performed). We have to have enough flexibility to make changes when what we are doing is not effective in our pursuit of the goal.

The next guiding principle for success is the letter **M,** which is to choose a **method** for executing tasks, a method within the plan to be implemented. **Choosing a mode or method of work** is fundamental and worth the efforts concentrated. If conducted with discipline, the correct method must "mechanically" lead us to fulfill our objective. The difference between the success of one company or another competing in the same industry is the method or mode with which they approach challenges or projects. The same happens with professionals. A better method or mode of performing tasks is what grants success. The manufacture of a new product may be similar at two different companies. However, one method or mode of performing may result in an efficient, practical, and cheap process, while the other is time-consuming and expensive. One student may take hours to prepare a school assignment and secure only 6/10 as a result, while another student may prepare the same assignment in merely one hour and secure 9/10, based on their study methods. There are many ways, modes, or methods of doing things, but there is one that beats the rest. It is worth spending some time defining what method to use. The more secure or reliable it is, and the fewer flaws it presents, the better. Not having a method wastes time, resources, and money and also makes any endeavor risky.

The third letter is **P**, which is what allows one to succeed once the objective has been defined. We must focus, choose a winning method, and devise a **plan** (without forgetting the virtuous circle or quality route provided by PDCA—plan, execute, verify, and act). We must **persist** and **persevere** until we have reached the goal and be **passionate** about what we are doing. It is also necessary to be **practical** (this ensures a speedy and quality execution and a reasonable cost).

Passion is a powerful engine that motivates us to defeat all those who perform activities because they have to, it is their obligation, they are ordered to, or they have to work. A person who puts passion into what they do guarantees 40% of their success. The other 60% is provided by the other three components of the

ACPM, at 20% each. If the PDCA quality route is planned and implemented, along with perseverance, there is no doubt that results will be seen.

Finally, what makes a difference in the face of the adversity that will always exist on our path toward meeting the goal or objective is our **attitude**, which saves us amid the greatest hardships, problems, or failures. We can have everything against us, but it is our attitude that saves us. It is also under our entire control in the face of adversity.

Let us consider a simple example. Suppose we are on the 13th floor of a building that is reported to have an ongoing fire on the 8th floor, and we realize that the fire is coming up. We can get scared and faint, become paralyzed, or prefer to jump from a window rather than die burned or suffocated—or we can find serenity for a few minutes to think or plan, alone or with others, a possible alternative for salvation. We may not be able to prevent the fire, but we can control the attitude we assume in the face of the incident, which can save us.

Attitude is then tied to several factors, such as courage, serenity, Columbus-style rule-breaking, boundary crossing, fearlessness, and decision-making. The letter "A" is also for **action**, which makes all the difference ("from words to actions"), and taking **risks** and overcoming the fears and mental barriers that inhibit action. Attitude makes the real difference between winning and losing in any circumstance that is not under our direct control. A final letter "A" is for **adaptation,** a complement to change, which enables us to leave behind the old rules that have governed us for some time and **acquire** new rules. Applying rules that are valid in a given situation to a different one can be fatal, which is why we have to adapt to new conditions.

Life will always challenge the objectives that we set for ourselves in any field. Passion—a powerful engine that drives us to love what we do—is not sufficient to overcome them. Attitude is a definitive factor in the achievement of goals. In the face of adversity, the wrong attitude can destroy all hopes and bury ideas.

There may be other formulas for success, but the ACPM is concrete and works wonderfully. Do not forget to throw some ACPM into your business, project, or life and always put it into practice. This will help us achieve success!

13

Connections in today's world, online communication

A few years ago, people talked about virtualization at work, which began as a trend in administrative matters, sometimes to save space and other times to avoid impractical long journeys. The technology available was mostly standard telephones and desktop computers when the idea began to be explored with trials at large companies and in large cities. This trend from 10 or 15 years ago is becoming more of a reality and usual practice for frequent travelers, people who work on clients' sites, those responsible for international areas, and those who can work from home or contribute their talent remotely.

The tools available today are obviously powerful: smartphones, tablets, wireless connections, mini laptops, web video conferencing, voiceover IP, high-speed internet, and cloud computing.

With the abovementioned technological support, in addition to others, if necessary, many professionals can stay connected at minimal cost and with extremely high quality in interactions. These may include those who live far from their offices, respond to international activities, travel constantly, or contribute their talent and express their valuable comments remotely or virtually. We have many examples to share, and some cases refer to experiences in today's modern world.

One example is the traveling father who connects every night from the hotel and talks to his children and his wife via web video conference as if he was at home. Another example would be business meetings between countries or people at different locations, without traveling.

A friend who attends three international video conferences weekly and shares presentations says that it feels as if they are all meeting physically, given the surprising quality of the image and audio.

This subject has come a long way, and the technology has become affordable for households and small businesses to have access to it.

Another friend says that he has delivered presentations to 80 or 90 people during an hour using the web and can answer questions and receive requests from many countries. He needs only the traditional internet connection, the conference coordinator and presenter in Canada, and an audience spread across nearly 30 countries. It seems incredible, but that is life today.

Another friend says that he reads the headlines of the most important newspapers and the most prominent magazines of his interest every day, and it does not cost him a dime. He becomes well-informed in less than 20 minutes. Most surprisingly, he does it in the taxi on his way to the office because he is reading the news from his cell phone.

Being online is essential today. In the modern world, the idea is the ability to be reached immediately and provide an opinion at a given time before it is too late or it no longer matters.

Chats have become frequent among young people and adults using cell phones. They use abbreviated or short text messages. The same is observed on Twitter. Chats are important because they do not interrupt the work or the task that is being conducted. After all, one answers when it is possible, and they have the advantage of being able to identify and determine what is important or urgent just by reading a short message.

As for meetings, chats have become frequent among attendees, especially if they are far away from one another at the table or in the room, if they want to offer help, or if they want to pass on some key or relevant information to the conversation.

The use of tablets, laptops, smartphones, and cloud computing has made the office, school or university, and home reachable at the touch of a screen. You can answer emails and key questions or send vital information instantly through them, such as photos of an important moment that is being lived in some part of the planet, in real time, or a recording or video of a meeting or an experience.

Internet access from cell phones has made it easy to answer questions merely by seeking the answers on the web. There are maps or locations, the meanings of terms or songs, the addresses of restaurants or businesses, or simply general knowledge and even instant translations. Owing to cloud computing, we can access vital files and applications from the office or home without physically being in those places. We can install an application, such as Skype, on our cell phones, making them work as video phones and allowing us to hold video and conference calls.

Being able to connect and communicate immediately with all the video and information tools available means that our physical presence is not required all the time, providing considerable agility and extraordinary productivity. Shortly, we will be almost omnipresent, and trips will be made only when strictly necessary, generating substantial savings in time, productivity, and money.

The best defense is a good offense

I will do to you whatever I please, and do not even think about doing something to me because then you will see the beast "inside me." The evil man seems to say this when making mischief against us.

For many years, I have been observing people's behavior in the business and family contexts with respect to their attitude toward failures or errors. I have to confess that, unfortunately, I have found a considerably high degree of immaturity, which causes people to reject or deny their mistakes.

The contradiction that sometimes generates confusion is that the person who commits the mistake or fails is content with not recognizing it or hiding it or pretending to be clueless like small children. They even become aggressive and moody, almost always adopting the position of those who should be concerned with the failure or mistake.

In terms of relationships, the person who committed the offense toward the other rather frequently ends up playing the indignant party and acting as if they had been offended. The world is upside down.

Companies, in turn, behave like human beings, with the offensive or attacking company acting as if it had suffered the offense or attack. In this sense, it attacks twice—the first time when offending and the second when defending itself as though it had suffered the offense. The bottom line here is that bad guys always attack because they remember the adage "the best defense is a good offense," and they use it intensely and frequently.

One is not prepared for the person who attacks to end the matter without making excuses and even acting as though they had been offended. As it frequently happens, through this reflection, we will look at some interesting defense methods.

The first thing to be aware of is that the most frequent reaction of those who make mistakes or commit offenses is to defend themselves through aggression. The aggressor or offender does not recognize their fault or error and does not apologize. Conversely, we see them acting as if they had suffered the offense or had been the victim of the error. That is, if we observe the bad guy's behavior, it seems as if it is us who must apologize. If you are not careful, you end up being the one at fault, or rather the person who has to resolve the faults because the actual culprit permanently plays the victim card. It is something like this: If you offend me, I will be angry, and if I offend you, I will also be angry. This is like the old story that says, "Heads I win, tails you lose."

Second, this type of person must be faced or confronted with strength or firmness to make them aware of their failures or offenses. We should send the correct message indicating our serious and cold position to demand that they repair their mistake or take back the offense. The aggressor must clearly feel the weight of the law on their shoulders and the consequences of the risks of not taking a step back.

Third, one must find an honorable way out for the aggressor or offender, such as helping them apologize or accept their failure so that they remain noble human beings and, to an extent, a brave hero. That is, instead of receiving punishment, they will be rewarded for their effort to face the situation. This exit helps people mature and lose their fear of punishment or failure and allows them to come out ahead. Making the aggressor feel like a hero instead of a victim by apologizing or acknowledging their failure is the best method or antidote for these types of characters.

Fourth, one must completely ignore these types of people, cutting them off and making them feel as if they no longer exist. This is a powerful method. Although it seems slow and painless, it leaves the adversary disoriented and "on the canvas," not only because of their confusion from being ignored, but also because the disconnection generates their concern for not knowing what is happening and how the other side will respond. It causes them to lose control of the situation and makes it impossible for them to attack again. The aggressor ends up getting desperate and punishing themselves. Since time immemorial, this type of attitude has been a deadly weapon for those who tend to think of themselves as major players by playing with the wrong method of defense, when they are the ones responsible for the failures or offenses.

The fifth method is to use witnesses when confronting the aggressor in such a way that it is difficult for them to lie when there is evidence of what one said and the aggressor's response. Pressure from people helps neutralize the aggressor's vicious outlets. These types of people tend to get so scared that they prefer to avoid facing a situation where they have to admit their mistakes. Imagine their fright when they have to face this situation in front of witnesses. These people are generally "chickens" who make excessive noise, but when push comes to shove, they are just strong words and nothing more.

Of course, there are other management alternatives for these cases, which arise as a result of this interesting evaluation and which I want to leave to the reader for meditation.

Recognizing mistakes and learning from them allow you to improve and develop as an individual or as a business. You start to get better the day you acknowledge that you are flawed and plan a solution or seek support.

Closer proximity, less attention

There is a high rate of reports indicating that the person closest to us is the last priority on the list when it comes to meeting an obligation.

Many of us have been taken by surprise and have learned our lesson with blood, sweat, and tears.

A friend once shared his sadness with me because his beloved brother had owed him money for more than a year and did not even give him hope as to when he would be paid. Instead, his brother had complied with the banks and other lenders without fail and on time, bought a new car, made trips abroad, and threw big parties.

Another friend was extremely close to the administrative manager of a company. Owing to this relationship, the manager abused their proximity to assign her desk or computer to other people when she was not in the office. Sometimes, she would arrive at work and have to wait for people to vacate her desk. The manager did not do the same to others because no one else would accept being treated like that.

Is it that being friends, siblings, or relatives means that "you are authorized to abuse me or treat me like the last priority"? Is proximity to a person like having a sign on your forehead that says, "I'm dumb; take advantage of me"? I have heard expressions such as "Do what you need to do, she will not complain. She is a good person."

"Leave it for later. He will understand the reason for the delay."

"Go for it. She will support you, no matter what."

"Do not worry. He is a good guy."

This is in line with the urban or popular saying, "because I love you, I beat you."

A new saying is coined for these cases: **You are the last priority in my life because I trust you.**

I think the big surprise in these cases is that helping someone close or dear to you is considered a voluntary act and even more so if they have not asked for the help. At the moment you say, "I helped you in the past, and now I expect reciprocity," the person you helped may believe that they have no moral debt to you, as they did not ask for the help, and if you did help, it was a voluntary act.

It is like saying, "if you helped me, it was because you wanted to. You did not have to do it. Now, do not complain. Nobody forced you."

A more modern way of saying it would be "help me so that I will never help you." When I ask you for something, I hope you give me a hand, but do not ask me for anything because you should not count on me. The relationship is one way. I use you to my liking and well, stop counting.

What I have shared with you happens often in the office. Camaraderie is not always reciprocal, although sometimes the "today you, tomorrow me" does apply, such as in shift work. Of course, we should not refrain from helping someone merely because of these comments and reflections.

We can and should help without expecting anything in return.

Remember that there will be times when, apart from not thanking you for your help, the situation may even harm you (opposite effect). If you are aware of that, it will not hurt or bother you.

I once helped a person who had been unemployed for months to find a job. Not even one year had passed when I received a call from them stating that they felt uncomfortable at work and that it was my fault for helping them get that job. They also expected me to find them another job to correct my mistake.

Sometimes people are like that, and it is surprising.

Another time, a person called me and asked if they could send me their resume because they wanted to find another job. I replied that I did not know where they might be hiring or needing someone with their profile but that if I knew of anything, I would gladly inform them and proceeded to accept their resume. Two weeks later, the person called me to ask what I had done with their resume. As I still did not know of any relevant opportunities, they insulted me and asked me why I had accepted the resume, making

them waste the effort and time in printing it out and sending it to me (I must clarify that I am not a headhunter).

The moral here is that if one accepts responsibility, even if voluntarily, we must face the potential consequences. You learn every day. You have to learn how to say "yes" or "no" with courage, even if it is to help someone voluntarily. If you say "yes," you must be fully aware to what and whom you say so. If you say "no," you must be gracious and almost get the other person to thank you for the refusal to stay on good terms and not generate enemies or resentments. We must also learn to command respect and, finally, to reverse the permissive or open conditions that we have left behind, authorized, or allowed by innocently saying "yes."

I leave you these reflections. I am sure you already have others in mind that are just as or even more interesting from which we can surely learn.

Bankruptcies, losses, divorces, high tension

L earning about the terminal illness of a loved one is a profound experience that makes us reflect on the meaning of life and the value of everything that surrounds us: friends, work, family, possessions, prestige, beauty, nature, politics, nation, enemies, achievements, and what we have not been able to accomplish.

If that loved one is your father, mother, brother, child, wife, husband, or even your pet, the process of accompanying them in the time before their death generates extreme reactions. Some face the situation with courage and considerable psychological maturity, whereas others cannot handle it and lose control of their senses and actions.

Finally, the denouement occurs, and the life of that loved one ends. We feel exhausted, but the weight of the tension has begun to decrease as it comes to an end. Grief will last days, months, or even years. We have to adapt to this new life with the *initial emptiness* that we feel. We have to begin to write a new chapter in our story, start from scratch, dream of a better future, and capitalize on the experiences and teachings that this person left us to honor their memory through actions and deeds on our new path.

Bankruptcies, divorces, or separations are considerably similar to what I have just described. The process begins slowly and then picks up speed until the situation gets more complicated and doors begin to close. The fuel of the company and the people, the air, the alternatives, and the possibilities of staying afloat start to run out. It is like being cornered in chess, queen check, king check. It is a highly tense process for all of those associated with the company, the organization, or the people. Everyone close to the administration sees that time is running out, and each solution arrives as a stumbling block. With every passing day, the company struggles to survive its last moments. Its people feel pain and suffer from stress because everyone senses the worst and does not know what else to do. They do not know if they should flee, shout, or curse. In these situations, it is valid for hope to live on until the last minute, which is precisely when one thinks that only a miracle or a stroke of luck will save them.

The sensation must be similar to what someone who has fallen in the sea and is exhausted from swimming feels, with nothing to eat and hypothermia slowly making them sleepy.

When the time comes, the company runs out of economic breath. Debts overwhelm it. There are bank blockades and a lack of cash. Here comes the "checkmate" or simply the "dead end." The END.

The same thing happens to people, not only in terms of health but also economically and emotionally. We endure moments of tremendous stress or high tension. We suffer a loss, get the catharsis needed to understand calmly what we have lost, learn from the positive and negative aspects of the experience, and, of course, become aware of who and where we are.

There are sudden deaths and relationships that end in a second. Theft financially destroys a person or an organization in minutes. There are accidental deaths. Interestingly, we are almost never alone. There is always someone with us giving advice or support. Of course, there are many who walk away because they are afraid of being close to those who experience these significant challenges in life. They distance themselves because of superstition or self-protection.

How about those who are saved because it was not their turn that day?

Miracles and good luck exist, and I have witnessed them many times. I have seen, and I believe that you have also been able to witness how, at the last instant, when everything seems lost, a person saves themselves, another wins a lottery, a company takes advantage of an opportunity to acquire another company, a new love arises at first sight, a misunderstanding gets clarified, or someone offers a hand to a drowning man. The threat is suddenly over, and the experience is like a resurrection, like seeing the shining light after the darkest night. It is happiness and the beginning of a new life or opportunity.

The possibilities are endless, and we have to be prepared to handle those challenging moments in the best way possible, with our heads held high, with intelligence, humility, courage, and dignity. I leave you with this reflection.

Business disloyalties and infidelities

A friend has a saying that is extremely graphic and applies to what I want to share on this occasion, "If you are looking for fidelity, buy a sound system because only it can offer high fidelity." Indeed, we see infidelity and disloyalty daily.

When my father worked in a bank, his idea was to spend his whole life at the institution until he retired. He joined the bank when he was only 21 and left with honors and several commemorative plaques and trays after having worked for 42 years.

Marriages were for life, and couples only separated when one of the spouses died.

Of course, there are still employees like my father and married couples like my parents, but they are now the minority.

Relationships have changed, and the glue is weaker in both human and business relationships. They say that people "endure less or are unwilling to endure." Today's marriages or business relationships have been compared with disposable cups—they have a short duration.

The bond is damaged when the relationship wears out, and people or companies do not express their discontent or do not strive to improve the relationship. It has become customary to do what monkeys do, which is "to release the rope only when they have a firm grip on another one" so that they do not fail or take risks. This metaphor describes a phenomenon of temporal and parallel simultaneity, in which work is performed quietly while seeking a replacement for the person or company, and the withdrawal is communicated only when the other opportunity has been ensured.

Based on the above, a kind of clandestine or hidden activity is generated, where a new relationship develops with another person or company that, from the perspective of the one about to be abandoned, is an apparent infidelity or disloyalty. In the case of companies, the disloyalty stings worse, especially if the person is switching to the competition. Some people or companies tend to get emotional and even threatening, and sometimes conduct offensive actions because they feel mocked or cheated. Others never forget the fact and go to the extreme of not forgiving or not understanding and declare the one who deceived them as their enemy.

What I just described is similar to what happens in many divorces. The man or woman, tired of the relationship, looks for another partner and develops the new relationship in secret until they decide to get a divorce or until the infidelity is discovered, and the battle begins. Some couples manage to handle the breaking of their bond with intelligence and maturity, but there are many who cannot speak with or forgive each other. If they have children, this situation makes it difficult to raise them and will affect them emotionally. I have a couple of friends who have handled their divorces in an excellent manner and have a superb relationship with their ex-wives for the benefit of the children. However, I know many more who do not even say hello to each other again.

I have had the experience of disloyalty in the company firsthand, and I must confess that it hurts because I felt cheated by the people in whom I had placed all my trust.

The story is always the same. They say that they are leaving and are in a hurry. They make up an excuse that does not make sense and sounds unhinged or illogical. Subsequently, you see them working for the competition and ultimately learn that they entered several months after having left the company (everyone knows that is not true and that they saw them go to work the next day after leaving).

With this reflection in mind, I know that you must be remembering other similar episodes or better ones with extraordinary teachings.

Youth are less loyal to companies and are eager to land better opportunities, more recognition, and a better work environment. Nowadays, the challenge of maintaining a relationship requires daily effort. We must constantly surprise our partner with sufficiently good details, as well as keep key employees happy, to maintain their interest and attract them, to retain them, or make them fall in love. The competition is increasingly aggressive and ingenious and goes *straight for the goal without hesitation.*

Appreciating simple acts makes the difference

A friend once shared with me his idea of marrying his girlfriend of many years. She was a beautiful, responsible, and hard-working woman, but the most important thing was the affection she had for my friend. He was extremely distrustful and did not want to commit, although he was in love, which made him plan, as modern couples often do, to invite his girlfriend to live with him without a prior civil or religious ceremony.

When I found out about his ideas, I invited him to go out for coffee and gave him the following lesson: Dear friend, you are going to embark on a new stage of your life in the company of the woman you love. How you do it matters little nowadays, as long as you achieve it, but later on, you will regret not having given the required significance to the act of marriage.

He was surprised and told me that he did not understand what I was suggesting. I emphasized that my advice sought to make him reflect on the need to "leave a mark as he walks."

I told him that in ten or twenty years or maybe in no more than five, he and his partner would try to remember what the beginning of their life together was like, and they would not easily find a beautiful memory, or at least one to make them feel proud. The lack of details and carelessness in them would cost them in the future.

I then recommended that he hold a small ceremony in his apartment and invite two or three mutual friends to join them and serve as witnesses to that special, unrepeatable moment in their lives. They did not have to make pre-printed cards or buy expensive champagne but to offer them something that the couple enjoyed, like some delicious empanadas or a tasty chicken dish. It could be anything that would make them feel happy in a loving and simple or uncomplicated celebration.

I also recommended that he tell one of their friends to bring a camera to take two or three commemorative photos of that day. Finally, I indicated that it would be good to dedicate some loving words that day in front of their tiny audience, something like, "We wanted to share with you our immense love and the decision we have made to start our life together today. You are our friends and also witnesses to the formal beginning of our new life."

What I have just described serves as a frame of reference for an issue that often goes unnoticed in offices and companies. I refer to the moments in which you have to stop for a minute and celebrate in a simple but unforgettable manner the important milestones, such as winning a big business, finishing a long project, remembering an anniversary, celebrating a promotion, saying goodbye, or receiving an award or memorial plaque.

Managers, employees, and even suppliers, regardless of hierarchy or rank, should be aware of this fine idea of appreciating seemingly simple but significant matters in life. Exercising the function of organizing a small celebration is an idea that should be embedded within work teams; it is not necessarily the intellectual property of human resource departments or managers. It is about learning to coexist with elegance and dignity, at minimal cost to us, and aiming to leave a trail and have the opportunity to share a pleasant or memorable time with colleagues. In the long run, the only thing that will remain will be the photos that were taken that day and some memento received from others as a reminder of the event. The rest will be filed away in oblivion.

Businesses seldom become aware of this pleasant and useful practice because they are busy with the pursuit of daily achievements and easily forget that human beings, like plants, need frequent affection and love.

Suppose a person who was ill has just returned to the office after a month-long absence. The person can enter and greet all their colleagues and bosses and then sit down to work and try to re-engage in everyday life. Such a return is common and takes a few minutes, while the person goes from one desk to another recounting their recovery experience. Alternatively, a group may form, and the person can comment on the details of their illness and recovery more simply and quickly, and thus, avoid repeating the story.

The point I am trying to make with this reflection is that this moment can serve a lasting memory. Given the joy of the colleague's return, a simple welcome back celebration with cake and a photo could be arranged to listen to their story and share other anecdotes, allowing everyone to leave the office for thirty minutes or one hour. Everyone can go home happy and share the event of the day and maybe even the best joke of the celebration. Thus, work is not the last memory in one's mind, with the stress or worry that it may represent. Conversely, we completely erase the difficulties or challenges that we faced during the day and exchange them for a celebratory cake and a note signed by all those celebrating the return of their colleague. Episodes like these are the ones that I refer to, and many of you at this time must be thinking that you have participated in them several times. I congratulate you for that. My invitation is for you to remember how many other episodes and opportunities you have missed, many of them more relevant than traditional birthdays.

Life is full of details. The important thing is to capture the most significant moments and cherish them forever through a small celebration. Life is about simple details, as usually occurs in marriage, where sometimes we go to bed and fall asleep without saying good night. However, a tender kiss and a "see you tomorrow, my love; I love you" make all the difference.

-19-

What to do with the 3HP factor

Someone has to tell the truth, once and for all, and I shall take that honor. Colombia is one of the best places to live in the world. Recently, efforts have been made to draw attention to Colombians who have succeeded abroad and the activities or products for which Colombia stands out worldwide. We have even been classified as the country with the happiest people on the planet. We are creative, resourceful, intelligent, and tireless workers and so much more. If we are the best in many areas, what causes us to fail in the end?

Why have we not grown like Korea, a country that 30 years ago was our size and was in a poor state and today is 10 times Colombia? Why are we not like the Asian tigers? Why in 500 years have we not achieved an inch of what the US achieved in just 250? Why can we not move forward like Chile has done? What is happening to us? Why have we been killing each other for 50 years? Why have we not stopped fighting since the time of Bolívar and Santander?

If we have it all, what is not working out? Do we need to learn teamwork? Do we have to change our religion?

The "3hp" factor inhabits all human beings, but there is a higher percentage in some. The normal value is 10% to 20%, but there are human beings whose 3hp factor presents values over 80%. Unfortunately, in our country, a significant number of people have a high value of this factor.

This factor generates individualism, lack of solidarity, envy, and immorality. The people who possess it to a high degree seem to be at an advantage. They want everything for themselves and nothing for others. They act as if the planet were theirs, and they are the only inhabitants, who only care about their world and their life, and they would be better off if others did not exist. The 3hp factor is the motivation behind "help me, but I will never help you, and if you are not careful, I will abuse you." Contracting the 3hp factor can be prevented, but once a person is infected and develops it to a high degree, they usually die with the 3hp embedded at 100%.

A friend told me that, some time ago, a couple of police officers had fined him for running a red traffic light on a Saturday, at around 3 AM, in Bogotá (stopping at a traffic light at that time is just asking for something unpleasant to occur). As they were issuing the fine, 20 other cars managed to run the red light without the police stopping them or doing anything. If he had stopped at the traffic light and had not seen cars coming, at 3 AM in the morning, no one would have fined him. In any case, he would have received a warning and would have had to take a course, but a fine would not have been issued. Was he looking for a "tip"? We will never know, but there was no money exchanged, and the 3hp factor came to the fore. Maybe that no longer happens today, but it happened on that occasion.

Another friend, who was involved in a car crash a few years ago, on a Sunday, at 1 AM, was taken to a police station to have their blood alcohol level tested despite being wounded and needing medical attention. At around 3 AM, when the police determined he had not ingested alcohol, he was told to look for a hospital because he looked badly hurt. Was his life not the first priority? Who would take him to the hospital at 3 AM, badly injured, and in a place far from where you can find any means of transportation? Why did the police not take him to the hospital? Had they been infected with the 3hp factor because my friend had a fine car? The police have improved considerably, but that is how it happened on that occasion.

An acquaintance had been awarded a business and had already signed it with his client and started working on the agreed plan when the organization was taken over. They decided to abandon the plan and hand over the business to another firm that belonged to a friend of theirs, for a value five times greater than the amount originally paid to my acquaintance. They then told him that his plan did not convince them and that it presented shortfalls. Not only did they take away the business from him, but they also spoke negatively of him and proceeded to pay five times more for an inferior plan. It made no sense. Was their 3hp factor active?

Many years ago, the apartment and salary of a relative who had served as a guarantor in the purchase of a car had been seized because his brother-in-law had missed a good number of the monthly payments. When the brother-in-law had to surrender the car to remove the liens on my relative, he said, "Because of you, I no longer have a car." Incredible! The person who trusted the brother-in-law had their property seized, and yet they are the ones to blame afterward. The world has turned upside down. Was there some 3hp factor in the brother-in-law?

The thesis supervisor of an acquaintance's son abandoned him in the middle of the semester, which delayed him from getting his degree by one more semester because he had withdrawn from a class that this lecturer delivered. Concerned about the boy's withdrawal, the administration investigated and discovered that the lecturer had not applied tests or exams for almost the entire semester, thereby failing to comply with the university's rules and validating the student's argument to withdraw from the class, a matter that the university authorized in light of the evidence gathered. The lecturer then took revenge on the boy who, without fault, made him appear incompetent. Nothing ever happened to the lecturer, apart from receiving a recommendation to be more judicious. Was he infected with the 3hp factor, causing an innocent person to be punished?

Sometimes in the work environment, bad colleagues or those who do not work are rewarded or given the best honor because they have sold themselves reasonably well to the bosses. There is the evil boss who treats everyone badly and abuses authority, engages in mental torture, and tramples on people, while everyone sticks it out and keeps quiet for fear of losing their job. No one from above notices the mistreatment and abuse, or if someone does, they do not take action for fear of having to look for a replacement for the bad boss, with the excuse that although they are a bad element, they produce results. Who has the 3hp factor?

What about credit-grabbing bosses who claim to have conducted a project or come up with an idea and attribute it to themselves as if it were their own?

What about those who say that nothing would be possible without them in the office, and when they go on vacation or travel, the results are seen in large proportions, without their intervention? What about those who worry about small savings like not spending on coffee but spend millions on hospitality and parties? Do they have the 3hp factor?

How about the character that crosses in front of us at the traffic lights just to go first? How many do the same in different scenarios of daily life and organizations? How about those who decide to pass the line of cars on a highway when all the cars are lined up, waiting to sneak in the moment someone delays their start or causes a second lane to be created and worsens the situation? Has the 3hp factor struck again?

How about those who abuse our name to pretend they are our friends and thus gain support from people who know us? In the office, there are those who frequently say that the boss gave an order that he has never given to get others to do what they need. If one checks with the boss, we will be surprised to hear that the order was never given. Is this not a legitimate 3hp factor?

What can we do to cure this disease? Unite and make demands in the face of abusers who have a high 3hp factor. We can counteract their actions only through solidarity and unity. We must become tough against those who have an elevated 3hp and demand respect from them. Simultaneously, we must make them understand, with courage and strength, that they are not welcome and that their behavior is unacceptable. We must reject them in society and also let others know who the people with a potentially high 3hp are so that they do not infect more people.

If you have a high 3hp factor, you should know that a limited future awaits you. If your 3hp factor is within normal parameters, help us with this noble cause to reduce its expansion and control the illness.

Dependence on the online
or virtual world

How about we turn off the computers for a day? What if we disconnect computers or cell phones from the internet? What if we turn off our cell phones or landlines or if there were no phone service at all? What if we turn off the power supply for a full day? What if there was no TV or if the TV command was damaged or lost? It would be as if we were in a jungle, desert, the middle of the sea, or living after an earthquake or a war. What happens to our work when there is no power, computers, or telephones? Can we continue with the tasks? Does the world temporarily end in that instant? Is productivity impacted? Does the company slow down? Do we have a sabbatical? Can anything be done? Everything we do depends on energy or computers or phones. Is everything virtualized?

These are some questions that help us think about the consequences of not having something that has become essential to many of us.

However, we must acknowledge that some people depend little or not on these things, enjoying a peaceful, less accelerated life.

I remember a friend who once came to my office and nervously told me that the third world war had started. I reassured him and asked him why he thought that. He told me that he had seen on TV that a war had begun in the Middle East. I asked him about his family, and he told me that he had already spoken with everyone and that they were fine. I recommended that he turn off the television and not worry until the war came to Colombia.

It has happened to me before that people could not communicate with me because they did not have cell phone minutes. Others say that they did not have internet the previous night and could not write or complete their task. Some others say that the power went out in their neighborhood and that there was no alternative other than to go to bed to sleep.

What if it happens to you when you are in a bank? The power goes out, and nothing can be done. You have to come back later or the next day. What if the power goes out as one is in the elevator? It has already happened to me, and I was stuck with two other people for over 20 long and dark minutes.

Take a deep breath, and take it easy.

I do not know if this has happened to someone who lives in a building, where power being out also means water being out. That is immensely harder!

What is the learning from this? I do not know about you, dear readers, because that is the idea with my writings—to generate movement of neurons in favor or against but adding value, nonetheless, through reflection. I understand that we should consider the foundations or fundamentals of life and not lose them. Sooner or later, we end up depending on something, and in its absence, we pay the consequences of that dependence. Nowadays, it is difficult not to depend on anything. There are tools or aids that have become indispensable and seem to be addictions. Others will say that you have to have a plan B, if possible.

Others will say that nothing affects them and that what I have just mentioned is not true. Go back to the time when nights were for stargazing or chatting when reading a good book or writing verses by hand used to be extremely enjoyable, in addition to making music with a good traditional instrument.

Candlelight has always generated mystery or charm. Becoming aware of old news, as if they had come by ship and were already history, has another effect on human beings. Going out for a walk, visiting friends at their homes, writing a letter by hand, going to a library, traveling, looking at old photos in albums, and many experiences of this kind can be obsolete or exciting, depending on who criticizes or appreciates them. Was the past better, or is the present better? I do not know. Each moment brings its flavor or its challenge.

Telephones, TVs, computers, and the internet, among others, have revolutionized our way of life, and even video games are now increasingly experiential and, in some cases, almost real. Our current world is richer in information and communications, as well as in tools and facilities.

Distances have shortened. Ages have grown closer. There is much more knowledge sharing, and speeds have increased. There is so much to see and learn that one of the problems is the limited time in the face of so much variety. We have great comforts, and the world, in many areas, strives for balance in our way of life with appliances, cars, airplanes, health, education, or at least with whatever is fundamental, basic, or essential. The big cities are similar in terms of standard facilities. Of course, there are still many people who do not have the minimum standard, but there are increasingly more people who gain access to it.

I do not know where life will take us, but today, it is difficult for people to answer mails or calls, watch TV, or navigate through websites of interest because there are many. They belong to various social networks and several international groups. I do not know how they manage to be in so many places simultaneously. I think the time has come to exercise choice with greater effort and focus because no lifetime can fit so much variety of information, so much opportunity for growth, development, interaction, research, or fun.

My apologies, I must leave you with these reflections because I have to answer some emails.

21

Hiring challenges for those over 40 years old

What if you have been working for more than 20 years for one or two companies, and when you turn 45 years old, you are told that your services are appreciated but you are invited to leave the institution because of reorganization, downsizing, automation, or something of this nature?

What if you neglected yourself, the years passed, and you became obsolete? How is the unemployment situation in the country or the industry or the specialty that you work in? How many young people aged 20 to 25 years do you compete against when seeking a job? How many candidates with more experience will you compete against for the position?

How many of your friends find themselves in this situation or something similar? How many relatives? What solution do you see?

This is a typical, frequent problem nowadays, and even more so in Colombia. The problem is worse if the person is aged 50 years or older, especially for positions from the middle range down. Senior or executive positions have more opportunities because they are reached at these ages, although there are a few positions or opportunities available.

What if you are a woman? Is it easier or more difficult to get a job after reaching 45 years or after 50 years? Something similar happens, but it may be more difficult if the woman's skills are not an exclusive vocation of her sex/gender. There are companies that seek and like to hire women who are the head of the family and have good experience. There are other companies that do not prioritize women in the recruitment process. It all depends on the moment and the circumstances. Nonetheless, it is a bit more difficult for older women to get a job.

Speaking of options and opportunities, it occurs to me that there may be at least three perspectives. The first is that of the company that wants to hire or fire personnel. The second is that of the headhunters who help in the search and selection or collaborate in the management of the exit or transition periods. The third perspective is of those directly involved, the potential employees or the unemployed.

Companies reduce staff to optimize processes, compete more efficiently, reduce costs, or make major reforms in the way they do things. A change in a company's strategic direction can lead to several surplus personnel because many are no longer experienced for the new tasks, a situation which makes it necessary to hire other type of personnel. It may not be easy to retrain or re-educate employees for new assignments. There are times when competition forces a company to make technological improvements to processes and procedures. This cannot wait and therefore causes reductions in personnel.

People over time become "expensive." As they get more experienced, their salary increases and so does their costs. Oftentimes, for the price of one senior employee, a business can hire two or three younger people who are enthusiastic, ready for change and challenges, collaborative, and qualified, albeit lacking experience. If there was an attractive offer of older people with the required profile and the willingness to work for a third of the salary and with the required flexibility, there would be no doubt that companies would hire them. The problem is that this is not the case most of the time.

Meanwhile, headhunters usually offer "fresh," well-screened personnel to their clients, or the clients request them. Therefore, clients pay a good amount of money for active (not unemployed), experienced, and young people between 25 and 35 years.

Headhunters do not offer people over 45 years old because they feel that they may portray a bad image to their customers and, consequently, companies would not rehire them for offering old-fashioned, old, or inactive people. Headhunters are required to work with limited age ranges. If you are over 45 years old, you can forget about a headhunter helping you with an opportunity in a mid-senior position or lower, unless it is an entry-level position that accepts people up until their 50s, or your specialization is such that there is a considerable demand for professionals in the market.

Word of mouth is usually an alternative method for those who seek employment. That is, ask all the people with whom you have a relationship to help you find a job or inform of any available opportunities. It works and is extremely effective sometimes, although it sounds a bit rudimentary. This method is similar to the situation where a person shouts when they perceive danger. By making themselves noticed, the probability that someone will help them increases. The only problem with this method is that we do not know when it may work owing to its informality.

These reflections allow us to think about various alternatives and some limitations in employment. The first idea to analyze is how flexible and friendly or adaptable we are or have become, regardless of our age. Are we the bearers of experience and wisdom? Are we or have we become hostile without noticing? Did we get stubborn? Conversely, are we the finest expression of rapid adaptability to all kinds of situations and people? Are we flexible? Do we positively accept that others think and act differently from what we believe to be correct or adequate or appropriate? Do we respect the ideas of others? Do we buy them? Do we make a joke of everything, and does nothing affect us emotionally? Are we in a good mood 100% of the time, regardless of whatever they say or whatever happens? Do we let others win frequently? Does it bother us to work day or night or on weekends? Does it bother us to work with younger bosses, either women or men?

The truth is that I have had to witness how several people over 40 years old are difficult to deal with in a modern, new ,or uncomplicated environment. Many times, I see that people in this age group are full of precautions, very procedural, irascible, complex, and distrustful. They possess the wisdom and accuracy in

99% of the cases, and the remaining 1% is subject to verification. They are excessively careful and reluctant to change or negotiate a position in which they do not come out on top.

The closer a person gets to 50 years old, the more difficult it is for them to deal with 25-year-old coworkers who seem irreverent, risky, messy, careless, rude, not very serious, and irresponsible.

There are few exceptions of people over 40 who retain the flexibility to learn from others, stay updated, enjoy the enthusiasm of youth, and work with the energy and speed of young people. Few fear failure or trying new ways of doing things. Few can stay up late, work on Saturdays and Sundays, and not fear moving forward despite not having the necessary knowledge or experience.

Now, let us talk about what they are willing to do at that age of 40 or 50 years and over. Will they accept an intern position? Are they ready to start from scratch? Would they work for a third or a fifth of the salary they had earned in their previous job? Young people switch from one job to another with no problem, and it is not difficult for them to start over because each new job is a rich experience that they can use to their advantage. For young people, everything is a learning experience, and as long as the salary is decent or reasonable, they do not worry too much about it. Those over 45 or 50 years old want the employer to pay them for the lifestyle that they are used to leading. Moreover, they consider their experience to be extremely valuable, which makes them expensive, at least two times more than young people.

Unemployment increases for people over 40 or 50 years old because they do not realize that each new work experience requires, in general, a willingness to start over from almost zero. Only a few get a job similar to the one they just left, and some get a better opportunity than before. As for the rest, if they do not moderate their requirements and become more flexible in their attitude and the way they relate to others, it will be difficult for them to find employment.

The point is simple: a person starts over in a new job, and over time, goes back to climbing positions by merit. Let us say that one person is useful because of their experience. Soon, they will begin to excel in tasks undertaken, and the recognition and rewards will not take long to come. However, these are not given in the first five minutes of a new job and even less in an interview.

I prefer to recommend people to erase from their minds the history of their many years tied to a job and start over from scratch with poise such that if things turn out as they wish or dream, everything will go well. If only minor opportunities appear, then they will not miss out on them.

Remember that there is nothing more destabilizing than being unemployed for many months and not having money. It is better to have a humble job with which one can buy essentials. It is better to have a humble job that allow us to sleep without so much stress, having confidence that something new or better may come along, but without feeling distressed. Therefore, in our 40s or 50s, a bird in the hand is worth two in the bush!

These reflections ought to lead us to demand more from ourselves as people and professionals because the competition is increasingly tough. For each job opportunity, 100 or more qualified people show up, and the best and least expensive candidate is chosen, unless one has a specialization that is hard to find, which ensures a long business life and is especially appealing in the market, regardless of the age (i.e., deep technical knowledge). The rest have to compete with young people who are more updated, have twice the desire, and do not have limits or vices. Additionally, hiring young people brings only a third of the cost of hiring an older worker. They have an immense capacity to adapt to new environments and have no problem being managed by a young male or female executive, as frequently occurs nowadays.

The positive aspect of this, apart from knowing that we have to stay updated, well-trained, flexible, adaptable, and economical to be able to be reemployed, is that if we do not find an opportunity after our 40s, we have no other choice than to assume our independence and establish our own business. In the long run, this helps create jobs and supports the country's growth. Every effort is welcome.

Many of us who have faced the challenge of becoming independent have ended up becoming entrepreneurs, with tremendous sacrifice and even pain, and without it being part of our objectives. We became entrepreneurs because of life circumstances and out of necessity.

The problem with entrepreneurship is that many fail. Those who do succeed remember to hire those over 40 years old. They offer an opportunity for start-up companies because they are already trained, and they can negotiate themselves at a reasonable cost if they are made aware of their condition. Most end up being extremely grateful to the organizations that give them the opportunity of starting a new business life, after going through the urgencies that unemployment brings. Older employees ultimately understand that the key is to have a decent job, stay active, and feel useful.

In short, there are lessons and challenges for everyone involved.

Companies should reconsider hiring those over 40 years old as long as they have the experience and are flexible and affordable. Headhunters should propose the alternative of using "seniors" more often as a "standard bonus" to the shortlist that they always present to their clients. Those over 40 years old must be willing to start over with the significant enthusiasm, flexibility, and strength of 25-year-olds. They should remember that they must be competitive in salary pricing.

If we rush to change, we will soon make those in their 40s and 50s more desirable, as is the case in many developed countries, where even retirees are an exquisite business commodity.

22

Sales, everyone's challenge

How many times have we dreamed of having an extraordinary sales manager? How many times have we wanted to be that outstanding sales manager? What would our company, department, or results look like if we had the "star" sales manager in our team? How much would we give to that sales manager for giving us the results we dream about? Conversely, other questions arise when sales do not happen or are unsatisfactory, complicated, or doubtful.

Great salesmen or saleswomen are considerably difficult to find or develop. When they are found, it is extremely difficult to retain them or keep them motivated because they are insatiable and volatile. They fear nothing and have a high level of self-confidence.

Great salespeople are people without limits. They go straight for the goal and achieve it with a high degree of creativity before each difficulty or obstacle. Their lives are hectic and full of hyperactivity. They are clear about who is first on their way to glory and decide everything around it. They are dangerously aggressive people and, simultaneously, great actors who handle diverse scenarios exceptionally. People who sell the most are admired and loved by almost everyone except by other salespeople who envy and hate them as they see them as competition in their careers.

Those who possess these characteristics or are sufficiently close to them are a kind of James Bond, agent 007, in sales. Successful salespeople stake it all every minute. Either they win the business, or they lose even their honor. There are no intermediate conditions when you are a "007" of sales. They always outperform results, regardless of the difficulty level.

I have known people who have managed to go to more than 35 sales conventions without missing any goals. That is, they have achieved the unthinkable, meeting every year all their sales quotas with excellence. They are impressive people and extremely sensitive to money and big challenges. They do not argue, only focus, make plans, and masterfully execute their sales tasks. They never, or rarely, fail. They are like a billiard expert who never misses a carom or a bowling expert who always rolls a strike. That is evident in them from the beginning.

It is beneficial for the company to have a "007" salesperson on the team, but it is clear that managing them is difficult and risky as well. Many times, we do not know what is better or worse: the incredible sales that these people bring to the company or the headaches that they generate in their daily conflicts with other team members and the management of their variable moods. The most stable, level-headed, and well-organized salespeople transition with some ease toward general management because this requires a well-rounded and self-controlled person who knows how to manage their overflowing energy adequately. Management can rest assured because these people can put everyone to work on their clients and the company itself without being anyone's boss. They have PhDs in management. In any case, good sales bring money to the business and overshadow the details related to management and variability, which are accepted or forgiven.

I still remember the example of the salesman who arrived after a late night, poorly dressed and with a drunken stink to work. His boss came out to fire him for violating the rules of the code of conduct and was surprised to find out that the salesman had stayed up late celebrating the signing of a multimillion dollar contract with a client, which he immediately handed over to his boss upon hearing the voice of authority. The excited boss decided to congratulate the employee and send him home to rest for a couple of days, as an anticipated reward for his heroism, to the astonishment of the rest of the members of the department. Of course, this story is more of a legend than reality, but it serves to demonstrate the anesthetic effect that contracts signed for a good sum of money have, as long as the business deal has been managed effectively.

Another person once said that the best sponsor you can have in life is "Mr. Results," and in most cases, this is true. Good results in the sales field allow permanence and give a strong voice and vote in many settings. People listen to and care more for this person. It is a matter of common sense. Even in serious offenses, some degree of attenuation is noted when considering the salesperson's historical success.

The bad or the good thing about this fascinating world of sales and management is the volatility of the results. Once a month, a quarter, or a year of work ends, everything becomes a past result, and the only thing that counts is the sales that are yet to be made. In this sense, I remember meeting a previous boss. It was January 2, and I reminded him of the extraordinary way in which I had closed the year, having sold 450% of my sales quota, and expressed to them the happiness that I felt. He looked at me in the eye and said, "I congratulate you, but that was last year. You have not sold anything this year yet, so stop dreaming and remembering old triumphs and get to work!"

Every good salesperson, the "007," fulfills extreme missions with prowess, which makes us think that they are worthy of admiration. However, we must not forget that this person has exceptional or extraordinary abilities that are incredible when they are used against the competition. Nevertheless, they are seriously dangerous when their feelings or objectives change, and they strike against us. In this regard, we must never forget that salespeople and sales managers are a group of "beasts," like lions and tigers, and although they look friendly and powerful or calm on certain occasions, they are still fierce. If given the opportunity or hungry, they can eat rabbits or giraffes. They can even kill the trainer who taught and cared for them or has known them forever.

I coined a phrase, the result of a book and a novel, and the phrase has acquired certain fame for its peculiarity. I changed it and made it positive for companies and mnemonics when we talk about sales. At a company where there are no sales, things become problematic, and the environment becomes seriously tense. Administrative and personnel difficulties are managed with some ease and facility when there is an abundance of sales, but without them, all activities become complicated: banks, referrals, hiring, and even business changes. Without sales, we get a desert-like environment; only cacti and camels can survive.

That is why I want to close this reflection with my phrase:

"Without sales, there is no paradise."

23

Executive assistant for various errands, All-in-one

We have one or more "all-in-ones" in the house, and they are also abundant in companies because of their usefulness.

There are partial or specialized "all-in-ones," which are the most commonly used and the most effective. There are "all-in-ones" with a broad spectrum of uses (the really good ones are very scarce) and almost infinite utility. I am going to give you a domestic example first so that we can get used to the importance and true meaning of the "all-in-ones."

What if we wake up in the morning and need breakfast for six people, but we do not have milk, fruit, juice, bread, coffee, or chocolate, and we only have two eggs? Who would save us? An "all-in-one" or an assistant who will run the errands for us and buy what we need. While we shower, the "all-in-one" can prepare breakfast, set the dining room table, make us all happy, and then wash the dishes and organize the kitchen to leave it as it was. This is then an "all-in-one" with four effective functions: runs errands, cooks, washes, and organizes.

In the house, there are triphasic "all-in-ones" that wash, iron, and clean. A husband at home is an "all-in-one" of various services, like a boy scout's knife (12 services, including saw, spoon, and fork).

An "all-in-one" in an office or company is the one who helps with the electricity, plumbing, errands (courier), car maintenance, and general maintenance (e.g., paints, fixes faulty appliances, fixes damaged walls).

There are two problems with the "all-in-ones." The first is that they are on the way to extinction because of specialization. It is similar to what is happening to doctors who have become so specialized that once I called our neighbor, who was a gynecologist and obstetrician, to help us because our son had a stomachache, to which he suggested, "Call a doctor or go to a hospital." I wondered, but is the neighbor not a doctor? It turns out that his specialization made him amnesiac and fearful to the point where if it is not his area of specialization, he will not attend the case. They call that professional responsibility.

The second problem with the "all-in-ones" is the opposite scenario to the one above because they are "generalists," and they do not do a single job well. Consequently, good "all-in-ones" are scarce and expensive, and whoever has one does not let them go. A friend of mine is, for example, a good multifunctional husband, an "all-in-one," and therefore, his wife does not recommend him to her friends. Wives are "all-in-ones," but they perform the tasks well and simultaneously (there are those who say otherwise). They are "stereophonic," while husbands do the tasks individually, making them "monophonic."

As they say, "Jack of all trades, master of none." The great disadvantage of the "all-in-one," whether at the office or at home, is that they perform the tasks with flaws. You have to discuss and clarify details to ensure the task is conducted satisfactorily. You have to provide every detail stepwise because the all-in-one may not have an imagination. If they do, they become a real danger.

I remember the constant explanations that the administrative and financial head had to give to the "all-in-one" in the office. She complained that he was distracted, did not present the accounts of the cash advances for transportation, did not present the invoices that helped justify the expense of the petty cash, and did not take advantage of the day because he did not program the tasks and their sequence well. Further, he did as he willed and did not listen to instructions and performed a poor task because he had not paid attention to what was being asked. Thus, each task had to be redone two or three times.

The "all-in-ones" have a special virtue: despite everything, people are fond of them because they are extremely kind owing to their natural limitations. If they were extraordinary, they would be our bosses, people say. People quickly note that an "all-in-one" is full of limitations, but mostly, they are very willing to perform services or tasks, regardless of what these may involve, even if they have no experience or idea of how to conduct such tasks. It is almost always a character who says to himself, "Let us see if I can do it," while he says to the boss, "Do not worry about what you need. Leave it to me."

The frequent failures of the "all-in-ones" upset their naive or trusting users, who are moved by their willingness to provide service and forgive them repeatedly in the hope that, in the future, they will stop making mistakes and perform the tasks well, even if they have to be repeated many times. This ends up costing time and money or trying the patience of everyone in the company or at home.

An "all-in-one" is like a "permanent adolescent" who believes that they can do everything. However, in reality, their disposition, lack of depth, lack of experience, and willingness to accept challenging tasks causes them to perform only half of what they say or think they can do. The trouble is that, mostly, they speak with authority and absolute conviction about what they think they can do or they know. Therein lies the risk and the source of the difficulties that later arise.

A friend has had several experiences with all kinds of "all-in-ones" he had hired throughout his life. One ended up damaging several office telephones. Another destroyed two cars. Another broke several decorative sculptures in the office. Another "ate" the money that it was given to pay some bills, and then it got "lost," leaving my friend in disbelief when his public utilities were cut off due to late payment. Another used to take his friends and family for rides in the car. To conceal the trips, this "all-in-one" said he was running time-consuming errands or procedures that ended up taking him all day. Another used so much transportation in the week, using up the company's petty cash, and the excuse was that he got lost in the city. He also "lost" invoices or payments or his suitcase with papers and money. Another damaged lamps, doors, locks, taps, and walls by being electrician, locksmith, plumber, and painter.

A friend reported so much loss with her house "all-in-ones." One broke her dinner set. Others destroyed the pots, used cleaning liquids on furniture, damaging the paint, broke several fine porcelain pieces, burned several of her husband's shirts, killed the ornamental plants by watering them every day, lost the cutlery frequently, bleached the color out of the bed covers and clothes, finished off the stock of food for the month in just 15 days, and no one knew where so much food ended up. Another made confetti that was in the room for visitors disappear. Another was bad with electrical appliances. Further, another would usually end up with handles in its hand or would manage to detach cabinet doors, bathroom faucets, or dishwasher parts.

The most surprising thing about everything I have detailed thus far is that when you ask an "all-in-one" about their faults, they allege that they have no explanation for the occurrence. Many times, it seems as if a ghost or bad luck follows them.

In any case, an "all-in-one" is a "necessary evil." Without them, either because of the tasks that they perform well or because of those at which they fail, the happiness and tranquility of the office or home are significantly affected given that the tasks left undone end up with the bosses, who are sent into despair and rage. No one can ensure the bosses' resulting foul temper for more than a week.

It is preferable to become upset or deal with the "all-in-one" than to put up with a grumpy boss every day.

I intentionally leave this reflection here to let your imagination fly, dear reader. May you find many more cases of one or another "all-in-one" in your daily life or your surroundings. May you find the true value of your closest all-in-one.

24

The appearance wizards

A famous phrase comes to my mind: "Caesar's wife must be above suspicion." In other words, it was not enough to be Caesar's wife. When people saw her, they had to believe. This lady must be Cesar's wife because that is the impression she gives based on what she says, how she looks, and how she behaves.

In all my years, I still have not learned to "seem more than what I am." I am who I am, and I like it, but I know that there are people who want to appear as something they are not, and they succeed.

In business and daily life, I have taken my hat off many times in front of characters, applauding them for being "masters of appearance," or "appearance wizards," because their performance skills were off the charts.

These famous performance characters seemed to only follow the second part of the saying on Caesar's wife, "It must seem…"

In terms of real, everyday life, I remember a couple who lived in an extraordinary, modern apartment. Each had a recent-model Mercedes with a powerful engine; beautiful, imported, branded clothes; expensive shoes; and great jobs in renowned companies. One day, the couple got into a fight and ultimately separated. Months later, I had the opportunity to speak with one of them; I found that as a result of the separation, they had sold their cars, the apartment, and the rest of their possessions and paid their debts, and each only had enough left to buy a pair of cheap sports shoes.

I have several examples from my work life that are worth sharing and analyzing owing to their different nuances.

An executive in a multinational company was promoted, thanks to his ability to deliver elegant presentations supported by half-truths that made them credible and to prepare good summaries of the meetings he attended (having the last word was his contribution). These two qualities, along with his serious and penetrating gaze that seemed to say, "shut up, stay out of this, do not say a word, I do not like interruptions," made him rise in the international hierarchies until he became a powerful vice president. The interesting thing about this man is that he never reached his annual objectives. With the abovementioned qualities, he convinced his bosses of the efforts he had made to resolve any impossibilities and made them value his poor results as something outstanding (he almost made people cry), given the circumstances faced. This executive was and is an "appearance wizard."

I also remember a co-worker when I began my managerial career in a large company. He always invested his salary in buying the best clothes, ties, and shoes for himself. He believed that a person should always demonstrate great presence to gain ground in any conversation (others always felt inferior in his overwhelming presence). During World War II, he said, the well-dressed Nazis in their dazzling uniforms and boots made the Jews, who wore dirty, threadbare clothing, feel inferior in the concentration camps.

My colleague had another "maxim." Every time his bosses or a client asked him about a task, he would always answer emphatically and enthusiastically, "The task is done. Let me know if you have any comments." He would then turn to whisper to me, "I need to run to complete the task. The truth is that I have not done it, but I will do it without them realizing that I had forgotten. It's all good." Lying with authority, strength, and conviction is one of the components of "keeping appearances."

What about the typical employee whose good ear is capable of perceiving someone coming from far, and they immediately start acting like they are working, even though all the other colleagues know that they were distracted with other unrelated activities? This reminds me of when I was in school, in one of those intervals between classes. Students engaged in the chalk war and other games.

Remember the typical asker? Every day, first thing in the morning, they would ask everyone a question and force people to do some work for them, as a favor. Once they have everyone doing something and made their presence felt, they leave and are not seen again until the next day, when they ask everyone for explanations, ask more questions, and order more work. This typical company actor believes that they are the generator of movement and the master of questions, but they do not contribute much to the actual work. This person is not even the boss.

Well, I will leave to your imagination other "appearance wizards," who, as shown thus far, work well for years without any obvious performance, except those who maintain appearances.

Behind the scenes, as they say in theater, the people who spend every day with the "appearance wizards" know them well and are aware that they are pure appearance. The bad part is that hardly anyone says something to expose the impostor. I think that another quality of these "appearance wizards" is to generate fear in their collaborators or in the people closest to them so that they do not give them away or, on the contrary, make them feel sorry. This is why they do not betray the "appearance wizards."

If you want to unmask the "appearance wizards," talk to the people who work under them, to their assistants, or to those in the lower ranks. You will be surprised to discover that what you believed to be true was only just appearance.

-25-

How much do I owe you?

I do not know if this has ever happened to you, dear reader, but it is very common to find people whom you have helped or supported, or for whom you have done some kind of professional or personal favor, and then once the deed is done, we still end up owing them.

We are talking about the "parasnobs," a cross between a parasite and a snob. They never lose and never appreciate a favor, because they think that everyone should do them hundreds of favors. Anything that happens to them or around them is anyone else's fault but their own. They never take responsibility for anything. They have never failed.

Such obnoxious people believe that their vision of the world and life is governed by rules that allow for "reverse engineering with opposite effect" (sounds great). In other words, they reconstruct everything, but in reverse. White is black, and black is white.

Let's consider a few examples. Two friends who have not seen each other in several months meet up, and the parasnob says to the other, "You have abandoned me. You have not called or written to me. You are a very bad friend." (Even though they are both in the same situation, the other loses from the get-go.)

The parasnob who borrowed money says to the person who lent it, "Because of you, I am in debt; you should have never lent me. You are a bad person. Look at what you have done to me. You have tormented me all these past months. You have caused me great harm. Your bad faith compelled you to orchestrate this crossroad, did it not? You just want to see me on my knees because of your money."

Some such people have come to surprise me, like the one who says, "We have not met up because you have never invited me for dinner or breakfast. When will you deign to do so?" The truth is that neither has ever extended an invitation to the other. They also tell the person who invited them once, "You did not invite me again. That speaks very negatively of you. You are becoming careless and stingy." The very person criticizing the other has never extended an invitation themselves.

The most infamous ones at work and in everyday life are those who say, "Because of you, this happened to me." "Why didn't you tell me?" "Why didn't you stop me?" "You should have reminded me." "You made me forget what I was going to say." "You scared me." "You convinced me." "You provoked me." "You confused me." "Because of you, I am mixed up in this." "You sold me out." "You betrayed me." "You do not trust me." "You have not given me a chance." "You want to trick me."

116

Anything that happens to such people is blamed on the country, government, boss, job, company, colleagues, project, task, objectives, system, clients, engineers, budget, laws or rules, religion, politics, friends, family, bad weather, good weather, abundance, scarcity, and so on.

The truth is that I have learned to avoid them, not necessarily to handle them. It is as if I have smeared oil all over my body so that their accusatory phrases or words slip right off. I do not respond to them. I ignore them. They do not exist.

They are bad-tempered. I do not like to come across them in my life or professional path; they are undesirable. If we take them seriously, they will make us feel bad, and we may begin to believe them. As per their classification, anyone is flawed. On a scale of 1 to 10, we all score less than 4 based on their criteria. Answering them logically only results in more aggression because they always have the last word.

The parasnobs are like gods. They think that the world should revolve around them, and they expect everyone to act accordingly, as if they were the boss or a celebrity that everyone wants to or must attend to. They will never perform an action without demanding recognition from others. That is why we will always be the sinner or guilty party, either by omission or by acting against them. We are the ones who should call them, invite them, attend to them, and take care of them. If not, we are guilty of being indifferent and rude. Remember, they are the center of attention. They are the important ones, and the rest of us are like their servants, and sometimes, we even seem like their slaves.

There is a good number of such notorious figures in business who seek to make life impossible or unpleasant for others with the way they think and act. There are people who make the mistake of paying attention to them and suffer because of it.

How do we deal with parasnobs? As mentioned earlier, the best way is to ignore them. Another is to figuratively smear ourselves with oil so that everything they say or do slips right off without hurting us. You have to perceive them as people who have a mental illness or who have never matured, or naughty children, and handle them as such.

If you are a parasnob, I do not care what you think about this reflection. If you have any comments, I assure you that I will not take them into account, because, for me, you do not exist.

Do presidents provide support or complicate things?

D o not even think about counting on the president, a friend once said to me.

But why? The president is the highest authority in a company. Presidents are the ones who give the instructions and orders. They are the ones who say what gets done, and how and when. They are the ones who give authorization, and ultimately, they are the leading voice, the one almost always with the last word.

Things are not the way you say they are, he told me. Presidents complicate everything. They have to enforce the rules and follow the procedures to the letter. They have to set an example. They have a harder time making exceptions. They authorize or reject potential options or risks or extraordinary situations, but they cannot self-authorize the exceptions; they have to go to the board of directors or the shareholders.

People listen to the president, and then each person does what they want while making the president believe that they are the person in charge. Under the president, another world is in motion—the world of possibility, the real world.

How many people have gone to the big boss's office to tell them that what the boss wanted or how they wanted it could not be executed exactly per their expectations, but a good approximation was accomplished with a similar, better, and cheaper solution. In other words, something else was done.

This can happen at home as well. The husband believes that his orders are carried out, and that is a lie. The wife, as well as the children, are the ones in charge, and the will of the father or husband is the last to be fulfilled, although he believes otherwise.

I remember I once told a friend that I knew a couple of notaries, and he mentioned that he had two friends who were at the third level at two different notary offices and that it was possible to streamline any procedure more effectively with them than with the notaries. It made me feel bad when he indicated that it was better to have mid-level managers as friends than top-level managers. Up until that moment, I had thought that it was essential to have acquaintances in high positions because one day they may be useful.

Based on these and similar experiences, I decided to create this quote: "If you want to use the power of the top-level management, you must first work the mid-level management."

An example is when the general manager tells a middle manager to look at a solution that they find interesting or useful for the company. That solution will not get anywhere. If the middle manager does not bring the idea to the top management for approval, the project will not take off, be delayed, or present problems. This is a curious matter wherein no one acts in bad faith or with bad intentions. It is human and natural. If a person has not bought an idea, it will be hard for them to bring it to fruition later.

In modern companies that practice participatory democracy, it is necessary to involve people from the beginning and let them come up with ideas so that they can work on the details. If the ideas come cut and dried from above, they might rebound because they are considered an imposition on middle management, which has, or believes to have, the power to formulate and choose the solutions that are under its direct competence or responsibility.

In matters of modern management, it is crucial to "be and appear to be" participatory in manner, in order to smoothly carry out projects.

In today's world, forced imposition does not work in our own homes. If you do not believe me, try imposing something on your partner or your children and watch their reaction.

The days when orders were given in companies, like in the military, and obeyed blindly by those with some management responsibility are ending. There are still companies that operate by the method of force, and their managers are true emperors, but they are fortunately becoming a minority. Of course, there are still great bosses who manage by generating fear in others and threatening with punishment or dismissal, but laws and styles have changed, and this has gradually become less frequent or less possible.

Going back to the point on middle and senior management, the conclusion is that both are needed if you want a project to be approved or streamlined. However, the order of the factors does alter the final product and, therefore, the project should be initiated from the bottom up and complemented from the top down. If the order is reversed and one knows how to work middle management, then we can facilitate things at the highest level. In this sense, it is useful to have access to the president.

Taking issue with a middle manager who does not want to allow the execution of tasks or projects because they did not bring them to the table or propose them can be a bumpy ride. One can accomplish something, but it would be necessary to climb to the top tier every time until the middle manager gives up. In any case, it is always better to avoid conflicts and better to develop an effective and close relationship with the middle management so that you can sell them a project and have them lead it.

Meanwhile, if we have already done the work with the middle management, access to the senior management (president) is also important because they are the ones who are going to give the go-ahead for the initiative presented by the middle management, and this is where reinforcements are important. Without a well-oiled middle management, a project or initiative will not take off at the highest speed and give the best possible result. Nonetheless, without the support of the senior management, a brilliant initiative may be left in the pipeline owing to lack of priority or budget.

It does not matter where we are—the manager or the supplier side. This reflection is key to understanding how to take advantage of the structures.

–27–

The reality is different. Very different.

There are experiences that demonstrate that reality is often contrary to what one imagines.

A colleague lived more than an hour and a half away from town, and for more than 10 years made efforts to manage his time and money to arrive always on time at the required destination, even if he needed to attend a meeting at 7 AM.

One fine day, his boss spoke privately and confidentially with my colleague's wife. She told him about the efforts her husband had made for many years to fulfill his work obligations. To improve my colleague's work conditions, the boss decided that from the following day onward, my colleague could arrive at work at 9 AM a particular location.

My colleague felt bad that his schedule and location were changed, and he interpreted this move as a threat to his job. Irritated and bewildered, he submitted his resignation and left the company.

My colleague did not allow himself to be helped but instead felt attacked by the change and left with a high degree of dissatisfaction with the company and his boss. He never told his wife his reasons for quitting.

This seems unbelievable, but it is true.

A friend accidentally bumped his car into his neighbor's. To avoid discussions, since his car had not suffered any damage, he told the neighbor that he was very sorry for what had happened. Given that it had only been a small scratch, my friend asked the neighbor to have it fixed and then send the bill, which my friend would reimburse.

The neighbor showed up 15 days later saying that he had gotten the car fixed and that, among other things, the car was not his but rather belonged to the company for which he worked. When he took it to the workshop, they had found more damage and mismatches in the car's body, and for this reason, the repair had cost the equivalent of USD 1,000. The neighbor gave my friend the invoice, which only specified the total value for the bodywork and paint, without any details regarding the repairs.

After a long and heated discussion, my friend paid the neighbor the equivalent of USD 500 (the most expensive scratch in the world), and they ended the matter. The neighbor was dissatisfied for not having received all the money for the bill he presented and because my friend did not trust him.

It was clear that the company had fixed the dent on my friend's neighbor's car, and that person had taken advantage of the trust placed in him to make a good amount of money for himself and also pretend to be offended.

Another friend's car was hit when it was parked in a public parking lot. Whoever did it had a BMW X5 SUV and despite the obvious damage done to my friend's new car, which would have cost the equivalent of USD 900 to fix, decided to play the poor, moody, and impatient driver who only had about USD 90. Since they had already moved the SUV and there were no witnesses, they forced my friend to accept the money offered, or get nothing at all. At least USD 90 was better than nothing.

On one occasion, a person managed to stay a little over a year in a friend's organization, telling lies about the tasks he performed, such as visiting prospective clients and following up on the proposals that he would submit to them. When the organization realised that, instead of proposing and visiting prospective clients and followed up on opportunities, the person disappeared. Not only did he leave the company in some difficulties owing to the negative effect on its image and the defaults with certain clients but he also took loans from several colleagues, alleging that he had a terrible emergency that he would resolve within a few days and compensate them generously for their support during that difficult time. They still do not know where to find him.

How many of you have lived or witnessed something similar? How many of you have changed the way you relate to people and have become cautious and distrustful as a consequence? Such cases transform people and make them close the doors of trust and turn them into protective walls against bad intentions and deception. Is the world in the hands of the bad guys or the good guys? Will the righteous pay for the sinners most of the time? In business and all organizations, we are exposed to similar situations. This is real life. This is the diversity we have, and we have to learn how to manage it without excessive naiveté or mistrust.

In this world, everything is possible, the good and the bad, the predictable and the unusual, transparency or deception, fair play and foul play. In the four aforementioned examples, my friends showed weakness in their decision making and in the handling of unexpected situations. In the first case, the decision made to benefit my friend was not communicated directly to him to make him aware of the advantages. Meanwhile, the employee decided to act rashly without thinking about the consequences or what motivated the change, letting himself be driven by emotion (emotion and decisions usually make for a dangerous, explosive bomb).

In the second case concerning the collision with the neighbor, it would have been better to go through the formal procedures. Informality leaves the door open for others to take advantage of the opportunity. Had my friend required the formal procedure, the result would have been different. The closer a person is, the greater the risk that they will take advantage of you.

In the third case, the parking lot crash has the characteristic of informality as well as the pressure of time, bad mood, and threats. Decisions must be made by taking a moment to pause amid the urgency. In such situations, ask for time to think and decide what is best. Taking a momentary pause disorients the opponent and improves your vision. Demand formality and do not cave into pressure. You were attacked. You take charge.

In the case involving the infiltrator who took advantage of the company, we have to be demanding in the selection process, by verifying references. There is nothing better than verifying the actions and results of new hires. The organization should not let go of the person until there is evidence of their behavior and reliable results.

We have to learn to navigate life and analyze human beings in different organizations. By understanding how to interpret each person's code, we can relate to others without risk, and we can even cultivate productive relationships or maintain a prudent distance.

Our future is determined favorably or unfavorably by the speed of our reaction to the new or unexpected and balanced way in which we assess the situation and make decisions in a moment of pressure.

Take a quiet minute in the heat of urgent matters and see how results improve. Like in basketball or volleyball games, ask for a time out. Ask for it. Give it to them.

28

You are the only one

You are the only one.

How many times have you been told this beautiful phrase in your life? How many times have you been made to feel like "the only one"? How many times have you believed that you were truly the only one?

I know that I made you reflect for a moment and even seriously question the truth. As they say, can so much beauty be real?

I remember the girlfriend I had when I was a teenager; she made me feel that I was the only one. I was, until the day I discovered her with another guy she had been going out with for more than a year. Her method was simple. She would demand dates and calls while keeping the boyfriends at bay. She would demand that we see or call each other every day, but the most interesting thing is that she would get upset whenever she would ask me if I could visit her that same day or the next, or the day after next, only to find that it was not possible because of study commitments. With that simple method, she could make a person feel like a failure or with limitations or as if they lacked desire or quality, while she was always ready for anything. It was her ingenious way of finding out when each of her boyfriends could actually visit her so that she could make preparations accordingly. It was great disappointment to find out the truth, but thankfully, it happened early in my life. What if that happens when you are in your 30s or 40s or 50s?

In the business context, it is a mandatory form of operation—you have to make everyone feel as if they are the only one. We all know that this is not the case, but we love to think that it might be. The good thing is that in business, no one bothers to check if they really are the only one or if there are ten others.

You may be asking yourself at this moment where or how this phenomenon that you have not identified occurs. The answer is very simple. The phenomenon occurs in almost every business activity.

Let us talk about clients. Have you ever been a client? Would you like to know that you are one of millions of clients? Would you like to feel like one of the masses, that is, generic? Let us start to understand the phrase, "You are the only one."

Every client deserves and wants to feel like they are cared for, appreciated, and pampered, as if they were "the only one." They come first, and the others have to wait. Have you noticed that vendors always offer you something exclusive, something special, something unique, something only for you? How many times have you felt that the discount you were given was not offered to anyone else? Your client will buy from you when you make them feel that they are offered something so exclusive, that they will be the first to receive the benefit of your product or service, that no one else before received the same good deal. Afterwards, thousands may receive the same benefit, but they will be behind you. "Whoever pays sets the conditions." This means for clients to be treated as if they are the only one, offered one-of-a-kind prices, one-of-a-kind services, one-of-a-kind quality.

What can we say about the bosses? In companies, each boss is "unique." When a boss gives an order, they assume that one has no other priority than to comply. For example, the boss does not check the schedules of their employees or subordinates or check the availability of their work team. They simply schedule a meeting whenever they want or can, and the others have to accommodate it. I feel sorry for the one who comes up with an excuse, because they do not understand that the boss likes to know that they are and feel like "the only one," even if clients are made to wait a little bit and the other hundred tasks have to be paused because of the unexpected meeting.

How about when we call the secretary to request an appointment with their important boss? What if you made them feel like one of the secretaries at the institution? The secretary is the boss's boss. Treat them as such. They are unique in the country, on the planet, in the galaxy, and in the universe. Poor you if you do not make them feel that way.

In the office, we all depend on others. One day you might need someone, no matter how junior their position is, to perform an urgent or crucial task for you. When that day comes, you will remember this reflection and apply the phrase, "You are unique," because, otherwise, your task will not get done on time. You will explain to the person that your future depends on them and that everything you have done in life will fall apart if they do not lend a hand and help you or if they do not abandon everything to assist you immediately. You will not skimp on kind and respectful phrases. You will watch the tone of your voice and even make the kind of promises that turn out to be expensive in the end. The truth is that the person you are depending on is unique. Otherwise, the task that you need could get done by someone else, and you would not be there begging in front of that person.

What about the company?

Do not even think about saying that there are better ones. You cannot look at the competition except to figure out how to gain business from them. You have to be loyal to the cause. You have to be as faithful as in a marriage. When you signed the employment contract, you practically promised and swore to give your life to the company (it may not seem that way to you because a contract is a contract), and this is what is expected of you. The company wants you to feel like it is the only one—like you have to live for it. You have to go to sleep thinking about your future in it. You have to wake up thinking about what you can do for it. Any plans not related to it conflict with it; you have to take your vacations as dictated by the company. If you dare say that your company is not unique, you will quickly see the trouble you will be in. While we are working as employees at a company, we have to work with the team and break our backs so that the team does well, because that will make the company and its owners happy and so we will also be happy.

Well, my dear reader, I hope that this short journey through the philosophical and practical importance of the phrase, "you are the only one," has been enlightening and reflective, even if I have not covered all the possible examples that you may have in mind. Remember that everything I wrote here is… just for you.

29

To great and frequent changes. Prudence makes true, wise people

Every day, we experience many changes across all areas of life and worldwide. Faced with change, people react very differently to their situations.

Let us say a fire suddenly breaks out in a building, and to make things more dramatic, let us say the fire starts on the 13th floor. There are people who, realizing the situation, would become completely paralyzed and not be able to speak, think, move, or walk. Other people would simply take the quickest and weakest route, which is to disconnect from the situation and probably faint. Nervous people might act as if they are a battery-powered bumper car zipping around everywhere, tripping over everything, and running to others without a definite plan and generally without positive results. One of the most common reactions is hysteria, where people scream until they have no voice left and are out of breath and strength, letting themselves fall gently on the floor. There are also the fatalists whose despair leads them to the conclusion that they would rather lose their life on their own terms rather than get burnt in a fire and decide to break the glass window and throw themselves into the void to end the problem. Finally, to extend the story further, there are the brave, patient people who calmly observe everything happening around them and effortlessly measure the risk while calculating the impact of people's despair. They then devise a plan that allows them to organize those left behind and find a way out, ensuring the evacuation of everyone from the building injury-free and alive.

When there is change, people like to be prepared. Perhaps that is why the phrase "get up early for change" was used a lot in the past, as a way to anticipate future phenomena. The idea was to perform mental exercises of intuition and anticipation to prevent change rather than manage it. Although "getting up early for change" is healthy, predictions do not always come true in real life. Life is more like the phrase, "It does not matter how early you wake up in the morning, the dawn will not come earlier." That is, we will still have to face and manage a good number of changes, since it is not possible to anticipate them or plan our reactions.

If everything I have said about change is true, a question immediately arises: What is the best advice on how to react when an avalanche of change falls on a person? I prefer to answer by using an excellent example in the management of change when it occurs suddenly and in great proportions.

Let us assume that a plane falls in the middle of the jungle, and a few minutes after the impact, you are the only survivor. Faced with a predicament as dramatic as this one, I assure you that the long introductory paragraph of this reflection has come to mind, and for a moment, you would go through several reactions that are very similar to those of the people in the burning building. If you manage to stay calm, after everything, the first thing you will do is try to begin to understand where you are and what condition you are in by carefully observing everything around you. You will feel motivated to enhance the capacity of all your senses and understand the new rules of the game that you are now playing to get out of the jungle alive and as quickly as possible.

When big changes occur in a company, for example, the best recommendation is to be patient or, better yet, if we remember the jungle scenario, to arm oneself with prudence and wait. Take the time to understand everything that the new change has brought in terms of the rules of performance, power dynamics, actors in the scenario, forbidden movements, established restrictions, as well as undefined or forgotten rules and new opportunities. Then, you may develop actions or tasks that have been made possible in light of the new rules.

Once the person understands their frame of reference well in the new environment and has a clear map indicating the permissible and prohibited paths, a second process that leads to the formulation of a strategy for their success in these new conditions should begin. It is comparable to someone who travels to a new country with a completely different culture. Upon arrival, the person will spend a reasonable amount of time learning about the behavior of the inhabitants of the region and their culture, what is acceptable and what is not. In summary, they will learn about everything they need to live happily in that new environment and to avoid fights, difficulties, misunderstandings, or risks that can be attributed to ignorance or tactlessness in actions or words. They will discover opportunities that will lead them to fame or success because they take advantage of the opportunity to understand something unknown to them or that is essential to know in that specific country.

It makes sense to think that people who live in a country where the average annual temperature is 35° C are unlikely to visit each other on a Saturday at 3 PM. Visits will most likely happen at around 9 PM, when the weather is cooler and everyone can get a breath of fresh air. For example, in a country where drinking water is scarce, something that may be in abundance in one's country of origin becomes an extraordinary business opportunity for a specialist in foreign trade; this person can become a millionaire very quickly by simply catering to their water needs.

In conclusion, I would like to remind everyone that the people who have managed to be successful under constantly changing and extremely difficult conditions have been those who, no matter how complex the various situations had been, made the decision to adapt quickly. They are able to do that with the speed with which sleeping habits of someone who travels from America to Asia or from Europe to America, or vice versa, change. If I go to sleep while others work and try to work while others sleep, in an unknown place, it will probably be very bad for me.

The old saying "When in Rome, do as the Romans do" serves as a very useful guide for managing dramatic and frequent change. Do not forget to treat the change as if you had just entered a completely unknown country. You will see that it will work well for you. When you arrive at the airport of the unknown country, ask what time it is. If it is 11 PM but your watch says it is 2 PM, my advice is to change the time on your watch to 11 PM and go to bed as soon as you can. Otherwise, you will stay up late.

Felons in business and personal life

Judas was good before he betrayed Jesus. Lucifer was a wondrous angel before becoming Satan. Cain killed Abel even though they were brothers. Betrayal comes from friends or people who are close to us, not from enemies. People are loyal to what you represent, not to you. Betrayal and disloyalty happen often and hurt the soul, cause significant damage, and even cause psychological or physical death.

Felony is a word that integrates treason and disloyalty.

It is difficult to uncover betrayal and disloyalty as well as the treacherous. When you realize that you have been betrayed or sold out because someone was disloyal, you are already being cooked in a large pot of boiling water, and there is little you can do except suffer the unpleasant surprise.

For the abovementioned reasons, it is important to know how to determine whom you can and cannot trust, who is and is not lying, who is an actor, and who is authentic and has only one face (they should only have side A, not side B or C). It is convenient to perform tests with small ideas, concepts, or secrets that do not affect anyone but serve to demonstrate evil intentions.

Treacherous and disloyal people are generally the champions of lies, falsehoods, and deception. They say whatever is convenient, regardless of the consequences and without limitations or pain. They are professional felons or fraudsters. Legally, felonies are also known as major or serious crimes. They are the most serious of all crimes, with different punishments in each state. A standard definition for felony is any crime punishable by more than one year in prison.

As for personal and business life, the "felons" do not go to jail, but they are known by the following synonyms: charlatan, liar, traitor, hypocrite, impostor, disloyal, Judas, unfaithful, false, and snitch. Since there are so many, I prefer to call them felons to identify them easily.

Every self-respecting felon has at least two faces, but they usually have many, one for each specific occasion. These people are capable of stabbing someone in the back with a dagger. If you are surrounded by felons in your personal life, it is best to move to a new house, neighborhood, city, or country, whichever you prefer, because sooner or later, you will end up being fried in a skillet. With such a negative surrounding environment, change departments or divisions or companies.

What do you do if you suspect that there are felons around you at work? First, perform an infiltration test. Make up a credible and naïve story about yourself, noting that it is confidential and private. Watch the story go around to verify the infiltration. Follow up to determine who the possible informants are, and once you have discovered the suspects, start sending some good lies through that channel. Over time, they will lose respect and credibility and will no longer be a problem.

Alternatively, once you identify such people, stay away from them and do not deal with them again. Cross them off or remove them from your circle. Again, take a moment to reflect and learn to keep your mouth shut or not make things public that you are not allowed to say or do. If you are not supposed to let everyone know, then do not do it.

If you want to play the hero against such people, expose them in public, in front of as many witnesses as you can, and confront them with the overwhelming truth of the facts. You are taking a risk in this confrontation, so it must be handled intelligently because the person will defend themselves vehemently. Remember that they are skilled at crafting lies. If you manage to defeat them before everyone's eyes, then the felon will retreat, having lost their credibility and good image.

Measure your strengths, your arguments, and your evidence. If they are not solid, a retreat or strategic withdrawal is preferable.

–31–

Becoming invisible or being blessed attracts the positive and repels the negative

O nce, in a taxi, I began a conversation with a wonderfully positive driver who told me the story of his life, his family, and the reasons behind success in many settings, including his own job.

The taxi driver had started and raised his family, a wife and three children, and they were all successful in their own trades and professions. He was already doing the same with his first two twin granddaughters; he had become a grandfather at the early age of 45 years. He was 57 years old when we had this conversation.

The taxi driver owned four public service vehicles. He had won two beautiful private cars in two raffles—one for his wife and one for himself. He had never been issued a fine despite having driven around with a restricted plate in the alternate-day travel system. He told me so many other surprising stories from his fascinating life.

He was a highly enthusiastic, cheerful, and knowledgeable person, and he was a true gentleman to his passengers.

I asked him about the reason for his success, and this is what he told me. The first game he played in school was the invisibility game. Every time he considered it necessary, he would say to himself, "I am invisible," and he would go unnoticed for seconds. The game began at school where he used to make himself invisible when he was engaged in some mischief or when he had not studied and the teacher was calling students to the board. No one ever saw him. The game continued into his adulthood, and in his work as a taxi driver, he often makes himself invisible when he has to make a forbidden turn in an emergency or when he drives past police in a car restricted by the alternate-day travel scheme. Since he knows how to make himself invisible, he is absolutely sure that he will never be issued a citation or fine. He called this quality the "gift of temporary invisibility."

His second key to success, called "the positivity magnet," is his assurance in attracting the positive and repelling the negative. He sees himself as a human magnet with the capacity to attract good people to support him or help him and to repel bad people who do not want to be even five meters from him. Being a "positivity magnet" has allowed him to win a significant number of raffles and contests effortlessly and repeatedly. His effect is so powerful that opportunities are offered or presented to him every day. It is almost like being blessed on a daily basis in every scenario. If he needs transportation, it turns up for him. If he needs a doctor, he runs into them. If he needs money, he wins it. If he needs a front row seat, it is given to him. This last quality of the magnet is so strong that everything the taxi driver needed in life materializes. The doors open as he walks.

The third key to his success is called "the law of taking advantage." It consists of taking advantage of every opportunity, no matter how small, that makes him a winner. In his own way, he gave me a practical example when he realized the traffic jam we were going to get into if we continued straight down the street. He looked everywhere and remarked that there were no policemen and no cameras and then made a forbidden turn to the left to get on a road that was completely free of traffic, as a faster alternative to our destination, claiming that he had a "Waze" incorporated into his brain and was able to get anywhere in record time (I almost fainted from fright). It reminded me of the "first-move advantage" in chess or in football where one takes advantage of the opponent's carelessness to come out ahead, just like in business and other kinds of negotiations.

I leave you with these three powerful reflections of popular knowledge. If you apply them, taking the positive and leaving aside some of the violations committed by the taxi driver, they may be useful in your personal and business life.

32

Why are your employees or collaborators still in the company?

Have you ever wondered, as a manager or owner, what your employees would do if they could do anything? An in-depth study and analysis of several of the best companies in the world found that 70% of the employees remain in their company because they had not found an opportunity that would facilitate a change.

This says a lot about the companies and the employees. It indicates that the company has certain conditions that the employee, even when they want to change, cannot find anywhere else. Consequently, the company comes to the conclusion that they are better off than they imagine.

As for the employee, the scenario suggests that there are issues that annoy them or make their life unpleasant, such as a bad boss or difficult colleagues and a boring or exhausting job. These are their reasons for wanting to explore opportunities to improve their current conditions.

Companies believe that their collaborators are happy and adore them, given that employee morale surveys provide results above 90%. However, the reality is that such survey results provide just a snapshot of one instant at the organization and that morale varies every day. In any case, despite the good survey results, there are always collaborators looking for new opportunities. It is as natural as someone who has a good car but thinks they would like to try out a better one, another brand or color, or different specifications or styles.

There is no sin in wanting to change; it is a natural characteristic in human beings. The important thing to understand is that we cannot fight against this reality, but a lot can be done to retain and attract collaborators in such a way that, most of the time, they come to the conclusion that they have the best possible job, after benchmarking.

The same happens in relationships where it is necessary to maintain enthusiasm and attraction for the relationship to last. There will always be very attractive competition, but the key is to work on maintaining the relationship so that the competition does not take people. There are many "opportunities" on the street—many men and women who might be more attractive than our partner. If the relationship has a good foundation and we cultivate it every day, then these other "opportunities" would not even be considered.

This reflection is for all of us and about our ability to appreciate and value what we have and the way in which we are built. There are people who like to change constantly, and they often seem

like they are eternally dissatisfied. There is no good remedy for such a feeling. The person who does not settle for anything and quickly gets bored or begins to see only the half-empty glass in each situation is one that no one can permanently attract or retain.

A friend who married for the fifth time and already wants to separate shared with me that he has begun to think that he is the problem. He finally reflected and realized that he is the complicated one.

The issue with the collaborator who is always dissatisfied in a company is that they are capable of "infecting" others or making others feel bad with their attitude. They are an electron in a world of protons. They are the negative charge who see the bad in everything, no matter what the company or organization does, which is exactly what happens when a couple is about to separate. They see and receive everything in a negative manner. The reflection in this case is to end things quickly to stop the suffering.

Finally, if both parties strive to do things right, and are willing, then any action taken, no matter how small, will be well received and add positive points to the relationship. It is, as always, a relationship where each person, company, or collaborator must do their part to maintain the enthusiasm and good vibes.

-33-

What is valuable to me is priceless

In today's world, the famous phrase "What is valuable to me is priceless, and if it has a price, it is of no value to me" has been forgotten.

I want to consider it and draw some examples. I invite you to work this phrase coined with great wisdom many years ago, so much so that it remains valid and powerful.

The first part of the phrase means that if something or someone is valuable to a person, company, or organization in terms of what they provide or mean to them, then they will be willing to do whatever it takes to preserve or continue their permanence or bond. There is no limit to what must be done to maintain or ensure the person or product or service, because they are significant or very useful or necessary, comparable to the value of the **oxygen we need to live.**

If a person or an organization feels that the only relationship that exists is the price, then the connection is very poor and, consequently, it is easy to change or phase out, because it is replaceable or useless. Their contribution has no added value or is not vital and may even be an obstacle or surplus.

When we talk about relationships between people or between companies, or between people and organizations, we ask the big question: What does that person or that organization mean in my life or in our company, or for our company? If I lose that person or company, or if they distance themselves or leave us, how much will it hurt, or how much will I lose in different ways, or how much will it cost me when I consider all the impacts of their absence?

Here, pride is worthless and not a sensible approach. Money is not a limitation. Telling the person or the organization what they mean to us and showing it in a tangible way can help retain them. Of course, we not only have to take care of the person or organization that adds value to the business or to our lives but also demonstrate our affection and warmth frequently. When the relationship goes through a rough patch, it is very difficult to express how we have failed in time.

Conversely, there are those that do not add value. Many times, we may lack the courage to recognize it and remove them from our inner orbit. They add more value when they leave us or when they are not around. For this reason, the second part of the phrase, "if it has a price, it is of no value to me," clearly communicates the importance of someone or something. When one has in mind the cost of something or someone, it is because, in reality, they are not that important or do not mean that much to us. The cost hurts us, and that is why we feel like we pay too much. In other words, it is expensive. In this vein, the saying, "cheap is expensive," is better understood. There are people or things that even at a cent are already expensive.

Many times, I have seen people wandering around in organizations who are obviously a negative contribution to the entity, and yet they are still there. They subtract more than add or divide more than multiply. How many personal relationships are toxic? How many people approach us to cause harm or take advantage of us and maintain proximity only while we are useful to them and then abandon us after we have served their purpose? Are these types of people worth it? It is convenient to monitor how many people add value and how many take advantage of us in our lives at any given time. It would be wise to surround ourselves with people who add to our value and to stay away from those who detract value from us—those "human electrons" or "business electrons."

Let us open our eyes and stay alert. Let us maintain and preserve or obtain and increase connections that add value. Let us accelerate the pace to distance ourselves from or end the connections that detract value and rob our energy.

34

Stages of modern management

A few years ago, it was a trend to talk about the stakeholders or constituents of a company. Now, the world has changed, and the subject has diversified and expanded significantly, making it dangerous and risky not to take into account the following 10 stages.

First, we have the traditional ones: ***stakeholders, employees, suppliers, community, and customers.*** These are the stakeholders or constituents that define a company's existence. The idea is to optimize the satisfaction or delight of these five key players by maximizing the possible level that each one could reach without anyone at an advantage or disadvantage.

Nowadays, management has become more challenging and complex. It is clear that there are key players who were not previously considered as actors in the equation of a company's success or failure, but now they are.

The five additional players are *the distributors or channels; the honorable competition* that distracts us, teaches us, and challenges us, in addition to being an ally or a client at times; *the government,* which is a large partner that takes a good chunk of the profits and sets the pace of business; our *society* that qualifies us, judges us, or makes demands from us, having as much or even more power than clients, channels, or suppliers; and *the digital world* that monitors us, accelerates our pace, qualifies us, gives or takes away prestige from us, gives us presence, harms us, destroy us, or empowers us.

In the world we live in today, any of the new players can make a company dance to a different rhythm. They can help the company grow or bring it to its knees and end it.

Sales are no longer made directly as before. We increasingly depend on third parties to reach all markets and corners of the world. Channels or distributors allow companies to cover the planet, reach directly where they could never have dreamed of. Some channels eventually become the vital vehicle for the existence of modern companies or organizations.

The government, which previously made demands on us, now knows us to a surprising level of precision. It increasingly demands more from us and imposes on us procedures, standards, processes, taxes, audits, rules, and laws for everything. Not planning this relationship and how to take advantage of it is suicide.

What about society? Earlier, a company did what it believed was fair, but now, society demands ethics and sets the rules. Society demands fair treatment and respect for the rules of coexistence and respect for minority groups, as well as for the environment, animals, women, LGBT people, minors, the elderly, and the sick. In the past, someone would have a breakdown and nothing happened. Now, it may be the result of overwork or harassment by the boss and have consequences. Bosses can no longer do what they want, because society and government impose a certain behavior on them. The same happens in schools or at home. Teachers or parents cannot mistreat, torture, threaten, or beat minors as before.

The digital world is like a great country of which we have to be citizens because it connects us with the planet, other companies, competitors, potential clients, and society. Not being in this world significantly affects progress. However, being in it requires discipline and proper observation and measurement tools. Make a mistake in the digital world and your reputation or that of your organization can end within hours. Similarly, a person or an organization can become famous within hours. It is a world with other rules and power. It is a world wherein one must learn to handle the pace and contents. There are already many great players or powers in this new world which we are all rapidly entering without exception. Observe what happens today in a meeting or on the streets where everyone is busy texting, where solving a query takes seconds, where you can instantly contact someone regardless of the distance, where barriers have changed and borders have ended.

What about today's competition? I have friends who have gone bankrupt because other countries drove them out and replaced them with better and cheaper products and services. Nowadays, there are gradually more alliances between long-time competitors, something that was unthinkable in the past.

I will let your thoughts wander because the 10 stages of modern management are worth considering, or else we will have a rough time.

-35-

Hard work produces incredible results

An acquaintance who did not make much progress in his professional life used to say, "Working is so boring that you get paid for it." With this kind of vision, he became perfectly mediocre as time went by, and although he held some leadership positions in the companies where he worked, he never stood out for anything other than being one more on the list of those who hardly give an average performance. Such people work or go through life at half the speed they can go and do only what is strictly necessary, never going above or beyond their duties, much less exerting themselves to be above average. In companies, they are the people who never perform tasks in such a way that they stand out either negatively or positively, and they can last years in an organization until someone realizes that they are a kind of passive burden and terminates them. Have you ever met a person like this? Are you like that? I will call them "Mediocrates," to sum it up easily. The name sounds somewhat Greek.

At one extreme, we have the pessimists and negative thinkers who, most of the time, see the bad in any situation and find a problem for each solution. Very close to these individuals are those who play the role of the permanently dissatisfied. Nothing is good enough for them, and nothing fulfills or pleases them. If they swallowed their own saliva, they would be poisoned. These are the individuals who can see two small, almost microscopic black dots on a huge white wall. The bacteriologists of life, with due respect to this profession that studies the chemistry of body fluids and waste, are likely bored in a world full of imperfections in which they have to live. If it is sunny, it is bad, but it is also bad if it rains. If there is only pasta for dinner, they prefer beef; if there is beef, they prefer fish; if there is fish, they want chicken; and if there is chicken, they prefer vegetables. They make anyone feel bad and they are the guardians of the unlocked truth. Have you ever met them? Are you one of them? I will call them "Bitterus" to make it sound a bit philosophical.

On the other extreme, we have the enthusiasts and positive thinkers who see possibilities and opportunities where others see problems. These people are always willing to carry out activities no matter how complex or difficult they are. They do not waste a minute dwelling on the past because they only see in the present the way to build the future. In the face of adversity, they focus on getting ahead by finding solutions and options, and of course, they are people of action and results. They are always ready to face new challenges. They are the first to understand, accept, and promote change. They propose ideas and innovations and radiate joy before each new challenge. These people clearly understand that nothing is achieved completely or quickly if you do not work hard or make alliances. They know that working as a team is good for the common good. I will call them "Positrons."

Are you the type of person who pushes or who has to be pushed? In our everyday lives, we find the three types of people I have just described. Which type would you talk to most often? To Bitterus, the perfectly dissatisfied and bitter person? To another Bitterus, the negative thinker who sees everything in gray and finds nothing fulfilling? To Mediocrates, the one who leaves everything for tomorrow, does nothing exceptional, puts in the least amount of effort, and achieves mediocrity? To Positrons, the positive enthusiasts overflowing with the will to execute and achieve, apart from being a good human being? By whom do you want to be influenced? Do you want to be on the winning team, or do you want to be a loser?

Of course, we always need people to *guide us, encourage us, help us, facilitate the way, advise us, instill confidence in us, provide constructive criticism, correct us, motivate us, enlighten us, accompany us, or lead us.* That person can be a boss, our best friend, a family member who loves us, our life partner, our colleague or co-worker, or all of the above (Positrons).

What is also clear is that we do not need a person who subtracts, who produces the opposite effect, and practices the inverse of the aforementioned verbs, causing us to slow down or back down, demotivating us, scaring us, making us lose confidence in ourselves, and guiding us to failure (Mediocrates and Bitterus).

Virtuous cycles exist, and these catapult our results and enable us to achieve what at first seems impossible and improbable. What do you think the results of a team formed mainly by Positrons will be, and how do you think the collaborators and leaders of that team will feel? Would a virtuous cycle be generated? Do they have a good chance of achieving or exceeding the planned objectives?

The boss is happy with their personnel and the results; the personnel are happy with the boss and the results; and the company is happy with that boss, the collaborators on that team, and the results. A growing positive spiral is generated where everyone contributes, and the more they do it and improve, the more they achieve and improve, and conditions improve for everyone and the company, and so on: the virtuous cycle. This facilitates leadership and generates a natural bond that brings about trust and tremendous commitment from each person to their tasks and the organization.

The greatest historical achievements in many scenarios of life have occurred in the most adverse and challenging conditions. When you have the greatest restrictions, the opportunity to grow and improve arises, and this is where the virtuous cycles and the enthusiastic contributions and commitments of everyone doing their best become key to those achievements.

How good to hear the bosses and collaborators say, "Tomorrow, I am leaving early for work because I have some challenging tasks that await me, and I am going to enjoy them with my colleagues, who are excellent professionals and add to my own value every day, and the bosses are the best part of it all. They allow us to learn, contribute, and grow, and they support and lead us with so much energy because they are part of a winning team." The bosses, of course, have similar remarks and indicate how wonderful it is to have collaborators who contribute ideas and results and go beyond the standard, who are always committed and devoted to the cause of facing the daily challenges with excellence. Everyone should be able to express, "I am proud to belong to this team and to this company, which I love with my soul."

We are the authors of our own destiny and of our own feelings and positions regarding any challenge or difficulty at work, in our profession, or in life. We cannot change what happens, but *we can change the way we react to, act upon, and think about what happens.*

-36-

The value of making mistakes and seeing opportunities for growth in them and the IDAE method

I was wrong. I admit it. I made a mistake. I apologize. I promise to learn from this experience and do better next time.

These are such wonderful statements. However, saying them in public hurts, but doing so strengthens us, helps us grow, and improves our self-image and the image others have of us. These are magical phrases with immediate and powerful consequences. Personally, I recognize that I make a good number of mistakes or omissions daily, but I also recognize that my reaction is so fast that the corrections and improvements go unnoticed. Therefore, only the positive final result is seen, as if I had done everything well from the start.

We make decisions and carry out actions on a daily basis, as we make our way to achieving a goal. Decisions and actions can be many or the sum of many. Some may be small, some large, some without risk and others risky, some urgent and others not at all. When one looks at the details, the path toward achieving an objective consists of a series of decisions and actions of all kinds, with some being good, some regular, and some bad. The key is our ability to analyze and react to each partial result.

It is surprising that one usually thinks that there is only one or two decisions to be made and one or two actions to be carried out. However, a detailed analysis demonstrates that there can be hundreds, and the more days go by, the more activities there are in between. The analysis that arises from this reflection leads us to ask ourselves the following questions: What did I do wrong, or what did I lack? What did I learn, and what should I do to avoid falling into the same situation or to do well or better next time?

Apart from correcting an error, it is worth using the rapid and constructive analysis and diagnostic method **IDAE**, which guides actions based on four questions: What can be **Increased**? What can be **Decreased**? What is worth **Adding**? What should we **Eliminate**?

Suppose you have decided to lose weight. Your weight is 75 kg, and coincidentally, on a particular month, you have to participate in celebrating the birthday of 10 people with cake and wine. At the end of this, you go from 75 kg to 79 kg. In such situations, first, recognize your mistakes: You ate a lot of sugar and drank a lot of alcohol. Then, use the IDAE method to help correct the four kilos of weight gain. **Increase** daily exercise by doing an additional half hour of cardio. **Decrease** the intake of sugars. **Add** water and protein to your daily diet. **Eliminate** carbs and a sedentary lifestyle.

Thus, the IDAE method does not fail to correct errors.

I remember the story of a boy who, during an internship, had been commissioned to make a backup copy of the electronic notebook of the boss in a multinational company. Instead of making the copy, he inadvertently deleted more than 2,000 key contacts of the company's president. In unison, all the executives of the company asked for his dismissal and request the university to not let him graduate. The president of the company told everyone, including the boy, that nothing was going to happen except the painful recovery of the information, since everyone has the right to fail and learn from their failures, especially a young man in an internship.

The people in the company never forgot that event, and from then on, everyone understood that there is a great opportunity to grow and learn from failure. The president also learned that sensitive information, such as his private address and contact book, should be handled by an expert and not by an apprentice (like the saying that goes, do not entrust a child with something that should be done by an adult). The intern, of course, was intelligent and very responsible, but he unfortunately pressed the wrong button, deleting all the information instead of saving it. He came out stronger from the situation, and his progress after that experience was spectacular. He is a very successful executive today.

In another organization, I remember a girl had to make a bank deposit of USD 1,600. She was conned at the bank branch by an expert thief who deceived her into exchanging her money for a wad of false bills with colored papers in the middle (at first glance, it looked like a wad of many bills and, of course, much more money than she had to deposit). The girl returned to the office crying, desperate and confused. She did not know how the deception had happened, although she did remember talking to a man who asked her the favor to exchange some money because he had an emergency (in Colombia, this deception is called the Chilean package). In such a situation, the girl could have lost her position and been made to pay the money that, in her case, represented almost four times her basic salary at that time. However, her bosses decided to teach from the experience and allowed her to learn from the incident; the company also changed its procedures to ensure more secure deposits on subsequent occasions. The lesson was learned by everyone. Of course, the girl was talented and very responsible but inexperienced and naïve because of her obvious youth. Today, she is the head of an administrative and financial department in a major multinational company.

Great inventors know perfectly well that only a long chain of failures can result in the creation of a new product that would revolutionize the market or the world. As adults, we forget that something as simple as driving a car took a large number of scares to both instructors and students as the latter learned to put the gears in place, brake smoothly, start the vehicle or brake without stalling, start the vehicle on a hill without it rolling backwards, and, certainly, stay on the road without drifting from the speed on a curve. While learning to drive, we make a significant number of mistakes before managing to master the skill.

Even as adults, we face something new every day and are apprentices in these new experiences. To err is legitimate, and without a doubt, it is the beginning of a path toward success. On one hand, it requires the will to learn and better ourselves. On the other, it demands patience, understanding, and support. Making mistakes is an opportunity for improvement and growth.

~37~

The goose that laid the golden eggs

The boss of a multinational I worked for once told me, "Nobody kills the goose that lays the golden eggs to make soup with it." He said this when I submitted my resignation in a prominent and important part of my professional life. I had been going to the sales convention for several years after gaining excellent annual results and had been an international sales champion for three consecutive years. When I resigned, he asked me to stay and told me that he was going to give me a promotion, a large office, a company car, a 50% increase in my salary, and other perks. When I asked him why he had not given me all that before, he said, "You produced 30% of the company's income. Nobody kills the goose to make soup with it." At that moment, I realized that I had lost the past 10 years of my life, in which I could have taken advantage of my talent and achievements to receive better recognition elsewhere, which indeed happened to me when I got the next job.

In everyday life, not only do the "geese" that lay the golden eggs produce money but they also provide us with happiness and joy, provide orientation or guidance, offer high-value company, generate peace when they are nearby, extend support of some kind, complement us, give us affection, make us feel important, make us reflect, offer a shoulder to lean on in the most difficult moments, enlighten us on the darkest days, and give meaning to our lives.

How many golden geese do we have in our company or our life? Have they been identified? How well protected are they? How do we treat them? Do we acknowledge their existence well? Have we lost them? Is it true that there are no more than five such people in a person's life? Are you a golden goose? If you are a goose that lays golden eggs, do they give you good food, treat you well, take care of you, respect you, and appreciate you? Do they tell you their feelings often? Do they make you feel good? As the goose that lays the golden eggs, do you feel exploited, abused, mistreated, threatened, or undervalued?

One final thought: The golden geese know their value and are tolerant, but they are not made of rubber. Do not neglect them. Worry about identifying and retaining them. Otherwise, you will regret it all your life and carry a bad memory that will cause you pain.

"You do not know what you have got until it is gone."

-38-

Failures in the millennial and current conquest

M any empires invaded and conquered other territories and wiped out their wealth and a good part of their original culture. Greedy conquerors were characters of different types, always driven by possession as well as economic, physical, and spiritual domination. Humanity was very primitive at that time and definitely not very bright. These settlers were, in a certain way, barbaric rapists of everything that appeared in their path. Invasions and conquests have been seen throughout the history of humanity, at the level of peoples, religions, and human genders for physical, economic, or political power.

There is a lot of evidence that conquerors enabled the conquered to flourish and elevated them to higher levels, being even admired and loved by the people they had conquered. Of course, history is written by the victors. There is also much more evidence of how the conquerors devastated everything and humiliated, robbed, brutally subdued, abused, enslaved, killed, and raped the conquered people.

We might ask the following questions: Did the people lack intelligence? Did they gain more from it? Did it allow them to grow more? Did it allow them to stay longer in power?

Meanwhile, the modern world seems to impose the opposite style: win/win, alliances, respect, mutual growth, mutual help, joint work, and mutual learning.

Domination by force is a method that has proven to be good in the short term; in the medium and long term, it usually ends in rebellion and violence that put an end to the domination and leave a permanent scar.

In a way, the modern method, which provides the greatest results at the level of communities, companies, and people, is characterized by a good form of seduction and treatment; this leads to "consensual domination" since the subdued sees the benefit, advantage, or convenience in being dominated, resulting in a positive bond or alliance where there is a leader and a follower, both with the same goal in mind. We live in a time where we seek to reach agreements with mutual convenience, where everyone wins, even if unequally (i.e., concessions).

The key to this whole process is that the approaches are a negotiation. It can be quick when cultural proximity and the objectives allow it. It can take longer when such cultural or objective differences are broad, and the parties have to be brought closer through side-by-side teaching or evangelization, when each has their reasons and validation in their assessments, customs, and perspectives.

Everything that I have mentioned in the previous reflections applies to the constitution of marriages, companies, partnerships, jobs in other countries or regions, the purchase of companies, territorial expansions, supplier management, channel or distribution management, gender and race relations, or relations with other political parties or other religions.

In some parts of the world, there are still some people who want to play emperor and be a tyrant in their empire. However, we are moving fast toward a modern scenario, like the one I have described, where higher-standard relationships are established, and where results that are 1000 times better, more productive, economical, and lasting can be achieved based on mutual respect and a win/win scenario.

Do you prefer the method of the tyrant or that of the seducer for your life, partner, work, businesses, region, and country?

-39-

Partnerships, marriage, eternal life, and good fortune

C hance accompanies us throughout our lives from the moment we are born. Many people do not believe in chance, but the truth is that even if one is not playing roulette, cards, or the lottery, life is a permanent game of chance that can surprise us every minute. The question is what do we do with the surprises that life throws at us every day? As we discuss some examples to support this reflection, we determine a possible response to this question.

A common and first surprise for many couples is pregnancy. How many people have shared with us that they did not plan it, either because they believed it would not happen or because they were using a contraception method that failed? I know several couples who had been married for years without children and suddenly became pregnant.

Let us reminisce about how we met our partner. How did you two meet? We will find incredible stories where chance played a role from the beginning to the end, and we can say that surprises almost always occur when you least expect them, that is, the "the least probable day." There are couples who met on a plane, on a bus, at a party, on a walk, in a choir, in a park, and on a visit to a friend's house. Most report that these were situations in which they had not expected to find or were not looking for a partner. Marriage, which is the culmination of courtship to begin creating a home, is a delicate and important event that begins by chance, and remains so as the couple stays together day after day, as it is a union of two people as "different as night and day," because they are not even related.

The passage to eternal life is another surprise. There is no expiration date made available to people. I do not know mine. Even more uncertain is how that passage to eternal life, or the next life, will be. Is it going to be a heart attack? An accident? Will it be while I am sleeping? An earthquake? A serious illness? A stray bullet? A fall? No one knows or can guess, but it will inevitably happen.

This happens with good fortune, as well. Although one can work hard all their life to be the best at something, several factors that are unrelated to preparation and willingness to do things play a role. It all depends on the moment, the competitors, our physical or mental state, and in general, on chance. A great athlete may not win a competition or become a champion. In some professions, people perform an activity and no one might listen to them, see them, or be interested. The same activity performed at a different time might be seen and appreciated by everyone. Why does this happen?

Let us consider a person who is working in a wonderful company and is appreciated and admired as an employee. Suddenly, the company is acquired by another that decides to downsize the staff that it considers redundant, including this employee. The lay-off happens to him by chance. I have often seen the opposite case, where the person is doing a job and is suddenly called and given a proposal to move to a totally different role, given that there is a vacancy where their profile may be the ideal fit. Life can turn 180 degrees overnight, and few can plan for it.

My parents' house had been rented out for a long time to a company. When my mother died, after being a widow for years, her children wanted to sell the house to the company that was renting it, but they turned out to be crooks and said they were going to keep the house in perpetuity by paying rent. We filed a lawsuit, and in the end, the owner had to occupy it for a minimum period of 12 months for the house to be handed back to us. That is how, after having left my parents' house 33 years ago, I found myself back in it, something that was unplanned and never considered.

Similarly, in business, chance is at play every day. One can work on an opportunity in depth, covering all the details, inside information, friendly clients, attractive prices, wonderful services or products, but nothing guarantees success. Anything can happen. I once landed a big tech contract with a bank, with the most difficult solution that was five times more expensive than that of the competitor.

My father played the lottery and, toward his 60s, began to win fractions of the lotteries. Two of them were big enough to buy apartments with the winnings. Chance is like that. You do not know why something happens, but it happens, good or bad.

Bad streaks are notorious, and you will remember the ones you have had or the people you have seen go through these difficult situations one after another. When I was 16, I was in an accident where a bus hit my father's car from behind in the morning. At noon, I was left stranded with the car, and it had to be taken to the garage. In the afternoon, as I was leaving, a car hit the driver's door. My father told me to stay in the house to prevent anything further happening to me. It was a streak of bad luck. There are people who have such days for years and end up being alone if others believe that it the tough luck be contagious. In companies, such a streak can lead to bankruptcy. In terms of health, it can be fatal.

Onto more positive and exciting topics, I married a beautiful woman whom I met in the least probable situation, and I formed a beautiful home with her. Looking back, I realize that I have won the jackpot with her, our children, and the long and happy years we have spent together. It was a surprise to meet her and a bigger surprise to get to marry her.

Business partnerships arise in the same way. You inadvertently meet someone, and in a conversation, you come up with the idea of starting a business. Many of the inventions that we know today are the result of mistakes or positive accidents. Columbus left for the Indies and ended up in America.

To answer the question of what to do with life's surprises and the chance that follows us, make the most of each experience, handle it as best as you can, and do everything that is required to be victorious or get out of it alive while you can. Otherwise, say "Ciao," goodbye!

Types of vendors based on tableware

A fork and a knife spot a spoon in the distance and try to give it a hug, but the spoon turns its back to them. The fork and the knife say to each other, I guess it feels like spooning. This story introduces a characteristic of spoons and its similarity to those who play the same role in the field of sales.

Vendors can be classified by comparing their actions and functions or characteristics to tableware. There are vendors who are only made to receive the merchandise, what people sometimes refer to as a store or counter salesperson. There are vendors who receive audiences in a large or small place, with people packed in rows or scattered about, which is exactly what dessert trays, soup bowls, mugs, and the like do: receive different amounts of food and contain it in different ways. If they have a quota, they keep receiving. Otherwise, another container must be used. The glasses or mugs are specialized and usually receive only one type of liquid or more, requiring the use of a stirrer. A typical example is that of vendors of men's or women's suits, sportswear, or shoes in specialized stores. Another typical tray-style vendor is one that sells automobiles of a specific make or multiple models of the same make.

There are vendors who operate like spoons, whose function is to facilitate the taste testing and to stir or mix ingredients. Of course, another function is to transfer contents from one place to another, as in the case of ladles and their function of transferring contents between pots and soup bowls or between the punch bowl and glasses, in the case of cocktails. The spoon-like vendors are a kind of distributor within an organization. They test the elements and transfer them from one place to another to the clients who are looking for elements in other sections; they constantly move the elements from one place to another, like someone stirring a soup or sugar into a cup of coffee. They maintain the interest in the client, by cooling them down or exciting them, but their function is more like maintaining an existing client, or accounts.

Knives come in different sizes and with different edges, but their function is clear: to cut. Large, sharp ones are used by butchers to cut raw meat and nerves. Knives are dangerous, as they can be used to kill. The function of the vendor is like that of the knife: they must have the permanent vocation to close the business, and if necessary, they have to kill to complete the sale.

The fork vendors are the hunters. They go out every day thinking about who they will skewer. Forks constantly perform the function of…piercing, piercing the potato, piercing the meat, piercing vegetables. They are the typical salesperson who gets new accounts or clients and brings them in to the knife-like salesperson to close the sale. The hunter does not let go of their prey or slip, which usually happens with spoons. The hunter catches the prey and punctures with force, so much so that they can destroy it. There are small and large forks, and their usefulness and effectiveness can be seen immediately, like the knife's effectiveness, whose function is clear from the get-go.

It is important to understand the different types of vendors that exist in order to understand which one fits best in a scenario: a deep-dish-like vendor, one who is a cross between a fork and knife, or simply a spoon-like vendor, who prefers to spoon out and stir up excitement. If you are a salesperson, ask yourself if you are a plate, fork, knife, or spoon. Each one has its function, utility, and application, and they can work in pairs or trios, like the plate, fork, and spoon in the dessert dish or the plate, fork, and knife in the main course.

Qualify Leads and Close Faster, A Quick Guide: RUDAC Method

Many sales do not occur because salespeople do not know how to identify potential clients, which is crucial in ensuring results and not wasting time and energy on what has no short- or medium-term future. The famous NDC method (which asks about what the client Needs, how they make Decisions, and what they are Capable of) is brilliant, but I want to complement it while maintaining its essence and simplicity.

The Basic Guide to Sales Qualification in the sale of a large project or solution is like the fingers of a hand. There are five key questions.

First, are there RESOURCES, money, or people to assign to a project or, in the case of an individual, are they available and do they have money (we will represent it with the letter R and involve the symbol $, to remember it as Re$ources)? If yes, then we are doing well. Otherwise, the task has to be postponed owing to the lack thereof, and this can leave the door open to competition or substitutes. The resource requirement is urgent; tomorrow may be too late. As for money, without a positive answer, the case presents no opportunity. If the client buys a dress but does not have cash or a credit card, or does not want store credit, what we have is a bystander or a voyeur. There are apprentices or timid salespeople who do not ask this question, and it is an essential one.

The second relates to the DECISION-MAKING process: Who makes the decision or who is involved to ensure that the right decision-makers are spoken to (let us represent it with the letter D for decision-makers) and not those who are only interested in asking or finding out information? The latter kind will never specify anything because they do not have the power or authority. Do not talk to the clowns; talk to the circus owner.

There are times when you have to talk to several people who act as decision-makers or advisers. There are processes where they will always require several quotes, look at several alternatives, or repeatedly ask for a lower price. You have to understand the process. In a personal sale, you can be talking to the brother or the husband or the father or a son. In a business sale, the decision-makers can be even more numerous, composed of the interested party, purchasing department, user vice president, technical vice president, president, board of directors, and advisers.

Third, by when do you need your order? Is it urgent? (Let us represent it with the letter U for urgency.) This is very important because one is usually caught by surprise. Clients might need a product by the end of the year or the middle of next year.

What if they need it for tonight or this Saturday or in 30 days at the latest? Each implies our position toward the potential client and opportunity. In the former case, you can come back later and nothing will happen. In the latter case, you must move fast for a potential and probable business. It is urgent when the need affects business or life or when a competitor is affecting the business. At such a moment, we will sell like there's no tomorrow.

The fourth relates to us in two ways. First, do we **have the SOLUTION that meets the client's needs, or can we provide it per their wishes and conditions but with most of our components. In other words, do we meet the compatibility demands? (Let us represent it with the letter C for compatibility.)** Can someone else do it? Sometimes, we struggle to try to sell what we do not have or cannot put together or specify. We could end up wasting time and money and hurting our image for failing to comply with or provide the goods or service. Second, **is the client for us or are we for that client?** Sometimes, the desire to sell blinds us, and it becomes a problem when we cannot deliver what the client needs or if the client is too big for us. A bad client brings risk that can destroy a good reputation.

Fifth, do we have good contacts on the client side (**let us represent it with the letter A for Amiable**) who can facilitate access to key information, provide guidance regarding our progress and possibilities, make recommendations, or support us. Not having friends within the potential client side means that we do not have a radar, and the chances of closing a key sale are slim or very fortuitous.

In summary, we have a new simplified method. It can be represented by only five letters that are easy to memorize. Compared with X, **RUDAC** is more powerful, more complete, and equally fast, and it does not fail. If you answer YES to the five questions, you can close the sale in record time.

R Re$ources (Do you have people, $$$, etc.?)

U Urgency (Does the client require something essential fast?)

D Decision-makers (Are all the decision-makers involved?)

A Amiable (Do you have friends or acquaintances or internal contacts?)

C Compatibility (Do we have the solution? Is this the client for us?)

Of course, apart from quickly obtaining clients, it is important that success in sales requires hard, constant, organized, strategic, and disciplined work. We must possess a good level of willpower or enthusiasm and carry out daily actions aimed at closing deals and monitoring progress so that we are aware of how to get to the client's inner circle. This way, we can take appropriate action, take care to not disclose anything we should not, and instead try to get as much information as possible. Finally, we must have something of a lucky star or, as the chefs would say, a pinch of good luck (sacks of salt are not sold).

Second half

The world we live in and humanity are constructed in a way that suggests that many key activities are carried out in two stages: plays and soccer games have a second half or act; school years have semesters; the months have the first fortnight and the second. We also find that there are occasions in which there are three acts, as in letters, books, or some plays, consisting of an introduction, body, and conclusion. There are situations that merit four stages, such as the seasons or the quarters of the year. There are also situations with five stages, such as human life: we are born, we grow, we reproduce, we age, and we die. Similarly, as per the bible, God made the world in seven days.

There are times when tasks are completed the first time around, but more often than not, the result is obtained after a sequence of events. For example, getting married is the result of a sequence of events, and it is very difficult to occur in the first event. You have to watch the second half.

In business or personal contexts, it is important to ensure a second half or a second time. We must establish connections that lead to a sequence. The key is to prolong the game as much as possible in our favor.

Speaking of sequences, partial results are interesting and important, but they are not critical. The vital element is the final result, the definitive one. It is like in high school: Each subject must be approved and contributes to the construction of the end result, but what counts is whether one graduates (final result).

The partial result of a boxing fight does not matter much if we knock out the opponent in the last round and win (remember Rocky?). The point to keep in mind is the end of the sequence. That is what really counts.

This way of looking at things improves our action plan. In chess, it is interesting to let the opponent take several pieces, provided that our plan foresees moves at the end to checkmate them.

We all have to go through bad moments in life. The interesting thing is that bad moments are temporary or an intermediate to good moments. Many times, they are a *mandatory* intermediate on the road to success.

In those difficult moments, where it seems as though one has everything to lose (and we are really losing or have lost) and the world is coming upon us, it is best to maintain serenity and endure the storm until it passes. Calm then settles in.

Think for a moment about what Hillary Clinton felt like when Bill's affair with Monica Lewinsky was discovered. Apart from discovering the deception, she had to endure the experience before global media, political pressures, the fate of the president of the United States of America, and the example she sets for her daughter. What would you have done in Hillary's shoes during those difficult times? Soon, the storm passed, and her stamina, strength, and intelligent response to the crisis allowed her to preserve her marriage, launch a best-selling book, and become a United States senator. The end result was the opposite of her conditions during the scandal, when everything was lost.

That is life. I myself have experienced many moments of great frustration, in which all had been lost, and then the sun rose in an impressive way. The second half has its charm. We experience everyday situations in which we seem to lose everything that is important. If we calmly handle the storm and fill ourselves with serenity, courage, and creativity to transform the negative into positive, everything changes, and we can be victorious.

A businessperson's life is full of such examples. One cannot be guided only by defeats. Everything can change. The business game is, like all games, subject to permanent risk, and it is sometimes like the old expression, "The difference between a deserter and a hero is only five minutes."

In business and in life, you win and you lose every day. The important thing is for the results to be good at the end of the period, the year, or in the long term. Executives and businesspeople, as well as people in general, bet to win. Everyone knows that there may be difficult times in which the most important thing is to survive, because there are many opportunities in the long term, if one is alive to bet on them.

Employees or people go through similar situations. There are times when everything goes wrong for a person. Days or months later, a bad employee may turn out to be the admired employee. I have seen it many times. I have seen an employee "threatened" by poor performance, and within a year, after being in total darkness, they were rewarded for being the star that saved the results of their department or organization. Others leave because they are bad or because of staff reductions and then find the triumph that had eluded them at another organization or job. We could almost say that they found success by exiting from the company.

Let us get back to soccer. It does not matter if the opponent scores a goal in the first half if we score two goals in the second half and one of them at the last minute. That is why they say that you cannot claim victory in a soccer match until the very end. The key is to stay active for 90 minutes and play to win. There is no sense in giving up after having played 15 minutes, even if we are losing. It is worth fighting and striving to change the bad streak. Remember, "in a long game, there is revenge," and life is a very long game, where the first five minutes may seem like 50 years have already gone by.

I am particularly a second-half player. I win all the wars there.

-43-

Survive amid continuous and inevitable change

The goal in any area of daily life is to preserve balance, calm, stability, love, affection, money, health, and joy. That is the key point and vital objective.

Life is full of unforeseen events and surprises, either because nature manifests itself with an uncontrollable force, such as through an earthquake, a downpour, an intense heatwave, or a landslide, or because of more typical, simple, but high-impact circumstances, like a crash, bomb, fire, illness, fall, mistake, a tendency for excessive words, robbery, stray bullet, pregnancy, headache, ill-timed sleep, bad-news phone call, lottery, lawsuit, accident, job offer or new business win, or failure with a key client.

What about your stability, reputation, and future? Are any of these points threatened? Everything can change in a second. Like the famous phrase, the darkest hour is just before dawn. Everything is at stake permanently. Life is a minute-by-minute gamble. How fast do you change and adapt to a sudden new situation? How fast do you react? How prepared are you to successfully navigate life's surprises or unforeseen and sudden events?

How quickly one adapts to unexpected changes can be the difference between life and death. A second in which we react positively and in time can be the definitive one that saves lives, closes a business, wins an audience or a competition or someone's heart, or prevents an accident. Our reaction speed to the unexpected is the key to success.

As a reflection, personally, I have been saved from death several times thanks to the adaptability I have had and the speed with which I reacted. On two occasions, a gun was pointed to my head, and a knife to my neck on another, like in the movies. Only that in my case, it was real life, and what I said or did save me from death.

Life events are constantly unforeseen. Learn to manage them, and you will live long.

A good leader listens, lets themselves be led, and makes decisions

When people are asked if the exemplary leader they have in mind heeds the advice given to them, the answer is usually NO. Experience shows that big leaders take into account what people tell them and almost always let themselves be led by the popular wisdom of the thinking majorities, like in the program "Who Wants to Be a Millionaire?" where the contestant has the option of consulting the audience or a friend.

Decisions are made based on inquiries and analyses that one makes in their mind, and based on the conclusions, we choose the one that fits best according to the analysis or preferences or structure of values and principles.

Normally, we ask others their opinion of what they would do in a certain situation or what they know about someone who has been in a similar situation, and we build in our minds a kind of history of "test flight" results of an idea that we have but which we are not sure could be the best alternative or best way out.

The minds of our leaders are not different from our own, but in their field, they can be more visionary, take more risks, or be more courageous when making decisions. Remember that the leader does the same as the thief; the only difference is that one is for a good and the other is for a bad reason. The two are similar in the sense that each one takes advantage of the opportunity that is presented to them and, consequently, performs a reckless and courageous action.

"A true leader is always led," said Carl Jung. It seems like a contradiction, but there is much depth and truth in that statement upon further analysis. Nevertheless, this statement by Carl Jung forces leaders to learn how to listen and pay close attention to what is advised or shown to them, so that they can take into account everything they have seen and received. With their best judgment and vision, make a decision that leads to a concrete action in favor of a community or group.

That is why I affirm, "A good leader listens, lets themselves be led, and makes decisions."

I have seen it in practice and how effective it is in leaders. It is the favorite and most effective tool of a good leader. I myself have practiced and recommended it when I had to be the leader or be close to a successful leader. History proves it.

If you are not a leader, keep in mind the above statement. If you are a leader right now, practice the statement, and you will see how well you do.

Do not just talk about it, do it. How much will not doing it cost?

A lot of conversation, explanation, and planning and little execution or action result in zero positive or negative progress. There are geniuses who enjoy delaying, entangling, or complicating actions, mostly out of fear that the result may not meet their expectations, but nothing is worse. I prefer movement, whether it is in reverse or a setback, because it generates action, which in turn allows us to move forward in the long run or make advances in the immediate future.

When you make a mistake or fail, you have no choice but to correct or fix it, which undoubtedly leads to real progress. Nevertheless, if the approach is correct, the result is twice as valuable, and it only generates more enthusiasm and motivation to keep moving or taking action.

Once, a friend was driving his car, and I was in the passenger seat. The route was long, and the road varied little. My friend fell asleep, and when I realized that the car was about to go off the road, I took control of the steering wheel. With a nudge, I woke up my friend. If I had not taken that action in those seconds, we would have crashed very badly, and we could have even killed ourselves that night. How much would it have cost, not taking control of the situation? I had to break our system of "you drive, I will be the passenger," because with the traditional rules and respect for these roles, we would have crashed. This is what I mean by "do not talk about it; do it."

Young children demand quick action and decision-making in their care because a moment of carelessness can result in someone eating something they should not, falling, or hurting themselves somehow. Children require immediate action, and not doing so can be painful. If the child hurts themselves and we do not act, what is the cost of inaction?

In companies, many people spend their time waiting for the boss to give their consent or authorization for an action that is important and urgent, when people want the risk to be assumed by the authority, so as not to expose themselves in case of failure. When an organization is civilized and advanced and fosters autonomous people, the decisions or key daily actions are mostly carried out autonomously. If an unexpected event occurs in the execution of an action, it is subsequently analyzed to learn from it and thus avoid failures in the future. However, no one is blamed or punished for having taken the initiative to go forward, acting in good faith, and with the best intentions in mind for the organization. The proverb "ask for forgiveness, not permission" is appropriate in this situation. It sounds aggressive, but in the end, it streamlines and turns the company into an active and mature organization.

In most cases, the form of operation we have just described is based on trust and autonomy, which in turn allow for productivity and speed. Such operation also ensures that collaborators act like mature, responsible people, rather than like immature employees who can make the company seem like a daycare center filled with young children who need to be taken care of and told what to do every minute. Although many employees have professional studies, extensive experience, and are of legal age, some companies end up treating them like children. In other words, employees are presumed to need an older, responsible adult to supervise them always.

This practice prevailed in most companies many years ago, and unfortunately, there is still a good number of organizations that operate centrally and with an authoritarian boss who authorizes everything. Without their approval, even a leaf cannot be moved. In today's world, where the competition is nimble and resourceful, and where clients are demanding and hungry for quick service, this centralized style is deadly for the organization, a result that is seen sooner rather than later.

"Do not talk, do it" is the embodiment of "empowerment." It is about concentrating on execution and the result without going round in thoughts and plans with no specific action. In other words, stop passing "the hot potato" from one to the other until we see who drops it. Go on and eat that potato all at once, even if you burn your tongue a little at first when carrying out the task.

How much will it cost not to make a timely decision? How much will it cost not to execute the task on time?

In the case of a disease where someone's life is at risk, not making a decision or executing it on time can mean losing the opportunity to save or attempt to save the person. There are also people who look at the positive side of the inaction and say, "We will let him die quietly."

There is no bad or good position here, but I will leave you with the following question for reflection: Which side are you on, that of taking action or that of remaining static?

The one who gives in wins
and vice versa

I have always had, like cars, five forward gears and one reverse gear. The reverse gear is meant to be used; without it, the driver would have difficulty parking and changing directions when the space is narrow. You have to use it many times if you want to use the car wherever you want. In life, it is essential to learn to use the reverse gear, not only when driving a car but also in relationships, negotiations, and everything in general.

I remember my professor in Investment Decision Analysis who taught us that there are times when the best decision is to stay put and do nothing. Staying still is a good option, especially if one is on the edge of a cliff. In this situation, the reverse is obviously another excellent option. Are you or were you on the edge of a figurative cliff or something similar in your life? What did you do? What are you going to do?

One tends to think that giving up something in a negotiation means lowering or diminishing one's criteria or losing in a certain way. It may be true in principle, but in the end, if the negotiation ends well and the objective of arriving at a reasonable agreement is met, then the sacrifice is equivalent to losing a knight or a rook in chess but ultimately achieving a checkmate.

A friend had a small company that was not growing owing to lack of investment in hiring good salespeople who would promote the product. One day, my friend decided to give in and found a partner who put up the money in exchange for 49% of the company's shares. Today, he sells 100 times what he was selling at the time he made the decision. He owns 51% of something 100 times bigger than what he had owned before. It was worth it.

On a highway, there was a car with a desperate driver who flashed their lights and was honking their horn for passage; we made way for him, and he was able to continue on his way to attend to his urgency. This also made the drive peaceful for us. Giving in solved the problem here, and we all won.

Once, we were lined up to go to a show, and my wife felt the need to go to the ladies' room. I gave up our place in line one by one to five people who were behind us, and they were very grateful. My wife arrived, and we were almost the first in line with no problem. Everybody won. In a situation where one gets into an argument with their wife or girlfriend or a woman, what do you have to do to get out of it alive with the least number of injuries? Give up space and rights and plead guilty even if you have not done anything wrong. Give in. Give up your rights, if you think you have them. Do not resist, because you have lost that battle; otherwise, it will be a very costly war. Take my advice, and you will come out alive, which is already a gain. Experts will agree with me, and novices will doubt me, but in time and after several drops of blood, they will remember this lesson. Give in, and you will win.

When a big business change comes, it is as if you are in the middle of the current of a mighty river. Do not resist, do not oppose the current, and give in to the change. Be part of the change; be an agent of change. You will see how well it goes, and you will outlive it. The greatest difficulty generated by a business change in terms of processes, or in a cultural change at a company, is people's resistance to the novelty. The best and wisest measure in these cases is to give in to change. Buy the change. Give in and win.

Finally, I cannot stress enough the importance of going in reverse. Apologizing and giving up power or prestige are strategies or initial fees for a substantial settlement that will come later. As the saying goes, "You do not get something for nothing."

Change, the one sure thing in life apart from death and taxes

Everything changes. Changes occur every second and even a fraction of it.

Who we were, what we did, or where we lived an hour ago no longer exists, much less who we were or what we did yesterday, and even less, last year. We can accept change as something natural and welcome it, or it can be something difficult and painful to swallow. Which way do you prefer? Pain or enjoyment?

I am going to use some examples of different types of change and their effects on our lives, as a brief reflection, as well as a general conclusion about our attitude toward change.

Let us say your boss calls and fires you. There are many reasons that come to your mind: incompatibility with your boss, your department, or the company culture; your failure to carry out the assigned tasks well; a plot against you; downsizing, as your expertise was no longer useful for the company, and there was no possible relocation; you have become obsolete; you are old; or you are a block that delays or complicates the work in the company. Although all such reasons cross your mind, when asked, you might only receive a standard response by the company: they have decided to do without your services because they need to make changes. You better accept the already painful reality. It is confusing, but in this way, you will avoid further pain in case they tell you the terrible truth. Now, what are you going to do? Lower your adrenaline, and then think coldly about the next step. Life has closed a path for you, but it has also opened a new one. New emotions await you.

What do you do when your wife tells you that she does not love you anymore and asks for a divorce. You are puzzled and confused because you were not expecting something like this. What will become of your children, assets, and mutual friends? Who will you live with from now on? You can ask for explanations, but they will surely add to the pain. You can simply accept your reality and, seeing that a door has closed, begin to plan the next step for a new life, a blank page, an unexpected gift.

There may be unexpected changes in companies, such as reductions in staff and even in salaries, which is something unusual, but I have seen it happen. Companies have requested and supported the authorization to perform these massive changes before the Ministry of Labor, leaving many people in dire straits, either unemployed or unable to meet their monthly financial obligations. What do you do if you are on that list of staff for salary reductions? Manage the change, they say.

The most frequent and one of the most painful changes in daily life is when a close relative becomes ill or suffers an accident, causing us to change our priorities, making health the top one, especially if it happens to one's child, wife, husband, partner, parent, or sibling. This change, which is painful to the soul, invites us to reflect on what is and what is not worthwhile. The conclusion is always that family or love is vital—it is the engine that drives all movement and leads us to have a profession, a job, a business. Without that engine, life largely loses its meaning. This type of change affects morale and destabilizes us, especially if the outcome is the death of the loved one. How do we handle these kinds of changes? Is there salvation?

Among the positive changes could be winning a big lottery, which invites one to reflect on and plan a new life, like with any change. Although in this case, what we did or who we were before hitting the jackpot is very different from who we are going to be afterward. Who am I now?

A vital change is the birth of a child. The whole family is transformed, especially if it is the firstborn. The new role as father or mother, as grandfather or grandmother, uncle or aunt implies a reordering of activities, duties, responsibilities, priorities, and customs.

What about a financially attractive and professionally challenging job offer that is impossible to turn down? A complete 180-degree change. Suddenly, you are facing a change of city or country and, of course, a different company or organization, and everything changes dramatically. It is a new route that opens in our life. What will my future be? What about my family?

What if an unexpected business, work, or emergency trip to another country happens? What do we get, apart from an instant change and a break from routine, with new rules, food, streets, schedules, people, challenges, and knowledge?

What do we do with change? Let yourself get carried away as safely as possible, like someone who is dragged by the current of a mighty river, or if you have a good engine, ride against the current, upstream. With a good engine, you get to wherever you want to go. If you do not have a good engine, you have to let yourself get carried away by the current. Protect yourself from the blows using your arms, and swim in favor of the current but looking for a shore so you can safely stop and plan your next step.

Have a good trip down the river of change.

Conflicts arising from differences in principles and values

One thinks that others have or are governed by the same principles or values. In daily life, however, the situations where we have to make fundamental decisions and respond to a situation or fulfill our word, be it verbal or written, highlight the differences among people. There are those who, in those moments, do not respect laws, rules, or agreements. On the contrary, they behave like the worst criminals, rigging the system to escape responsibility or to abuse or violate trust while turning things around to become victims, when they are the perpetrators, or to bully or shamelessly steal before our own eyes, to the amazement of all the people who perceive them as shameless or hard faced. I am going to reference some situations that will serve as examples for reflection, and then I will finish with some recommendations.

Someone was hired to install a fence two meters tall in front of a house. The man arrived with his assistants to fix the fence and at around 9 AM, they used a drill to pierce the floor. However, it made a hole in an underground clean water pipe and water gushed out more than a meter high. At about noon, the water pipes for the entire block were shut off, leaving all the houses without water. The man tried to cover the hole in the pipe in different ways and nothing worked. At 4 PM, a desperate neighbor suggested to bring in a plumber and, in fact, called her trusted plumber because no one knew of one, specially one who worked on Sundays.

The neighbor managed to get hold of the plumber, who came with the proper tools and materials to fix the problem. Of course, the owner of the house asked how much the repair would cost before proceeding, and although it was not much, the contractor installing the fence said that he would not pay because he was innocent. If he had punctured the pipe, it had been an accident, and although he did not ask for service drawings, he would have never punctured the pipe if he had them. He said that the owner of the house should pay the plumber and a minute later, he said that his employee should contribute to the payment, and to put the cherry on top, he blamed the neighbor for calling the plumber and said that she should pay for having made the call. In the end, after a long argument among everyone, they managed to get the person responsible for the incident to pay at least half the cost of the repair. The contractor was able to say everything he said because he clearly had another set of values or principles, and it seemed normal or logical for him to think and propose what he proposed, as well as avoid his responsibility.

There are many people who plan to fall in love and marry once in their whole life and to constitute an exemplary and stable home with well-behaved children. Meanwhile, I know a man who has never married but has five children, one each with different women who he had lived with throughout the years. From the many separations, he gain a house, a farm, cars, and an apartment on the coast. He proudly calls himself a responsible father because he has a mother for each child—a glorious man of somewhat rigged and crooked values.

There are people who decide in their life to stay away from any type of vice, such as alcohol or cigarettes. In contrast, an acquaintance of mine has declared marijuana a great remedy that relieves pain and even helps him sexually because he feels that it makes him concentrate on his role of lover, isolating himself from noise and distractions and giving the best possible performance. He mentions it openly and feels very good about his achievements with that extraordinary remedy. These are interesting principles.

In many companies, corporate values and principles comprise practice, and their violation can lead to dismissal. Other companies do not even establish principles or values, and anything is valid. There are also some whose principles and values are displayed on boards hanging on the walls. They never practice them, and if there is non-compliance, nothing happens except for the jokes about violating those principles. Agreements are not fulfilled. The given word is not reliable. Ethics are too permissive, and the rules are adjusted or changed often, based on convenience. Double standards prevail, bad examples thrive, and innovations in these missteps are welcome. The reader who follows me knows that I am telling a great truth and that reality is different from the theory or the exemplary code of conduct that some companies establish but have not achieved in decades.

There are people who reserve their intimacy for a single person and in private, preferably with very dim lighting. There are others, however, who are capable of recording videos of having sex alone, with someone else, or in group. They say that it is great because they even get paid to do something they like. These are interesting principles.

The key point here is that differences in principles will cause some disagreements, which could lead to bad times or cause mental and spiritual suffering. Thus, it is important for us to be clear about our values and principles so that we can get involved with people who share similar views.

Someone suggested that I verify the principles and values of people and companies before entering unto a relationship with them, to ensure that their principles are similar to mine—an intelligent suggestion, although difficult to achieve in practice. You do not always have the time to verify, and you end up living life at a faster speed than you require. However, if one can prevent their involvement with people or institutions whose principles or values are incompatible with their own, that would be great.

If you have already gotten involved with the wrong person or with a company or institution that is not for you, my recommendation is to get the courage to leave that situation soon. Otherwise, you will have a hard time and it will hurt your soul, or it can leave lasting mental scars. Canceling what is not healthy for you is a matter of life, and it is non-negotiable because it is a transcendental life decision.

-49-

Qualify Leads and Close Faster, A Quick Guide: The RUDAC Method

M any sales do not occur because salespeople do not know how to identify potential clients, which is crucial in ensuring results and not wasting time and energy on what has no short- or medium-term future. The famous NDC method (which asks about what the client Needs, how they make Decisions, and what they are Capable of) is brilliant, but I want to complement it while maintaining its essence and simplicity.

The Basic Guide to Sales Qualification in the sale of a large project or solution is like the fingers of a hand. There are five key questions.

First, are there RESOURCES, money, or people to assign to a project or, in the case of an individual, are they available and do they have money (we will represent it with the letter R and involve the symbol $, to remember it as Re$ources)? If yes, then we are doing well. Otherwise, the task has to be postponed

owing to the lack thereof, and this can leave the door open to competition or substitutes. The resource requirement is urgent; tomorrow may be too late. As for money, without a positive answer, the case presents no opportunity. If the client buys a dress but does not have cash or a credit card, or does not want store credit, what we have is a bystander or a voyeur. There are apprentices or timid salespeople who do not ask this question, and it is an essential one.

The second relates to the DECISION-MAKING process: Who makes the decision or who is involved to ensure that the right decision-makers are spoken to (let us represent it with the letter D for decision-makers) and not those who are only

interested in asking or finding out information? The latter kind will never specify anything because they do not have the power or authority. Do not talk to the clowns; talk to the circus owner.

There are times when you have to talk to several people who act as decision-makers or advisers. There are processes where they will always require several quotes, look at several alternatives, or repeatedly ask for a lower price. You have to understand the process. In a personal sale, you can be talking to the brother or the husband or the father or a son. In a business sale, the decision-makers can be even more numerous, composed of the interested party, purchasing department, user vice president, technical vice president, president, board of directors, and advisers.

Third, by when do you need your order? Is it urgent? (Let us represent it with the letter U for urgency.) This is very important because one is usually caught by surprise. Clients might need a product by the end of the year or the middle of next year. What if they need it for tonight or this Saturday or in 30 days at the latest? Each implies our position toward the potential client and opportunity. In the former case, you can come back later and nothing will happen. In the latter case, you must move fast for a potential and probable business. It is urgent when the need affects business or life or when a competitor is affecting the business. At such a moment, we will sell like there's no tomorrow.

The fourth relates to us in two ways. First, do we **have the SOLUTION that meets the client's needs, or can we provide it per their wishes and conditions but with most of our components. In other words, do we meet the compatibility demands? (Let us represent it with the letter C for compatibility.)** Can someone else do it? Sometimes, we struggle to try to sell what we do not have or cannot put together or specify. We could end up wasting time and money and hurting our image for failing to comply with or provide the goods or service. Second, **is the client for us or are we for that client?** Sometimes, the desire to sell blinds us, and it becomes a problem when we cannot deliver what the client needs or if the client is too big for us. A bad client brings risk that can destroy a good reputation.

Fifth, do we have good contacts on the client side **(let us represent it with the letter A for Amiable)** who can facilitate access to key information, provide guidance regarding our progress and possibilities, make recommendations, or support us.

Not having friends within the potential client side means that we do not have a radar, and the chances of closing a key sale are slim or very fortuitous.

In summary, we have a new simplified method. It can be represented by only five letters that are easy to memorize. Compared with X, **RUDAC** is more powerful, more complete, and equally fast, and it does not fail. If you answer YES to the five questions, you can close the sale in record time.

R Re$ources (Do you have people, $$$, etc.?)

U Urgency (Does the client require something essential fast?)

D Decision-makers (Are all the decision-makers involved?)

A Amiable (Do you have friends or acquaintances or internal contacts?)

C Compatibility (Do we have the solution? Is this the client for us?)

Of course, apart from quickly obtaining clients, it is important that success in sales requires hard, constant, organized, strategic, and disciplined work. We must possess a good level of willpower or enthusiasm and carry out daily actions aimed at closing deals and monitoring progress so that we are aware of how to get to the client's inner circle. This way, we can take appropriate action, take care to not disclose anything we should not, and instead try to get as much information as possible. Finally, we must have something of a lucky star or, as the chefs would say, a pinch of good luck (sacks of salt are not sold).

Challenging standards methodically leads to success

"Ifyou keep doing the same thing, you will get the same results." "Every improvement is a change, and the opposite is not necessarily valid." "Improvements or positive changes generate progress, and the opposite generates delays."

Do you have the courage to overcome your fears and act? Do you have what it takes to see the future through a telescope or observe the panorama from above and then act on the details at the micro level?

The two previous approaches are the key to success and the way to challenge the standards to move clearly toward new scenarios for exciting results or positive quantum changes. It is like visualizing the future or seeing the right way out of a maze.

What else do we have to do? If you still lack some courage and assurance about what you believe needs to be done, you can run a trial, a pilot test or a concept test, or you can look for a reference, if there is one, and thereby quickly secure your path to success by confirming the approach. It is simple, clear, and concrete.

The driver for everything is the desire to change and overcome the greatest obstacles on the way—the fear of the new or the unknown and being out of our comfort zone. If you can overcome that natural obstacle and jump toward positive change, then the chain reaction that leads to success immediately follows.

To ensure whether the path is the right one, we must visualize the future scenario, that is, to envisage ourselves in 5, 10, or 20 years, and from there, go back and do whatever is needed to reach that goal. Trace the route to get to where we want to. It is similar to getting on a helicopter and finding our exit from the maze. Looking from above lets us know where we are and the way to a safe destination. It is as if we could see the forest at the ideal height and then, knowing where we are, get down to take the right path toward freedom.

The third formula is for those who want to follow a set path, despite having visualized the future. It involves performing a pilot test, having a reference or testimonial that allows one to verify whether the visualization is possible, and then taking on the risk, which is minimal.

Sometimes, it is better and cheaper to verify the actual testimonial of someone who has already left the maze or is simply 10 years ahead of us. If there are success stories, the easiest way is to replicate the path traveled and thus accelerate our own achievement. If there are no cases to replicate, it is advisable to perform a pilot or concept test, or a simulation that allows you to visualize or verify whether the path is the right one to follow.

Conquer your fears. Visualize your future or the probable panorama from above. Verify whether someone else has done it, and replicate their formula, or simply conduct a simulation and go ahead. Change successfully.

Hire the best and gather forces in an optimized manner

I worked with IBM for 15 years, my first multinational job, and I learned a lot about the business life, good business practices, and dealing with clear rules and respect. It was not paradise, but it was a very good alma mater. Part of who I am is thanks to that company.

Fate then took me to another multinational, NCR, where I also worked for 15 years and learned to flourish and help others flourish. I multiplied myself by a hundred. It was a tremendous organization.

From these two experiences, I drew a simple but very useful conclusion for those who plan to hire staff for cheap, which in the long run turns out to be, like the old saying, expensive.

Both IBM and NCR were always looking for the best at the best price. My father told me to buy the best brands when they are on sale. Always look for the best and wait patiently until you find it at a good price.

Finding an excellent collaborator who has wisdom, autonomy, and influence is investing appropriately in the organization's present and future. With the best, we provide the company with transformative and innovative capabilities, in addition to speed and quality, which may not be easy to accomplish since the latter two qualities are in opposition to each other. However, skillful and/or expert collaborators achieve the seemingly magical result of high quality and opportunity.

Aside from getting the best, another thing that I learned in these multinationals is to get the star employees to collaborate on initiatives that can be very high-level, impactful projects.
The key to having the best is to make them work together with common purpose, ideals, language, values, and shared feelings. Teamwork joins forces, and collaboration can occur in earnest—a result that makes a group produce as if it were the sum of millions. If there is collaboration and coordination with integration, the result will entail evident dramatic change.

If people do not understand and block one another, the result may be inferior to the one that a regular person could obtain. However, the situation might disintegrate dramatically. I have seen many organizations that failed as they did not clearly understand these two concepts. "Hire the best and integrate them well" may be the phrase that summarizes the key to business success.

The good quality of hires can be quickly seen through their results. Bad hires are noticed by the absence of good and abundant results. Integration is noticeable when problems are minimized and everything is operating on time or is ahead of schedule. When there is no integration, everything is delayed or complicated, and there is a prevalence of delays and fights or misunderstandings.

The third lesson relates to the opportunity to take action with the right people at the right time. You have to come up with innovative positions or solutions and services when there is a gap in the market. Developing a business idea that no one perceives as a solution or feels is needed leads to bankruptcy. Doing it when others have already taken advantage of the opportunity reduces our strength and diminishes our presence, image, and monetary gains.

Opportunity is key, as are people and teamwork. You have to be at the right time with the right people and the right solution, as the saying goes. The timing of these three elements is what ensures success.

Friends in life

We can count our true friends with the fingers of a single hand, or two at most, and no more.

One such friend of mine told me when I asked him about friends: From among my childhood and adolescence friends, there is one I still hang out with, and we now spend unforgettable hours in the company of his family and mine. We remember the songs we sang, the parties we went to, the dates we had, the friends we never saw again.

Of the friends from school, he told me, I keep in touch with about 20 and maintain a close relationship with about 5 and their families. They are great, fun, and always full of nostalgia and anecdotes, as if time had not gone by and we were still in the classroom having chalk wars and copying test answers. We remember the disorder, the class trips, and the comments about the good and bad teachers, the crazy and nerdy classmates, the soccer games, the exams, the discipline. A good number of us meet every five years to celebrate the anniversary of our class, and we have a great time. There is a lot of sincerity, respect, and, above all, great admiration for who we were and the lives we lived. It is quite a crystal clear, and sometimes, innocently sincere bond.

Of my college friends, I maintain direct contact with about 10, and we meet up almost every year. We are all colleagues united by the memory of our studies, and, in general, we did not have to compete in supplier companies or have supplier–client relationships that distanced us, as happened to many others who had to find out the cruel reality of the meaning of colleagues, which is a mix between partner, friend, enemy, and interested party. Of these honorable colleagues, there are two or three who are good friends, and I have a friendly but distant relationship with the rest. A good number turned their backs on me when I needed them, the friend told me.

We have neighbors that we visit every day or on weekends, or during vacations, because they either live in the same neighborhood or are our neighbors at the vacation home where we go to relax. We have spent unforgettable moments with them. There is only one problem: when we move residences or sell the vacation home, the familiarity gradually cools down because it becomes difficult to see one another (where earlier, it was effortless and natural). Nonetheless, as the song goes, nobody can take the dance we had away from us.

Growing up, I discovered that there are people who will approach us because we are worthwhile to them at a given moment or we represent an interest to them. There are some people with whom we only share good times socially. We could help them many times, but when we need something from them, we will discover that a true relationship did not exist and that they were only close because we were useful to them. Especially in matters related to money, business, and health, we are bound to find out that the friendship disappears with high volatility and speed. There are very few—fewer than five—who remain close when you really need them. These include business partners, co-workers, neighbors, fellow parents of the children at school, and friends of friends.

How many of our former neighbors are still close to us or remain our friends? How many of our college classmates are still close to us and offer help? How many of our primary and secondary school classmates are still close to us and offer support? How many former co-workers are still close and are our friends? A harder question is this: how many of our cousins and siblings are still close to us and support us or are there for us as friends?

Once, a true friend asked himself the above questions and concluded that he had very few friends and family who deserved the title of true friends. There were no more than 10 among his friends and family. I then conducted a similar analysis and arrived at a number that does not exceed 10. That is my real family. My real friends. People who are always with me unconditionally and who have helped me without reservations or limitations the times I needed help. As for my part, I have also helped them as much as I could, and they are like brothers and sisters to me. My two brothers are on that list, and they are great because of how loving and united we are. This is not usually the case. My friend, who made his list of family before I did, had to remove several of his 10 brothers and sisters because they did not fulfill the concept of close family at all.

Make your list and keep in mind that true friends are far and few. They are like brothers or sisters who are always around in both happy and difficult times without conditions or restrictions. They accept you as you are and treat you as a human being, whether you have money, success, or titles. When you fall, they are there to help you get up, heal your wounds, and support you in your recovery.

-53-

Painful deceptions

They are everywhere and in abundance, in business and in personal affairs.

Throughout my life, I have had many partners in different types of organizations, and, except on very few and honorable occasions, I have always had to experience some kind of deception related to something wrong with the company, something bad that was about to happen and nobody saying anything, promises of variable payments, ownership interest to be recognized, shares to be sold, or dreams of profits or objectives to be met. Everything has its little tricks, and one falls innocently into all those traps, which I prefer to think people do in good faith because they were raised in that way or it is their nature.

False promises, such as the typical, "Help me, and I will give you a percentage of the company." You help them time after time, and they give you nothing. Or the typical promise, "There is no problem with your pay because it comes from the results you produce. There is no limit to the payment considered for the person or people who produce good results. The straps come out of the same leather." When the result is achieved and it is time to pay, the amount of money, which exceeds all normal salaries and standards, is questioned. It all finally ends in the deception that leads to a negotiation of the supposedly obvious and unquestionable pay, even though it is in writing, had been agreed upon, or had been published. A lot of creativity emerges in the stories and tales to blatantly sustain the meager reason for paying less. They renege and break promises, agreements, and contracts, ultimately damaging a good relationship because of an unrecognized excellent result. Other innocent people will come along and will be used again and again because that is the strategy: I will take everything from you. I will cheat on you. I will not be fair to you, and then I will upset you so that you leave, or I will get rid of you. (You have already served your purpose; I have already used you. I no longer care if you are not there because I have completed my mission).

A partner I had used me so that she could get all my high-level business contacts out of me and then ended the relationship. She began by telling me that I would be her successor, but I became suspicious when I noticed that she was not leaving. I then spoke with a former collaborator of hers, who informed me that she had applied this trick with everyone, and that I was victim number seven. I then protected my contacts. By then, I had only used 50 out of almost 5,000, and I was the one who ended that relationship, but not before telling her what I had discovered. She never gave me any of the 20% of her company, which she had promised to me in writing, and the fixed pay was getting further delayed. Variable pay was never given.

A friend created a form of analysis that would allow companies to reduce their logistics expenses considerably. For this service, my friend charged a basic fee plus a percentage of the actual savings. After the third contract in which the clients played dumb regarding the variable pay and contract, despite the good results, my friend realized that this way of payment is a dream that results in cruel deception in the long run. Thus, he decided to charge a higher fee from the beginning and thereby avoid the difficulties involved with charging variable pay.

People play with variable pay because they know that a lawsuit would be long, controversial, and expensive. They simply assume that the victim is not going to sue them, which is why they trust their own judgment and almost always win, unless they come across a meticulous brave soul that puts them up against the wall, in which case, they loosen up and negotiate, but always knowing that they will end up paying less. One is almost grateful for some kind of recognition at the end of the lawsuit so as not to continue the dispute, which is a financial and mental drain.

Apart from feeling cheated, feeling used and abused is a condition that deeply hurts the soul for a long time. When we are deceived by strangers or by people whose only relationship with us is business, it is not as painful as being deceived by a friend or someone dear to us. You must now be thinking about the times that a family member or loved one has done something like that to you and made you feel like the bad guy in the end, when in reality, the other person is the bad guy. Who has not been deceived by a friend? Who has not been deceived by a partner? Who has not been deceived by a colleague? Who has not been deceived by a cousin? Whoever has not been deceived in life, let them cast the first stone.

I was very young when I experienced my first deception. I discovered that the girl I loved was cheating on me with another guy who was younger than me. She would go out with him when I was busy taking exams at the university. She used to ask me if I was going to visit her, and if I told her that I could not because I had to study, she would take advantage to arrange her appointments with my honorable competitor. Very ingenious. "When the cat is away, the mice will play."

Once, I bought an extraordinary business that turned out to be a perfect scam. Nothing belonged to the owners, and no one bought or valued the services despite having spent many years selling them. Along with me, 50 other innocent idiots, who were tricked in the same way, also bought in, and there could surely be another 50. It was a foreign company that claimed to sell franchises. It changed its business name and location when the sales issue began to grow more complicated with deceived users. It was a formal deception machine, created to steal between USD 50,000 and 100,000 from each naive character with a well-told tale, which demanded prior payment and a selection process more complex than the one to enter the Pentagon—a first-class setup. You would find out about the deception once you had paid and begun to try to use what you were supposedly sold, but by then, it would already be too late. One was already in too deep.

A friend hired an accountant for his company, and by the fourth month, the accounts were delayed and in disarray. I remember that I had the opportunity to ask the accountant a couple of basic questions, and on both occasions, he told me that he would give me an answer the next day because he wanted to be sure to give me a well-structured response. When he had to be fired, my friend learned that the infamous accountant had three siblings who were also accountants and had helped him graduate from college. They did everything for him because he was absolutely terrible with numbers but very skilled in making people believe that he was an expert. A thorough verification of his references led my friend to discover that the accountant he had hired was a fraud.

Another friend told me that in his youth, an ex-girlfriend he had not seen in a long time showed up suddenly to see whether they could rekindle the old flame; the affair resulted in a disaster, and in the end, nothing of the old love remained. Three months later, the ex-girlfriend appeared claiming that she was pregnant. At the beginning, she claimed that my friend was the father, but over the years, the ex-girlfriend's son developed an undeniable resemblance to his true father, who had an unusual eye color. The boy had intense gray eyes. At the time he told me this story, there were no DNA tests (the 1970s). Although my friend had been deceived, the truth came out some time later, when it was too late. It was an old, highly effective trick used by girls of that time. This lady had deceived my friend several times. The first time was when she assured him that she had never taken a lover, and it turned out that a lot of water had already passed under the bridge. The second time was when she fell in love with an underage boy, with whom she betrayed my friend, and then left my friend for him. She then got pregnant, but the minor would not respond to her. She was eight years older than him and two years older than my friend.

Bandits carry crime in their blood since birth. I know this story very well because it happened to my best friend from youth. He suffered greatly because of this young lady.

It is difficult to protect yourself from so much evil because life requires managing some risk to move forward. Everything is possible. In practical terms, my advice is DO NOT TRUST ANYONE and to check out who you are dealing with prior to the first action. Talk to former acquaintances, employees, or relatives and look thoroughly into a person's track record in terms of relationships, business, or life. Buy time to perform this review calmly and find out what the person is like in formalities away from social visits and gatherings, settings in which they are usually admired. In private settings or within their organizations, people are aware of the great truths and the monsters that they really are. If we inform ourselves thoroughly and verify the warnings given to us, we can prevent ourselves from becoming the next victim. Remember that those who cheat are professionals and they will go over you and your written or verbal contracts and agreements without compassion. Do not be so naive as to believe that we live in a world surrounded by little angels.

I will leave you with this reflection on deception and the antidote of choice.

Imaginary verbal commitments generate conflict; resolve them

"Hello, I would love to be able to count on your key support for a new company or project that I plan to start and whose future is bright. Your talent and experience are of vital importance to the company, and I want to know if you can help me."

The person naively answers that they will gladly see how to take some time to collaborate with the initiative that sounds attractive and fun. A week later, the person with the project proposal calls and assigns various tasks to their expert, and that is when the expert realizes that the person had not clarified absolutely anything about the project and the company and how the relationship will be established or acknowledged. The brilliant creator of the idea then says that they only know that the project is going to be very successful but that they can only have some certainty about the arrangement once the expert performs the initially assigned tasks. On the other hand, says the person with the project, your contribution to this company is your talent and experience, and I will recognize your contribution in the end with a small percentage of the company. I need your task urgently because time is running out. You made a commitment to work with me, and that is what I expect from you—results.

The expert reflects and feels as if they have acquired a new boss overnight, who gives orders and demands compliance and, worst of all, will not pay them. They will not be grateful for the help their potential partner has willingly offered. They propose to the expert shares in a company in which they do not necessarily want involvement and whose risks they do not necessarily want to assume, all without establishing any contract or agreement beyond an informal chat that was probably over the telephone. What do you think? Does this remind you of a similar experience?

What about when they call and tell you that they have an unemployed son, a brother, or a friend, and that they will send you their CV or resume so that you can help them look for a position, and the next day, they are already asking what you have done, to whom you have sent the CV, and what else you are going to do to place the person in a good position? Worst of all, they get upset because they think you have not done enough to find something for that person. When that happens, one wonders, "At what time did I establish a recruitment agency? Who said that I have the time to put myself through the task of investigating where someone with that profile is needed and even promoting them, in addition to reporting on the progress of the search process? Are they abusing me? Who hired me? How much will they pay me? Will they thank me? Do I have any obligation?" It is easy to get tangled up with people and verbal agreements that are made in minutes. People assume that one understands in 60 seconds everything that they have been plotting for months or days; they believe they have been sharing their ideas during all that time and jump to conclusions, and that is how one gets involved only by looking at them or listening to them.

I remember a friend in his early teenage days who used to get in trouble with girls because they would remember his answers to their questions verbatim. My friend used to say yes to requests because he was very positive and enthusiastic, and easily engaged in tasks that he did not know he had to do. He would unwittingly end up committed to the girl in a relationship. When they got angry, he realized that something bad or some misunderstanding had occurred. But you told me, they would say.

People automatically assume that you understand what they are proposing and that you would know all the details and pros and cons, and would be willing to do what they ask without verifying whether you really understood the arrangements, the time to be committed, and the expectations or implications in terms of responsibility over time or money. They end up thinking they have a slave who surrenders at their feet.

Another friend told me that a person in his office once asked for permission to use the bathroom. My friend agreed, and then the person asked for directions to and the key to the bathroom. My friend got the key for them and showed them where to find the bathroom. After a while, the person came back and asked him to go with them because they could not open the door. My friend went to open the door and clearly told them that he could only help them up until that point and to not ask for any more help. How is it that a simple request to use the bathroom becomes a verbal commitment that is more complicated than a contract?

To avoid this type of problem, my advice is to ask the other person to write down what they are telling you as a project proposal so that it can be analyzed with the attention that it deserves. This way also allows us to better understand what is being requested or what is missing, and thus, evaluate whether we are interested and capable of meeting the requirements. Of course, it is necessary to demonstrate what the gains are and who gains from the project, as well as the risks entailed.

If it cannot be done in writing, because it is something more informal, always ask for more time to analyze the matter in depth. Do not get carried away by emergencies that belong to those who want you to get involved in their problems. They need everything by yesterday—that is a red flag. Beware of strangers, opportunists who barely know you and ask you if you want to get involved, or people you have not seen in many years and suddenly appear. In my experience, little good comes out of them.

Go at your own pace, document everything, study, consult others, and then come back with a well-researched and confident "yes" or an elegant but courageous "no." If you do not clearly understand or see what they are asking, say firmly but elegantly: "My schedule is very busy this year. I would need resources that I assume you are going to provide, because I am short even on time. Clearly, you gain something, and what do I gain? Thank you for your fine consideration, but this is for someone else. I do or did something similar, but you are asking me for something else." Be careful. Do not make a commitment. If you have absolute clarity, and you are sure you like it, then do it fearlessly and enthusiastically. If you do not see it clearly or do not think it is viable, say no without saying the word, like in the aforementioned examples, and remember, "it takes courage to be courteous."

Make others do it; do not do it yourself

asier said than done. Your child has homework to do, and we know that they will either do it badly or will not finish it on time. Temptation overcomes us, and we complete the homework in 20 minutes with the highest quality, which would have taken the child hours, and the assignment would not have been completed apart from being of poor quality.

What is the right thing to do? What do we do in a case like this? Does the same happen in the office? If a collaborator or employee has just joined or is not very experienced, do we perform their task by way of "we are a team, and your results are all our results"?

The previous reflection calls for an extremely clear definition of what you want to achieve in the present and future. If there is no future to contemplate, and it is a unique and isolated occasion, the answer is that it is convenient to complete the other person's task. However, most of the time, the future is involved, and it is not a single occasion, which leads us to believe that we are facing a learning process that we know is slow and painful but it is the only way we can ensure that people learn and mature.

The dilemma is, what do we want? Good instant results, thanks to our existence and skills, or the development of people, which will ensure for us a better future? At its core, it is a profound subject that lies between bravery and selfishness.

Many of us experience the dilemma that I have just described, and the decision is delicate and difficult because it is a life policy or a company policy facing the challenges of nature, time, market, competition, quality, contractual commitments, or training for development. There are many variables at stake, and some of them are very delicate and have their own risks.

I particularly recommend making the effort to overcome the urge to violate the learning and development process of individuals and courageously refrain from working on a task that someone else must perform. It is always better to observe how people manage to get ahead in the face of their challenges in life or at work, which generates a lot of value for their future and that of the organization. If we get others to develop their assignments and do not get involved, individuals or organizations grow and become autonomous. If we do the opposite, that is, if we perform the tasks assigned to others so that they are done perfectly, we support mediocrity and irresponsibility or permanent immaturity.

Freeloaders are the product of parents or bosses who do everything directly themselves so that things run smoothly. Thus, they generate drones or eternal teenagers incapable of doing anything well for themselves. They foster a dependency that ends up being a funnel for the organization or the family in the long run. Nothing gets done without the great boss's knowledge and authorization or questioning, or without the father's or mother's blessing.

Let others do what they have to do. Do not do it yourself.

Managing "NO" brilliantly

He says to her, "My love, let us go for a walk. The day is beautiful." She answers, "I am not in the mood for walks." The result: the couple stays home.

In a meeting, one of five participants says, "I like what they have proposed for the company party. Shall we decide on it?" Another person, who had not provided an opinion, says, "I am not sure, I would like to think about it calmly first. I propose that we look into it in the next meeting."

"I want to put on record that I disagree and vote against it" is the typical departure of some honorable directors. Some threaten permanent dissatisfaction if what they have forbidden goes ahead. "I am resolutely opposed to it, and they will have to pass over my dead body before I tell them something in favor of that initiative."

At home, when we go for lunch with the children, the conversation could go something as follows. "How does a good piece of meat sound to you?" "Dad, I am tired of meat." What about the infamous phrase, "Let us stay quiet, my love, because I have a headache."?

Other infamous ones are as follows: "Let me further study what you are proposing because I do not understand it well enough, and this deserves further attention." "I wish I could look at this carefully because it is a matter that requires attention." "I would like to give you my suggestions regarding the issue you just raised or presented, so let us look into the matter at our next meeting." "I do not feel safe or secure making a decision on this issue today. Something tells me that we should be more cautious with such a delicate matter, and I do not feel comfortable.

Let us defer this matter to a more prudent time." "I am not prepared to make a decision today. Please send me the detailed documentation so that I can study it. I want to complement my analysis with other materials and thus be able to contribute my best professionally." "Excuse me, but I feel harassed and I need time. I am not as fast or as intelligent as you." "A delicate and strategic matter like this deserves testing before taking such an important step."

When one has to suffer the consequences of a NO, it is terrible because they are destructive, decelerating, or powerful blockers. When you are the one who uses the powerful, intelligent NO, it is wonderful. Little can be done when the intelligent NO appears the first time, but it can be attacked the second time by indicating that we should not continue delaying decisions, because it is harmful and we cannot indulge one single factor. This way, we can unblock the barrier. As a strategy, the application of the intelligent NO is like the Eighth Wonder, and it is worth learning how to use to delay, block, entangle, complicate, or weaken.

Happy reflection.

Influencing management is more important than being very good

With all the due respect that Lionel Messi deserves, nobody understood why he was awarded the best player in the last World Cup. Although there is no doubt that Messi is an excellent player, there is also no doubt that, for the purposes of the current World Cup, he did not generate results that merited such recognition. Many other players were on the list before him. Meanwhile, a player like James Rodríguez, an evident scorer by concrete and visible results, was awarded a month later and in private in recognition of being the player who scored the most goals in the World Cup.

The reflection is simple. Which is more important, to be very good and obtain the best results, or to have the influence that enables one to stand out and be rewarded regardless of the results?

How many times have we witnessed and experienced similar situations in other contexts of our lives? How many of our acquaintances had sufficient merit and remained in second or third, or fifth place, even though the figures and evidence showed that they were number one? What other factors influence the fact that even when you have the best results, someone else is chosen for the award? Remember, the lowest price does not always win the bid. The prettiest is not always the queen.

Other factors add value to the decisions made. The best company does not always win the award for quality. Sometimes, it is better to have a name, recognition, continuity, proximity, style, charisma, specific weight, or one or more of these characteristics, than to have the best possible figures. It is about looking harmonious or shining even if we are not made of gold. Therein lies the key: shine brighter than gold, without being gold.

You have to shine. That is the objective. To do so, you must have a good combination of factors, like the ones I mentioned earlier, or others, along with some kind of result. Businesspeople often prefer a person's loyalty than the results they may have contributed to the organization, because tranquility and control tend to be given top priority over pure results without trust. Of course, integrity is essential, but loyalty and trust have a very high value, regardless of the result, because they offer security.

Another important factor is style. You must have style to present a topic or say something. There are styles that people like, and there are styles that are dismissed or scary, or that seem ordinary; they lack height, or they lack class. A person who lacks class might have very good results; this attribute in a person with average results might catapult them to stardom, shining brighter than those with very good results.

I have seen many people who are not the best rise and succeed in business, because their style, figure, or manner of speaking and presenting is likeable; this generates an 80% probability of success. We see it every day in movies or on television. There are people who are not necessarily talented or who are just average in what they do, but an attractive or cute figure magnifies them, causing people to see them with different eyes, and they seem wonderful. The same happens with average people with a likeable style. People like the way they speak or present or argue. This phenomenon is like physical beauty, which provide people an advantage from the start.

If someone who is very good at something ever wonders why someone else, who is not as good, ends up being more recognized or awarded, it is because of the reasons I have given above. You often hear about people who win others over with a smooth tongue, which is the outstanding quality of some politicians and some notorious seducers of the heart.

Given all of the above, if you are very good at something, try to complement your skills with a good style, good presentation or conversational skills, and good friends and/or relations, to ensure your success or, at least, broaden your options. Remember, it is not enough to be good or to be the best. If you are not so good at something or if you are not pretty or good-looking, develop other types of charm, like the ones we have shared, and you will see that your chances of success will rise. There are successful ugly people.

Not all beautiful people succeed. One single outstanding quality is not enough to succeed; you have to complement your portfolio to improve your chances of success.

In organizations, politics moves around axes of power, which is where those who are the most skillful, rather than being the best, manage to win the trust of the boss by selling themselves as loyalists, informants, or collaborators. They are able to whisper into the boss's ear and end up calling the shots and doing more than the boss themselves, becoming something like the boss's boss. They become the advisors who tell the boss what to do and what not to do, the power behind the throne or the first lady. There are famous cases in world history about the leaders of a country or a kingdom who were influenced and manipulated by characters who, in the eyes of the world, were the ones who truly held the power.

Gaining the trust of someone important is key, and that is the goal of those who are aware that they are not very good and have to choose other complementary methods to succeed. I will leave the reflection here, because I do not know if the person reading this is the best and is now aware that they have to complement their qualities, or if the person is an average character who has just seen a light at the end of the tunnel in the race to gain confidence. A person can write several books on this topic.

There is no trip without gasoline

Have you invested? Then we can start the business. Do we think big or the opposite? Do we act bravely or the opposite? Are we sure about what we are doing? Do we trust ourselves or our people? Where are you? Where is your company?

I bet you have never answered differently to several of the questions, although the truth is that most of the time, you are the opposite of the opposite. Do you understand why you have not grown? Why you have not made progress? Why you have not gone at the necessary speed? Why is the honorable competition beating you?

Women have a very intelligent saying, "A woman who does not spend, a man who does not progress." It is true.

That is, "There is no trip without gasoline."

Let us get into the details. People ask which came first, the chicken or the egg. The chicken did. Noah did not put eggs in the Ark. First, the egg is laid, and then the chick is born.

Do we want a party? Let us get sponsorship. We want a contest. Let us get sponsorship. We want a concert. Let us get sponsorship.

We want a parade. Let us get sponsorship, and so on. "There is no trip without gasoline."

It is common sense.

In any case, people forget very quickly, and after a few days, they begin to make demands as if the tasks had taken years. This applies when it had only been months since the start of any endeavor, be it having a child, being married, being friends, or being partners. Within a few days, people begin to feel as if it has been years.

There is an old proverb that goes, "Do not assign to a child a task that should be performed by an adult." Every time we initiate or start something, we are like children. We have no experience, no vision; we are delicate, defenseless, and at risk. Life perspective is different at five, 15, 40, and 70 years old.

Investments and efforts are constant. It does not matter if we are talking about a walk, a marriage, a party, a business, or a company. Ignorance of their similarity upsets people when they have to invest more, because they do not understand that this is the way the world is. A typical example is when one goes on a long trip by car. The first tank of gasoline runs out, and you have to refill it several times. You have to pay road tolls. You have to stop to eat, and if the trip is really long, you have to pay for a hotel. Not to mention facing mechanical problems or someone getting sick, which will involve expenses that go far beyond putting in money to fill up the tank to start the trip.

The same occurs in the business world. The start-up investment given by the partners for a company is not enough, and that is just the beginning of a long journey in which many things can happen. The most typical occurrence is that the business would not materialize as quickly as expected or gets delayed. In addition, the period allowed to reach the point of equilibrium moves from that naive dream of the person who does not know or has forgotten these fundamental principles: to start recovering the investment at six months, to see if everything shifted, and reinvest the money repeatedly until, finally, after three years, the person achieves their goal. The problem is the mental toll and stress on the company and its members owing to the urgency of the investors who did not consider these basic principles. What if we were just as demanding with a child? The results can be traumatic and serious for that human being in training. How fast do you have to go, and how far do you have to push?

The same happens in real life or in a marriage. Quickly, the couple forgets that they had only been married for six months, and the demands begin as if the couple had been married for 25 years. Life is built step by step. A child is born, and only after a year has gone by will the baby begin to walk, with considerable challenges to their balance. They may then speak little words. It is clear that it will take a long time for the baby to give up the diapers, and even more time to learn how to get dressed and bathe on their own, not to mention being aware of their own acts—something that parents forget is only achieved after many years. MATURITY.

Children are not at fault for being born with limitations and for costing a lot. Relationships are not at fault for their limitations and slow progress. Companies are not at fault for being created. Life is not built in a day or even in the first year.

Based on everything that I have shared with you in this reflection, it is worth observing our patience or impatience. Demanding maturity from a child when they are barely two years old is absurd; the same is true with companies and relationships. There is a lot to support, guide, and do to reach maturity, and one can make demands and try to speed up the process, but "it does not matter how early you wake up in the morning, the dawn will not come earlier."

Remember, there is no trip without gasoline.

59

Prize for the wrongdoer, punishment for the do-gooder

The universe seems to conspire against logic.

Throughout my life, I have repeatedly witnessed that the inverse of what logic dictates is true. The do-gooder should be rewarded, and the wrongdoer should be punished, but it is easy to demonstrate that this is not the case. Look around you, and you will see the cases I am referring to. How many people have you seen get promoted to important positions after everyone had seen that they had not performed the tasks or achieved the results?

How many people have lost years in their studies or in their jobs because they had not met their objectives, but were still awarded, promoted, and even applauded because they are so ingenious that they managed to demonstrate that they had everything against them and that not even Superman or Wonder Woman could have accomplished what they had? The little they achieved deserved honors.

The most notorious cases in humanity are in the Bible, which, with all due respect, is a history book. It says that the famous prophet Jesus was tried, sentenced, and killed in a couple of days even though he was innocent. On the contrary, Barabbas, who was a known criminal, was released. If this happened to a famous person, surely it can happen to any simple person.

How about the well-known popular belief: when a man is abandoned by his wife, he is the culprit, and when a man abandons his wife, he is the culprit. It is a joke, but it serves to clarify the point we are trying to make.

Many years ago, the general manager of a renowned multinational told one of his young employees that he was a promising star. Every year, the employee exceeded his sales quota by more than 300%, and the manager would promote several of his co-workers because the employee produced 30% of the company's revenue, and "nobody kills the goose that lays the golden eggs to make soup." Nevertheless, after this over-performing employee announced his resignation, it was time to grant him any request—a company car, a large office, a 50% raise, work abroad. The employee told the manager that they had not killed the goose but that they had lost it forever. His promoted co-workers undoubtedly had less credentials than him, and although some of them had merits, none had merits like his. Months later, another multinational company rewarded the employee's talent and elevated him to the position of general manager. A truly incredible ending that is nonetheless true.

The universe only collected the debt, but it is clear that it had originally punished the good guy.

Think of how many bad people you have seen occupy undeserved managerial positions and how many outstanding professionals are still on the waiting list. Does one need to be bad to get promoted? Do you and I have the wrong concept? Have we wasted our lives being good? Is the world upside down? Does being good not get us far? Are there other factors that get us far that go beyond being good at something or being very good?

Unfortunately, the answer is almost always YES.

Savings that impoverish,
expenses that enrich

Companies and ordinary people often make blunders by cutting expenses in areas that they believe will save money or by giving up investments or expenses in areas that will generate significant profit or keep them alive for a long time. As the popular belief goes, "There are savings that impoverish and expenses that enrich."

Some expenses are like the plug of a drain or a trap for a bathtub or swimming pool. When the plug is removed, the pool or tub is emptied. All you had to do was remove a simple plug, and you emptied out all the water from the pool. It seemed to be in the way and not very useful, but it was vital.

Some organizations do not want to spend money on a low-ranking administrative employee who is going to perform the paperwork tasks involving banks or notaries, chambers of commerce or registries, and communication. Instead, the various professionals and expensive executives have to allocate their valuable time on these tasks, which ends up costing the organization 10 times the value of the clerk. Executives occupy their time with routine operational issues and leave aside what is important to the organization's growth, which is vital for the business.

A small area for employees to heat up and eat their lunches seems like an expense that should not be incurred, but it just so happens that with such a facility, people feel happier and more comfortable, and spend less time for their meals. Camaraderie and personal or family savings are fostered, and in the long run, the company ends up gaining productivity and improving the availability of their personnel. Curious, is it not?

Payroll processing is a task that has been outsourced for many years, and it is very cheap. There are companies that have several employees dedicated to registering, preparing, and processing a payroll, which ends up costing three or four times the value of outsourced services. Outsourcing companies process hundreds of payrolls per month and have the experience of recording and processing collateral issues, such as tax contributions, and understand the constantly changing laws. Outsourced services execute the task with a high level of quality, reliability, and confidentiality, which internal personnel cannot fully guarantee. Not spending on these types of services implies spending much more money, which is clearly an example of savings that impoverish.

The example above is similar to having an insurance in place for serious and large cases in which an accident would have forced a company to sell or shut down had it not been for the insurance.

Several years ago in Bogotá, Colombia, a bomb was planted in an emblematic club, Club El Nogal. It practically destroyed a good part of the club. Had it not been for the insurers who paid the salaries of the employees who could not work for more than a year, and who gave the money to rebuild the club, the institution would not exist. Not investing in insurance is an example of savings that impoverish.

Paying for a good salesperson is priceless. You only need a little patience while they manage to seal the first deals. Those same deals will pay for the investment, and there will still be money left over. However, you have to recognize the achievement of salespersons so that they will keep bringing in more business and do not get bored and leave you. The good salesperson brings in business, clients, a good image, and growth. Not rewarding a good salesperson brings customer attrition and ruin.

An example for Latin American countries is the support that is needed in a house, particularly in a home with small children who require a lot of care, soil significant amounts of clothes, demand special food and, of course, exhaust anyone, even the bravest. What if the husband decides to cut the babysitter's services because of the high costs, alleging that the services can be perfectly done by the housewife (the truth is that the services do not cost that much, and they help a lot)? The consequence of these impoverishing savings is a bitter wife for the rest of this man's life and a finished marriage. How much does the tranquility or happiness of a home cost, USD 1,000 or USD 2,000? Are we willing to have an expense that enriches or to generate savings that impoverish? Do you want happiness or permanent conflict?

What about spending on health insurance? An illness occurs at the least expected moment. I have seen families without insurance having to sell their cars and houses to pay hospital and medical bills. These families often go into ruin. For context, the monthly insurance payment is generally worth the equivalent of USD 300 and covers the entire family. Savings that impoverish.

I recommended to a company that they spend on an expert salesperson to help them jumpstart a new line of business. I insisted for several years, but they were against spending money on this person. Finally, the risk of a drop in the sales of their traditional and highly popular lines pressured them to accept my recommendation. In only six months, they recovered the equivalent of USD 3,500 of the salesperson's base salary, and from then on, everything was profit, thanks to the salesperson, who produced enough to cover their own salary and also generated the equivalent of that expense in pure profit. Expenses that enrich.

Think it over before you decide to spend or save money. Surely, you have already remembered the times you have made the mistake of cutting out key expenses and keeping the bad ones.

Two-headed coin

Some people are like a two-headed coin. On one side, the coin is 500 pesos, and on the other, it is 100 pesos, as they say. Perpetually false.

Why does this happen? Is it a mistake of nature? Are they born or are they made? What do we do to discover who they are? What do we do so as not to be fooled? What do we do to neutralize them? These are some questions that we face when we realize that there are people like counterfeit two-headed coins.

We encounter this type of people among those friends who, in a moment of truth, and when we really need them, run away or turn their backs on us. We naively believed that they were our best friends. Much worse is when we discover that they kept pointing out or amplifying all our defects and envying us for our good qualities behind our backs.

As for couples, how about when we discover that our partner is not the saint we believed them to be, not even in the slightest, and has deceived us many times for a long time, either by cheating on us with another person or several people, or by telling us a story or several stories that were ultimately lies? At the beginning of the 20th century, a great-aunt of mine married a man who made her believe that he was the owner of a soft drink cap factory and was somewhat of a millionaire. Days after the marriage, he confessed that he was neither a manager nor the owner but a simple operator at the lowest level. My poor aunt lived a life full of love and great financial limitations.

What happens in companies? Two-faced people present in different conditions, such as the co-worker who tells the boss about group confidences, the infamous snitch. How many times have we been "snitched on"? The competition is unfair with a character who, within a group, acts as an infiltrator.

Another typical two-faced person is the boss or the colleague who never does even half a task but manages to sell the idea that nothing is possible without them. I bet you know this person well and have had to put up with them. The one who steals others' successes and sells the idea that they are Superman to the boss, who swallows up that story and is "blindly in love" with our very proficient, shrewd, and opportunistic manager or co-worker. How do these things happen in companies? How do very smart and important bosses look like idiots at the hands of scheming, abusive, and creative masters of appearance?

What I have shared with you happens quite often, and I am sure you are thinking about the time it happened to you, or maybe it is happening to you. The person who does not obtain results but is able to develop arguments that lead people to believe that they are incredible because they achieved 20% of what they had to do in spite of the 1,000 obstacles and catastrophes they had to encounter and endure. Thank goodness it was not the 180% (minus one hundred and eighty percent) that could have occurred. These characters even receive honors and awards because they find bosses who believe their stories, which we all know are just that—stories.

I have just described magicians, who create illusions, and the audience who buys into them as irrefutable realities. This ability to tell stories and to provide a foundation that makes them seem credible is how some politicians manage to get people to vote for them, and there are millions of voters who believe them. The same happens in companies with "corporate politicians."

What do we do? Exposing the phony in public with concrete evidence that uncovers their lies is like revealing a magician's trick to the audience and making the magician repeat the trick so that everyone sees that it is a lie, a trick, an illusion. It is also using the power of many or the power of evidence to unmask the liar.

It is easy to say, but doing so requires courage and tenacity, something that many people do not have, and is the reason they prefer to put up with two-faced characters. I believe that people come into the world with the DNA of deception and lies, and some develop it early while others develop it later, but once they develop it, there is no turning back. That is why it seems as though they become this way, but in reality, they are born this way. One observes from a young age that tendency in some people. Nature presents its errors, and this is an obvious one. Fortunately, they are not very many.

I hope you have identified your two-headed coins and are managing them properly so they do not hurt you.

What great bosses do not see

S occer team captains are strategists of each game, when everyone else is on the field playing against the opponent. Without the captain, the team normally exhibits diminished energy and probably has a high chance of losing. A good coach is aware of this. They know that the captain sets up the plays and turns plans into reality because the captain is the one who initiates or develops the plays or passes that lead to the goal.

In business, there are captains who play the same role but do not carry the title. They are the ones who make the team function and resolve the most complex situations by getting the team to think and act—by moving people. One can normally find this type of player in executive committees, on Boards of Directors, in simple management committees, or in normal groups within a department, unit, or division. Each group has its captain, apart from an official coach, who is the top head of each unit.

Now that I have offered you this reflection, all of you reading this passage must have realized that captains exist in all human teams and that they play a vital but barely recognized role in companies.

In the moment of truth, these team captains in different areas are the ones who ensure the timely and proper execution of crucial tasks in the company. They are the ones who wear the organization's shirt and seek the best for it. As often occurs in soccer, the captains are not necessarily the ones who score the most goals, which is why the scorers are remembered the most. However, these scorers would not have the glory or half of their success if it was not for the captains who set up the plays for them.

In business, the captain's silent work receives little to no recognition. When there is no good captain in a given area of the company, new ideas do not flow, plans do not materialize, and oftentimes, even the simplest plan gets entangled or complicated. When the different activities in an organization are facilitated, the decisions taken, and the activities executed, you will realize that there is a good captain on board. When the captain leaves the team and is not replaced, or no one takes their place, their absence is soon felt, and the equivalent to the team's coach begins to realize that the person who left was vital—but it is too late. The damage is done. The problem is that pride and arrogance hardly allow one to take a step back to acknowledge mistakes publicly. They simply suffer from their mistakes in silence and in the results.

I have seen many excellent corporate captains leave because they got tired of fighting against a bad coach. Remember, in the long run, the captain may be one player in the team, but he is the player who sets up the winning plays, giving the team rhythm and speed, who inspires tranquility and confidence, or the one who encourages growth in the face of adversity. Of course, successful teams must have a good coach, a good captain, and good players, but the two heads must be of excellent quality to deliver results, and they must be perfectly synchronized. Finding a good coach is as difficult as finding a good captain.

Personally, I have often witnessed what I have shared herein throughout my life, which is why I decided to make it public. I have lived it firsthand, either as a player or as a captain, or as a coach, and I know how essential it is to consider these reflections.

I suggest that each person discover or detect the person who acts as the silent but effective captain in their work group or organization, and help maintain or protect the captain so that the group or organization may have many years of good results and satisfaction.

Remember, this applies to any human group, even families. The issue is that great bosses almost never see the captains, and they generally disqualify their significant contribution to the organization.

A huge hug for our beloved, selfless captains.

63

Who do the great "white feather" bosses listen to?

Great bosses are constantly told stories because they are removed from the day-to-day liaison with clients, suppliers, and employees. I think this is a big mistake.

The foregoing situation gives the second-in-command the opportunity to manipulate and filter, in good or bad faith, information based on what is most convenient and, thus, block the great boss from talking to others and getting to know viewpoints other than the one that a single person of extreme confidence can provide, who, no matter how well-intentioned, has only two eyes and two ears. My advice has always been to meet up with clients, employees, and suppliers often so as not to lose purpose and to map the situation on the ground. Making the right decisions greatly depends on the level of reliability of the information we have about a case, project, opportunity, or problem. Therefore, it is better to have several perspectives that can be collated, based on which we can draw conclusions and make decisions.

"Do not swallow whole" a single source, regardless of their trustworthiness or good intention. The problem lies in the "white feather's" forgetfulness when they become the great bosses. They act as if they do not know these pieces of advice, and despite their great vision and extraordinary talent, they fall like small children into the trap of believing 100% of the information provided by their trusted person, whom they love blindly. They allow themselves to be manipulated by a person who ultimately ends up having their power amplified by 300% in the great boss's shadow, since they are the only valid interlocutor and the only channel through which information flows to and from the great white feather boss.

When the trusted person or the various trusted people have good judgment and good ears and are fairly open, the information that reaches the great boss is filtered, but its quality is good. However, when the trusted people are short-sighted and of "poor hearing," the quality of the information that reaches the big boss is low, leading to the risk of failure, given that the boss will make decisions based on misinformation or will not act in time because they do not perceive the urgency. They may also take actions based on monsters that do not exist and ghosts that are misinterpretations or bad visions of the trusted sidekicks.

I have often seen the second-in-command falling out with a client and attributing to them the responsibility for the disagreement, something that should set off the great boss's alarm bells. However, the opposite occurs, and the boss ends up losing their temper with the client because they swallow the trusted advisor's whole story.

Another thing I have noticed is that the second-in-command becomes the hero, the one who does everything. Superman is no match for them. This should, again, set off the big boss's alarm bells, but the opposite happens. The boss swallows the tale whole and believes they are lost without their trusted person, because nothing would get done or accomplished without them. It seems unbelievable, but it happens. This is how things work in real life.

What do you do if you are the Big Boss? You already know. Wake up and get in touch with clients, suppliers, and employees or collaborators. Listen to other sources.

What do you do if you are a trusted person who manipulates the boss? Make sure that the big boss does not read this because things may start going wrong for you.

If you are neither a great boss nor a trusted person, help others awaken the great boss so that the organization does not collapse. Be persistent in motivating the great boss to come into direct contact with reality so that they will wake up.

Judas, Pilate, and Caiaphas in real life

Judas (the traitorous fool), Pilate (the power that kills because it does not support the good), and Caiaphas (the manipulative enemy and mastermind)—in real life, in personal affairs, and in companies or organizations, you will always find this infamous trio of characters. Think for a moment about what happened when you were betrayed. If you analyze the case, apart from the traitor, you will find a Caiaphas, and if you analyze even more deeply, you will be surprised to find that the person you believed was the powerful authority did not support you and, instead, ended up condemning you (Pilate). The matter is not only religious, as happened to Jesus, who ended up on the cross because of a traitor and a powerful man who allowed himself to be manipulated by the real murderer with the face of an angel (Caiaphas, the high priest).

I have had to suffer Caiaphas's existence several times—people who devised a plan to get me out of the way because of envy or fear and, thus, continue to reign over their domain. I have been surprised to find out that the person I believed was going to help me, because they seemed to be a level-headed leader, ended up withdrawing their support and trust, punishing me and rewarding those with the least merit (extremely unfair). It is painful to know that the people we had by our side as trusted allies were the ones who sold us to the enemy to finish us off. We get taken by a tremendous surprise and disappointment when we realize that the world is like this. It has not changed, and it will not change.

Typically, the one we most often detect is Caiaphas, the person who clearly envies us and criticizes us in public or highlights our defects. They attack us and make us feel bad, as if we have violated some rule or law because we are not, or do not want to be, under their control and manipulation. The key point of this reflection is that a Caiaphas is never alone and is always in the company of a Judas, the traitor or the disloyal, and a Pilate, who never makes decisions for himself and expects others to advise them or tell them what to do.

Pilate is the character who legitimately holds the maximum power in the community, organization, company, city, or country, and waits until they are forced to define a situation, in which they will make it clear that if they kill, it is not their fault, but are merely complying with someone else's will. In reality, however, we all know that Pilate does not need to comply with anything and has perfect autonomy and unquestionable authority to make decisions. The problem with Pilate is that he ends up killing the good guy and publicly washing his hands of the situation by stating, "I had to, I was forced."

We can never trust everyone. Remember, these characters always form a trio. Always. If you encounter one of them in any situation, immediately find out where the other two are, and watch your back, because they are going to stab you.

The daughter of a good friend of mine fell victim to a Caiaphas, who charmed her and took her to another country under the belief that she would have a better future there. He then manipulated her into cutting off her relationship with her parents. He literally kidnapped their daughter. The powerful figure who was Caiaphas's husband washed his hands of the situation and only dared to say that he would not interfere because he respected the decision that the girl, of legal age, had made regarding her parents. In the end, they were "stabbed" and left without a daughter.

Another friend came up with an idea and formed a partnership with three others. The closest partner, who was his lifelong friend, sold him to a Caiaphas, a manipulative and dangerous character, an opportunist, who, out of envy, hatched a plan from day one to gatekeep the ideas and the organization. Caiaphas was the one who finally ended up keeping the company. The Pilate characters, those who knew about the matter and the facts in depth, washed their hands of the situation and left, but they never made a decision. They did not defend the creator. They let him get stabbed.

In another organization, the fighter and generous leader confronted the Caiaphas ideologically (Caiaphas is never right but he wants everyone to bow to his will. He declares those who go against him as his enemy; he looks for Judas to betray the leader and has the latter executed by Pilate). The Caiaphas character immediately looked for someone weak who could be a potential informant within the organization, and tried to make the leader look bad in Pilate's eyes (the great corporate boss), who, ultimately, as often happens, did not defend the good guy. He agreed with Caiaphas and ended up stabbing the innocent leader who had started the business.

You must be remembering your own experiences by now, and you must have realized that the trio always coexist. It is not a religious or biblical issue; it is a reality that occurs, without fail, in families, friend groups, companies, and any human group. It seems incredible, but that is how it is.

Look for these characters and protect yourself or flee before you get stabbed.

Pay attention: The story of the NOYENADA and NOVENADA

This is a famous and very didactic dialogue of an interview between a boss and a future employee.

Boss: What can you do?

Employee: I can pay attention.

Boss: You are hired.

How difficult it is to get people to pay attention.

I have heard countless stories of bosses who spend hours giving advice and guidance to a collaborator, and many times, it is as if they are throwing words in the air. The words go in one ear and come out the other, and they never stay long enough to enact the change required, achieve the objective desired, or straighten the course of events. When that happens, one knows that the task or assignment is going to go wrong, and in the end, the collaborator will end up leaving the organization for disobedience and for failing to fulfill the objectives.

Adolescence is a period in life that is commonly observed in companies, in employees who are no longer between the ages of 13 and 19 years. Although people are older and more mature, they do not pay attention and end up either not doing or doing other activities that lead to different results, or simply not producing results. It is like someone's mature and conscious behavior of silly rebellion of attempting to kick the lunchbox and ending up getting fired or dismissed for not listening or not diligently meeting the recommendations or instructions of the boss, friend, or colleague, who generally seek the best for the person and the organization.

None so deaf as those who will not hear, goes the saying. In the modern world, where threats are not used and management is participatory, many people misunderstand instructions because they are not given in a strong or military voice. These people forget that the boss is the boss or that the advisor is the advisor—the leaders who make sure things happen and tasks are executed. The difference is that in these modern times, we assume that people have discipline, self-control, and a sense of responsibility. Basically, we assume that they are mature from an early age and know that they have to perform and anticipate tasks, rather than wait for someone to call their attention and breathe down their necks for not doing them.

In organizations, there are many people who behave like adolescents. They do not pay attention and then say that no one listens or helps them. They play at being rebels and are occasionally aggressive to the people who guide them to perform the required tasks in the correct way. No matter how many times they are asked to perform a task or job, or how many times they are told how to do it and the benefits of doing it a certain way, they will never pay attention because they only do what they want.

The issue is simple when dealing with a person of a low rank within the organization: all you have to do is dismiss them, and the matter is settled. However, it is especially difficult when the person who behaves like a teenager is in a position of responsibility or, even worse, in a position of leadership, which clearly impacts the results of the company in the end. Although this problem ends in a dismissal, the disruption it produces is great, and the cost is high. The evidence is easy to find and verify, given that the expected results do not occur in the required timeframe, and "death" occurs owing to non-compliance.

The NOYENADA, as I have decided to call them, abound, and they generally delay, complicate, question, hinder, or impede an objective, task, plan, idea, decision, action, or initiative. How many NOYENADA are around you? Does your work depend on any of them? What would the organization be like if the NOYENADA did not exist?

People put up with the NOYENADA because they prefer to find alternative ways to overcome the difficulties the NOYENADA generate or because it is exhausting to enter into long, meaningless discussions with them. Other times, people avoid the NOYENADA because they become a nightmare. They argue or talk, but nothing concrete is set because they are always against any proposal, and the dreamy alternative that they propose rarely takes off or works. They are blindly convinced that it will, however. Should they also be called the NOVENADA?

The solution is to detect them and to have the courage to call them out with facts so that the organization becomes aware and dismisses them.

Pay attention.

Five organizational elements

At the end of the 90s, I had the opportunity to devise an organizational model that has spread and become truly successful owing to its practicality and simplicity and, best of all, its results. In the multinational company where we first implemented it in 1998, it was called the pentagon because of its five aspects. It is about five elements that an organizational team must have to ensure balanced operation. The absence or redundancy of one element can end up taking the organization to an undesirable or even fatal end. The five elements are creative, grounded, bold, fixer, and human.

The model has a very simple philosophy. If we lack the creative element in an organization, we will run out of innovation until the market and the competition finish us off. If the grounded element is missing, then the machine would have no brakes, and we run the risk of losing control or crashing. Without the bold element, the organization is excessively prudent and shy, which slows us down. Without the fixer, we will not be able to overcome the inconveniences that arise, and without the human element, there will be no people who will stick around or serve us.

If we have two grounded elements and no creative element, or if we are missing the bold element, the organization will make very slow progress. What if we have three grounded elements, the human, and the fixer? What if they were all human and sensitive? What about just creative elements? Just bold elements? If we are talking about a single person, we have to find a balance between the five elements so that it does not end badly in some respects. If there are two people on the executive team of an organization, each one should exercise a couple or three of the vital elements, depending on the case.

Even in a foundation or non-profit organization, there must be a blend of the five elements. It cannot be all about humanity and helping others or only sensitivity; otherwise, who will be in charge of creating financial options or obtaining funds? Who will be in charge of controlling expenses and investments? Who will be in charge of getting donations or exploring possible grants? Who will be in charge of resolving the difficulties that arise? The key is in rotating leadership, or determining who exercises the leadership in that team of five elements.

Of course, minimum operating rules must be established, as in all high-performance teams, so that the members come closer, make decisions, take action, resolve differences within the five elements, and maintain the indispensable unity and trust. Another important factor to understand is that we do not achieve the five elements purely or uniquely by vocation. It is clear that each of us has more or less of one element than the others. We decide what role to play in case we have to perform several elements at the same level. It is a matter of self-organization.

As in soccer teams, we cannot only take defense positions. The team cannot be all goalkeepers or all forwards, although some of these extreme ideas do not sound bad. What if we all want to be the coach?

The five elements are very similar to those found in nature: air, earth, fire, and water, plus a fifth element: the human (heart), as proclaimed in a very old cartoon with an ecological purpose (Captain Planet in the 90s). Today we realize that the cartoon had a lot of depth, more than its creators had, not as a story but as a serious and vital business practice, which is what I turned it into. It went from a cartoon to an organizational tool of great practical power and common sense, albeit not obvious.

Now that you know what can be accomplished with well-equipped and balanced human teams as well as the risks that you run when they do not have the appropriate characteristics, do not forget that "the power is yours."

Rhythms in life and the vitality of their synchronism

C ompanies, as well as people, have their own varied daily rhythm. The challenge is to keep the similar rhythms in parallel. When the rhythms oppose one another at a given moment and are very distant, breaks occur. Either the company decides to liquidate the worker or the worker resigns. Among people, friends, partners, and marriages, the divergences of rhythms cool down relationships, whereas the proximity of rhythms improve them.

My daughter studied at a school whose purpose was for girls to be happy as they learned and made good friends. At one point, a new principal was assigned, and the new school's guidelines were to achieve the best averages on state exams. The school became an environment where all the girls competed. They became enemies, and the stress from the pressure to be the best became unbearable.

My daughter changed schools because the school's rhythm diverged from what she was looking for and from what she liked.

A friend got an important position in an American organization in Texas. His wife disliked going to the United States and loved being in the company of her siblings and parents. My friend left for the United States after separating from his wife. The rhythms changed, and the couple dissolved and drifted apart.

Two friends shared a weekly golf game on Saturdays, which caused a proximity between the families and countless happy reunions. One day, one of the two friends decided to dedicate themselves to tennis, and the proximity reached its climax. The rhythms changed and they drifted apart.

Sometimes, the distance is because of greater events, such as the death of a relative or a couple's divorce, which generate significant changes in the circle of friends that surround those homes. Ties are broken, rhythms change, and people drift apart because what united them no longer exists.

A company manufactures a certain type of product, but the market forces the company to migrate to other types of products to survive in the face of competition and to address client requests. The experts in the production of one product are usually different from the experts for the new product. Consequently, many employees have to leave the company. It is a constant turn of events. Inevitably, the rhythm changes, and everything else changes.

Changes in rhythm require heroic decisions if you want to maintain proximity. A specific case is marriage. People's rhythms change every day, and it is a real challenge to keep up, just like in a dance. We are dancing salsa, and your partner suddenly begins to dance rock. If we do not follow her, we lose her.

I knew a person who had been working in an ever-changing company for more than 35 years. When I asked them how they had managed to stay in the organization, they replied that whenever a change came, they would raise their hand and say aloud that they wanted to play an active role in helping to bring about that change. I invite you to be an agent of change or, at least, to stop suffering, abandon the present, and seek new directions.

Following the path that life is forming is the key to staying together

Surely it has happened to you where you enter a company and over time, you realize that what you had initially known begins to disappear. The company starts making changes to its structure, its culture, its strategies, and even the people that compose it. It ends up being a very different company from the one that originally attracted and seduced us. We feel as if we are in another company.

The same happens with our partners. At the beginning, we felt attracted to their personality or to what they did. We were seduced by many very striking characteristics that, when you realize, have changed over the years, and one ends up with a partner who seems nothing like or hardly resembles the original person with whom we initiated the relationship. This is simply because we have grown up or matured, we do other things, or we devote our time to other endeavors, jobs, or responsibilities, and we even find that our tastes are different from those we had in the past. In other words, we are with another person.

Everything changes, and this is normal and natural. Life is an adventure film with continuous challenges, but we are left with the photograph of the first day. What do we do? What is life's game? The challenge is to follow the route despite the changes and keep the attraction alive, not through past events that no longer exist but by falling in love daily with the new company or the new person that accompanies us, who is the same as always but has evolved. That is the real challenge—building a relationship day by day with the same enthusiasm of the first day. The easiest thing is to follow different routes and end the relationship owing to incompatibility in the face of changes.

The construction of a good building is a challenge that requires care, careful step-by-step execution, patience, time, and quality. Meanwhile, the demolition of a building that had been standing for a while takes seconds with strategically placed explosives.

The same happens with a good name. A reputation takes many years to build, and it is done step by step with great dedication and quality. Destroying a reputation can be in a matter of minutes with a malicious comment made in public by any of the communication channels that exist today. Rebuilding the image is very difficult because trust has been destroyed. As the famous phrase goes, "I am where you are, and you are where I am," but this is easier said than done.

In any case, there are people who change significantly or very drastically in life, making it almost impossible to follow them. In those moments, you have to see and evaluate how to follow them, if possible, and try to do so.

There are organizations that make drastic turns when they merge with others, which generates a change in culture, management, services, or products offered, as well as goals or direction. Those on the inside must evaluate whether they want to or are able to continue, while the organization does the same and terminates some relationships, particularly those who will not follow the new route or will not be of use to the company, which now requires different talent.

Companies also evolve after a change in ownership or owing to different market demands, and people on the inside suffer or become confused because they feel like they are in another organization. Here, too, people must evaluate the effort in following the route, which sometimes becomes difficult because other skills and dispositions are required, and it is not enough to be eager or willing.

If it was easy, there would be no challenges, and life would lose a bit of its flavor.

You have to try to stay together or close despite the changes and clearly understand that changes are normal or natural and frequent. Consequently, our ability to adapt and how quickly we do it will allow us to stay alive and remain united with people or organizations.

Following the daily path of life is a great challenge, and although it hurts sometimes, because we significantly distance ourselves from our objectives and visions or styles, it is worth trying. Change is good for all of us, not only for the person or organization that changed.

Change is a perpetual constant in all life scenarios, and aside from death, it is the only sure thing that will happen in every context. Everything changes at all times. Based on this, I do not understand why we humans sometimes forget this aspect. We dislike the fact that there are changes, or we do not tolerate or cannot handle them.

Following the route, either as people or between people, and as organizations or between organizations, can be demanding, just as training to become a good athlete is. It will hurt and it will cost us, but we can do it if we want to and work on it.

The challenge is worth fighting for if we still want to and are willing to face it. "I am where you are, and you are where I am."

-69-

Key characteristics in a collaborator or partner

I t is very important for the person at our side to be intelligent and to have self-control and autonomy. However, two people in the same category often end up competing with each other or hurting themselves; it is better for them to complement each other: the active and the passive, the cranky and the good-humored, the fast and the slow, the creative dreamer and the grounded and cautious, the focused and the distracted.

Most of the time, people do not think about the benefits of opposites or the benefits of equals, and they end up fighting because they are either very different or very similar. The important thing is how we take advantage of the differences or similarities and how we overcome the different challenges of daily life, by using these characteristics in our favor to obtain the best results. Many people spend their lives arguing about differences or similarities instead of building on the enormous possibilities of having double or opposite capabilities.

Apart from intelligence, self-control, drive, and affinities or complements, the key to everything is the attitude toward change or daily challenges. Our ability to survive or succeed, or fail or die as a team, in our company or in our relationships, is in our attitude toward the realities of the problems, restrictions, mistakes, or difficulties.

The same applies to companies. It is not enough to be intelligent or proactive, to have knowledge or experience, or to be compatible with the internal culture. Although these are essential aspects that cannot be lacking in a job, attitude toward daily challenges and changes is vital, and it can make everything else fall apart. One must analyze and consider six points when choosing a collaborator. If any of the six are missing, we will feel the effect, but three are vital: intelligence, compatibility, and attitude.

It is not a minor detail, but commitment and loyalty to the cause, to the leader, to the partner or the organization are indispensable elements. They are definitely not achieved on the first day, but when they are attained, they are the glue that ensures a long-lasting relationship, or they are able to accelerate an abrupt ending.

The ninth element is strong principles and values, which are formed by our upbringing. They ensure that the person is incorruptible or displays impeccable behavior regardless of any stressful situation. I often say that when a person is in a bad temper, it is important to make sure that they do not take a screwdriver and poke us in the eye, to put it somewhat dramatically. If they have strong values and principles, there will be no inappropriate behavior.

In summary, the key characteristics of a collaborator or partner are intelligence, self-control, proactivity, knowledge, experience, compatibility, commitment, loyalty, and solid principles or values.

Experts, apprentices, selling ourselves or internal sale

"The expert makes something difficult look easy, and the inexperienced makes something easy look difficult." (Hugo F. Valderrama)

"The key is to sell the reliability and quality of the best product that we ourselves are." (Hugo F. Valderrama)

The difference in the quality and speed with which a project or task is carried out depends largely on the person in charge of it. In the hands of an apprentice, we will experience delays and reprocesses because of their inexperience. We are guaranteed to encounter many errors and problems. In the hands of an expert, there will be minimal problems, evident good quality, and the task will be completed in a short time.

This all seems logical and common sense, but it is not actually practiced when companies focus on savings. This ultimately results in a loss of time and money, as well as the learning that we should have placed an expert from the beginning. The high initial cost would have translated into less time and impeccable quality, which costs the same or less in the long run and is less painful, of course.

Sales happen when a product or service is performed with the excellence of an expert along with the trust that the person or company provides to the client. Therefore, it is crucial to generate that trust to make a difference. During the sale process and once the deal has been sealed, trust in the leader moves people internally so that everything is organized around providing the best solution and the best customer service based on the quality of the negotiation and the capacity to fulfill the commitment. The latter is called internal selling, and it is much more challenging and more demanding than selling to the client. Of course, I am referring to the professional sale of large solutions in large accounts, but the example serves to illustrate the importance of selling your own image of trust, which is vital in any process and an important asset for present and future accomplishments. The image of trust and reliability or seriousness and compliance is the greatest asset that a person or an organization can have.

In the hands of the experts, great challenges seem simple, and one is amazed at the clarity and speed with which these people or companies carry out tasks or projects. One hires a certified expert in a vocation, and their actions are evident from day one. This characteristic of experts can be appreciated in every aspect of daily life. When we hire a person who knows little, we see how they report problems, limitations, difficulties, delays, and conflicts from the very beginning. It seems as if life runs them over because they do not have the ability to anticipate or react. Another thing is that we pretend to be blind, or we do not want to see the obvious.

The reflection that I want to share is related to a medical question that elucidates the importance of experts. If your mother had a heart disease, would you take your mother to a general practitioner or a beginner cardiologist?

The importance of the reverse gear and the elegant finish

The reverse gear is not limited to cars, but few people or institutions use it, even though it is an essential and necessary change to resolve "dead ends." When they have to go in reverse, they do not know how to do it or what lever to move, figuratively speaking.

People and companies know perfectly well how to start a relationship in a fine and elegant manner, but very few prepare or know how to approach a termination of employment in a way that generates a good reaction and makes people content. Moreover, many have never thought about terminations and when they occur, they make so many mistakes that they end up generating conflicts, leaving scars. Unremovable and unforgettable. People do not prepare for either of the two previous cases, which are ultimately related to ending a relationship.

Lawyers usually offer a few clues with a couple of notorious phrases about terminations and reversals. "Things are unmade the way they are made," and "a bad settlement is better than a good lawsuit." My father taught me another key phrase for these cases: in any case, enter by leaving. How are we going to end up or how are we going to return from having entered a relationship, partnership, or business or having entered a car, boat, or building. How do we get out unscathed if the need arises?

Let us consider various cases to support this reflection. A friend's son's checking account had been seized because he had not paid a traffic violation penalty that he did not know he had in his name (because it was one of those placed by a hidden camera). Although he immediately paid the amount, which was very small, it took several months to get the embargo removed, which kept him financially blocked. Not knowing how to use the reverse gear presents serious consequences.

Another friend was told that the IMEI of his fine cell phone had been "cloned"—another person registered another device with the same number, causing his service to be blocked and his cell phone rendered useless. He presented the original invoice for the purchase of the cell phone to the company and asked seven times for the issue to be resolved. By the end of the eighth month, he decided to write off the unusable cell phone and bought a new, quality cell phone, in addition to the cheap one that he had been using as months went by without a solution. Of course, he switched to another operator since the former one knew how to suspend the service but was unable to re-enable it—a measure that was established to block stolen cell phones, thereby rendering them useless forever. They were unable to go in reverse.

A friend was traveling on a plane in first class, in a fine white suit, when a flight attendant accidentally spilled a glass of red wine on her. Although they helped her remove the stain in the restroom and gave her a complimentary ticket, among other things, aside from an apology, which mitigated the incident, my friend lost her suit forever. Reversals are not easy.

A friend was fired from an institution through the infamous "pink slip." It was necessary to terminate the relationship unilaterally. My friend had done nothing wrong, but he suddenly fell off with the boss, either because he was made for another time or he was not doing his job properly. However, the effective management of an exit can make this moment, which is certainly unpleasant, less painful as long as the termination is conducted kindly, cordially, and appreciatively. Every person contributes something positive during their relationship with another person or organization, and these contributions can be acknowledged and appreciated while the person is being told that the relationship has sadly come to an end, without bad faith on any of the parties. The ending can be arranged or adapted to be elegant and pleasant. It is a perfectly manageable process even though it is a termination. The person does not have to be made to feel bad, disrespected, or unappreciated as a human being, as a professional, or as an ally. It is not about pursuing a "bloody death"; it is about how to achieve a "beautiful death."

Reversals in business, institutional, or personal relationships are always difficult. The start may be a honeymoon, and so the ending becomes a challenging matter. Many times, it is like trying to disarm a bomb, where you have to know the sequence in which to cut the wires so that the bomb does not explode in your hands, apart from having the courage and the will to reverse decisions and agreements. The elegant end is closely tied to this reversal moment because "it is at the exit that the gentleman is met," which is difficult to handle because, upon termination, people get tense or moody, or are not interested in elegance for maintaining the height of the resulting relationship, despite the circumstances. Oftentimes, emotions win over reason. You just want to end things so you do not have to see each other again, like an adolescent or immature overreaction. My suggestion is to plan those moments of reversal or the end of a path along a given direction and try to act with maturity and intelligence to achieve an elegant and pleasant ending, despite how difficult that moment is. You have to leave your emotions in the freezer and consider all the positive experiences, instead of concentrating on the defects and errors or shortcomings.

I recommend maintaining the balance between good and bad if you want to conduct a historical analysis to reach a conclusion that justifies the reversal, as well as handle the termination with elegance and even with gratitude, because nobody in their right mind will seek to complete their assignments badly on purpose as a means to end everything. Finishing and going in reverse are natural acts that we must learn to handle with due elegance and serenity.

I invite you to plan your reversals and to practice how to achieve an elegant ending, where despite the harshness or complexity of the situation, the relationship is not destroyed and both parties are grateful for the way the difficulty was addressed and a successful conclusion reached. Of course, you can.

-72-

Forgiveness or reversal solves 99.9% of life's problems

Acknowledging mistakes and asking for forgiveness in a legitimate and sincere way are the fastest and most effective way to defuse a relational bomb.

Not taking this fine action of acknowledging and asking for forgiveness as soon as possible allows the indignation of the one who feels attacked or wronged to grow. Reversing that condition as time passes becomes very difficult, and its consequences are usually more painful than losing a bit of your pride and lowering your head in recognition of a mistake or oversight.

It hurts to face your mistakes, and in a certain way, you feel you lose some dignity as well as a bit of humiliation. However, it should be the opposite. About 99.9% of the time, asking for forgiveness or reversing a badly executed action makes others appreciate us even more than they did before. Our image improves as they see the generosity of our actions in the face of adversity. Recognizing our mistakes is an act of maturity. Not recognizing them when we have made them is an emotional response of little common sense and some adolescent behavior. Ultimately, I believe that *"Reversal or forgiveness erase the errors on the blackboard of life."*

In my case, I learned to take responsibility and accept my mistakes from an early age, even in public. I have had to apologize many times in my life, and I have observed that people end up applauding my reaction; I have also gained more favorable points, greater credibility, and admiration. It is difficult to say, "I was wrong, sorry" or "It was my fault, sorry," but the final effect is truly incredible, because people perceive this action as an act of responsibility, integrity, and generosity. In the vast majority of cases, it erases the grievance and even generates greater proximity and admiration.

Only a couple of times have I come across people who are closed to all kinds of excuses, who do not accept that mistakes can be made, and do not accept apologies. They come up with feelings or emotions. They utter the infamous, "I forgive, but I do not forget," a catchphrase that has made some people's careers, but which does not make sense, except to be used as an excuse not to forgive. If people forgive, they will forget, as when one has a debt and pays it. The account goes back to zero. People cannot argue that you paid the debt but that they will never forget that you had it. Nonetheless, there are people who do not forgive when someone asks for forgiveness. These people have a lot of pent-up emotions. They are prone to adolescent or childish reactions, or they believe that we committed our error or mistake in bad faith or with bad intentions. In any case, asking for forgiveness or reversing an error or a mistake closes the cycle, at least on our end.

Of course, there are situations that leave mental scars and that are very difficult to erase because the consequences of our actions harmed the other person in such a way that it is not possible to return to the way things were before. In addition to asking for forgiveness or reversing the situation, if we can try to compensate in some way for the failure, we will have a better chance of erasing from the blackboard of life what we wrote in indelible ink.

I know that some will be in favor of this reflection and this method, and others will be against it, but it is worth taking the risk because this way, we will be saved from many difficult situations and conditions in our personal or corporate lives. Without this reflection and invitation to action, our errors will continue to exist.

If someone does not like what I have said, I beg your pardon.

-73-

Low-battery moments

Have you ever had those days when you would have preferred not to get up because, from the very first minute, everything starts to turn out badly? Those day when you do not have a single bar of energy left in your personal battery? I am talking about those days when one is too clumsy to act and cannot even think straight.

I remember when I was about 14 years old, and I was with my older sister. A bus crashed into the back of our car while we were waiting for the traffic light to change. Then, our car broke down on the way to the garage, and a bit later, a truck ran a red light and crashed into our car door. My father sent for the mechanics to take the car and told us to sit tight for three days so that we would not take more risks, given that things were going very badly.

There are people who are able to fall out or get upset with four or five different people on the same day as a result of different altercations, and several of the episodes end up being irreversible owing to the damage caused by the hurtful words or phrases exchanged in the heat of the moment. Friends, family, co-workers, partners, and clients are lost at such times. Even when the party at fault apologizes, and there is forgiveness, the relationship will not be the same again.

Low-battery days are deadly for relationships or work with clients because there is a high risk of ruining current or future business. On those days, the opposite to the King Midas effect occurs to us, and instead of turning everything into gold, we turn everything into ash. We destroy everything we touch.

The truth is that it is common to have bad or very challenging days in life, as we would say from a positive point of view. When one sees an opportunity in each problem, which is the enthusiastic way in which we must face our harsh reality, then we can say that those are days that come fully loaded with opportunities. We must assess if we can endure or if it is better to manage such opportunities in parts, or to delay.

I often hide in my private office or look for a place to be alone for several hours to collect my thoughts before setting myself to a low-frequency or zero-current day. Without these spaces to calm myself down and be creative, it would often be impossible for me to face my daily challenges. One has to take the load off. Doctors who see patients with mental problems or serious difficulties every day have a routine and space for unloading everything they accumulate; otherwise, they will end up just like their patients. We have to unload all these negative energies, bring the meter down to zero, and then return with clean energy to face what lies ahead.

Someone once told me that their problems overwhelm them and last a long time because they do not see an easy solution. I told them that unless they go into withdrawal or isolation and wait until the storm is clear to put the pole to the ground and achieve the necessary calm, it will hardly be possible to see an exit or light at the end of the tunnel.

David and Goliath

The ancient story of the fight between David and Goliath is an excellent lesson that teaches us how ingenuity and resourcefulness can overcome strength and great size. This is a fact that occurs daily in all scenarios of life. The great and powerful lose competitions or wars against the seemingly small and defenseless. There are many historical examples that remind us of nearly incredible or impossible feats; these teach us that there is no small or harmless rival. On the contrary, every rival deserves respect, and we must not trust, neglect, or be confused by appearances.

Oftentimes, strategy is what enables the person with the least strength or ability to win. We are reminded of this by the famous Trojan horse, which allowed the Greeks to infiltrate and take the city that up until that moment was impossible. Guerrilla warfare has proven to be a strategy that has overwhelmed powerful armies, surprised by the small groups taking unexpected action, often in camouflage or disguise so as not to be detected before or after their attacks. Let us remember the famous ETA in Spain, Vietnam and the United States, Colombia and Farc, and M19 or ELN. Colombia was liberated by a poorly armed and dressed army, thanks to military strategies.

In the business context, we have often seen small companies acquiring or defeating large companies with bold and innovative business strategies. The Banco de Colombia was bought by the small Medellín BIC. The technological changes that have allowed small companies or nascent inventions to outstrip powerful companies with a recognized trajectory are notable. Let us take a moment to remember some of the "Goliath" brands that lost the battle and the war against the "David" ones: Kodak, Blockbuster, BlackBerry, Nokia, Olivetti, Sega, Atari. There is a phrase that speaks well of David vs. Goliath: "It is better to be a big fish in a small pond." This means that a human being can shine more in a small company than in a large one, and if they lead, they will be even more noticed. This is very true in many cases.

When you are a "David," you apply your brain more effectively because you know that you do not have either the strength or the size to compete and win. Therefore, creativity reigns until we can find a way to achieve victory. We see it daily in competitive games' strategies, and we appreciate how an underdog team surprises everyone and ends up winning.

My recommendation is that one should always keep the "David" mentality, which will stop us from getting too confident and help us to stay alert, as well as devise different alternatives when facing our very respectable competitors.

Trust, a vital ingredient in personal and business relationships

Trust facilitates, accelerates, minimizes, and simplifies processes. It eliminates and prevents doubts. It builds and lets us work or act without harassment. Trust shows the positive side of any initiative and allows growth. When trust is lost, the relationship is damaged, and co-existence is seriously threatened, whether between friends, couples, partners, companies, or countries.

A small and simple example among countries is that when there is trust, there is no requirement for visas. When there is no trust, however, the process of issuing visas requires many documents and lengthy verification procedures through references and interviews that often end in rejection, even for a simple tourist. This serves to point out how a natural procedure tends to be infinitely complicated when there is no trust.

Couples are formed and consolidated when trust is strengthened. Couples separate when trust is lost, often owing to infidelity or excessive jealousy, which are clear indications of mistrust and insecurity on the partner's behavior. If you do not trust your partner or your partner does not trust you, the relationship is dead. It is that simple.

In personal or business contexts, money is lent if there is a history of trust in the credit behavior or seriousness of the entity or the person in the payment and fulfillment of their financial obligations. If there is mistrust or if their history indicates some defaults, there is no possibility that a loan will be given, and there is no compensation that can be paid to resolve the mistrust generated. In the business context, deliveries of merchandise or services to debtors are suspended, only delivered once they have caught up on all the payments. These entities will be required to make the payments in advance. They have zero credit for losing trust.

You do not leave your house or your car in the care of someone you do not trust, because they can steal or cause damage. They may take advantage of the situation to use the property inappropriately. They may even allow others to use it.

There are people who never place their trust in any human being or institution. Those people only trust themselves and no one else. They do not trust their partner, siblings, parents, or friends. They may request a polygraph test and demand collateral or mortgages as well as verify references just to lend USD 1000 to their own mother.

When trust is blindly placed in another, it is done regardless of whether the other is the best, the most skilled, the most beautiful, or the most competent. Trust is granted no matter what. The key is that the person or institution in charge is completely trusted, and the rest is forgiven, does not matter, or gets handled. The same happens with lovers. Love is blind—it does not see anything, it does not hear anything, or at least it does not want to.

In business deals between companies, when there is trust, all standard processes and procedures are bypassed to facilitate and maintain the relationship. All the fine print in the requirements and commitments applies to the rest of the suppliers.

I am reminded of the lady who comes to my house to help us with the house chores. She has four children and a granddaughter, and for that reason, she comes to work at 10 in the morning every day. She leaves her house running and her children attended before leaving for work at our house. She has the keys to our house and has been loyal and honest for many years, which is worth more than her late arrival in the mornings. My wife will not swap her for another lady who can arrive at 6:30 or 7:00 AM, which, for this purpose, would be more useful, and she prefers to take on the vital tasks herself before the lady arrives, at which point all the morning chores have been completed: beds arranged and breakfasts served, apart from the fact that we have all gone to work.

How about when you need to trust someone with a secret, and that person does not keep it and discloses it, causing us irreparable damage from the social impact or shame of public exposure?

When we are children or when we behave like children, we are not subjects of trust. We cannot be left alone because we might do something wrong or cause some damage. We are risky subjects. Anything can happen when we are unsupervised. As we mature, we become reliable for a good number of tasks, and we may be assigned tasks that we will complete with a high level of certainty. When we repeatedly demonstrate that we are correctly performing the tasks entrusted to us, we gain the trust of people. From then on, there is no doubt that they will always assign us more.

With regard to ourselves, self-confidence will allow us to face all kinds of challenges and get ahead. It is like a hopeful security that whatever we have in mind or in our hands will happen, and it will happen as we wish or plan. Without self-confidence or trust, it will be difficult to achieve something positive. I would even say that sometimes, nothing is possible without trust.

Using reason: what it consists of and at what ages one acquires it in life and in business

My mother told me that when I reached the age of seven, I would have the ability to "use reason," which was something like realizing or being responsible for the acts carried out, or like being a beginner adult who is aware of what they do and, consequently, are responsible for their actions.

I had always thought that this idea was not true, because in reality, at the age of seven, I had no idea what life was, nor did I understand a significant number of fundamental concepts. I believe that "using reason" is something that is acquired in stages. In other words, one matures in different aspects of life, and at different ages, via events that awaken us and make us be conscious.

I have seen people reach 50 or 60 years old, but in certain behaviors and criteria, they are still children or adolescents. An example is the person who is dominated by a vice. There are vices like the infamous Deadly Sins: gluttony, lust, greed, sloth, envy, and anger. They all lose or have lost control.

Another is the person who continues to depend on their parents despite them being quite old. Those who assume that everything they are and their limitations, shortcomings, or suffering can be blamed on others. Those who are emotionally dependent on others, on religion, or on their psychiatrist. Those who are financially dependent on others despite having the faculty to be productive. Those who are afraid to be alone; the eternal "Don Juan Tenorio." Those who continue to think that they are just going to turn 18, and they do not grow up or look in the mirror and realize that they are already mature. Those who have never used their judgment.

The truth is that one matures by section, according to one's vocations or specialties, like the divisions or areas of a company. Maturity is not uniform, comparable to regions of a country, each of which has its advances, progress, limitations, and characteristics. It is like being very good at math but having trouble with literature or being good at gymnastics but terrible at drawing or music. Maturity is similar to the growth of our physical parts. Some grow short because their legs or torso did not measure up to the normal size, while others exceed the standard and have to sleep doubled over in traditional beds or cannot find shoes in their size.

Maturity in different areas or dimensions of life varies greatly among people. Human nature is uneven, just like the parts of the body. A person may have long legs and short arms, a small head and a large body, or a large mouth and a small nose. There are multiple configurations that are not very well proportioned. It is very natural.

The same happens with degrees of consciousness in the different areas of our life experience, such as knowledge, relationships, environmental view, and our perception or understanding of life, our mission, the value of different elements in our surroundings, the importance of priorities, and the management of emergencies. We could have different degrees of consciousness of the value of family, friendships, time, places, colleagues, neighbors, the country, the planet, the economy or money, intellect or knowledge, and differences in race, age, or gender. The list further includes spirituality, religions, profession, trades, lifestyle, money making, being authentic, or happiness.

There are people who do not become deeply aware in any of the abovementioned areas. They become aware only in some areas, and they certainly do not mature in all of them, or their level of consciousness or maturity is different in each one.

The point is that only when you become aware can you act, pay attention, or take responsibility, but not before. Nothing or very little is achieved for the person to take proper action and act autonomously and conscientiously as an adult in a certain field.

The key in life is to recognize the areas where we have not matured enough and work on the most important ones, or on those that can affect or help us daily to accelerate our progress and results.

Patience is necessary. Developing the right level of awareness and responsibility in a specific area takes time. The most difficult thing is to acknowledge the areas where adequate development has not been achieved, and then prepare a development plan. Once we discover the specific areas where we fall short, we can work hard to become aware and grow where we have fallen short. It takes work to grow, and it may even hurt, but it is worth trying to mature in the key areas where we have not made advances—if we become aware of them.

Surgeries or Treatments in personal life and in organizations

W hen do we have surgery or get treatment? It all depends on the urgency or the method you want to apply, if you have the possibility to choose.

A decision that illustrates the importance of having clarity over which path to take relates to the foot of a diabetic with an infected wound. Can they be treated with antibiotics and be saved, or is their life at risk, and is it better to amputate?

On the positive side, the question in an organization will be, "Does the solution to the problem allow for the learning curve of a junior employee in the face of a commitment with the client, or should we hire and pay an expert to solve the problems and avoid losing the client for bad service?"

Returning to health, if your mother were seriously ill, would you let her be treated by a medical apprentice? Or would you look for a specialist with certified experience? How much is the life of your mother worth?

With this reflection, one can understand whether a responsibility can endure the long learning curve, or a slow but safe treatment or, on the contrary, whether it is necessary to go to the topmost expert urgently, like when you are faced with a life-threatening situation and the only option is a surgery that brings risk but also provides speedy recovery, if everything goes well.

Here, the well-known expression, "Do not assign to a child a task that should be done by an adult," is the key to success or failure, if we are talking about junior or expert employees for a certain mission. There are savings or trials that can cost a life, a client, or a business. What is your case?

In medicine, there is the long-standing confrontation between allopathic or conventional doctors and homeopaths. The former often uses surgery or drugs of immediate and focused action with the consequent side effects. The latter consists of a supposedly systemic treatment that repairs the interactions and levels of the body to bring it into balance, similar to the vaccine effect. This system follows the logic of "being cured in small doses." The treatment requires time and patience but is reported to work. There are also the so-called alternative medicines, relatives of homeopathy in a certain way, such as acupuncture, neural therapy, and other practices that treat the spirit.

It is clear at this point that there is no single solution or path to achieving a goal or finding a cure. It is also clear that there are fast and slow methods, each with its own effects and risks.

This reflection is vital, as the speed in achieving a goal or an objective is often tied to surviving or dying, or winning or losing. The path of construction or repair applies pressures with respect to the variable time we must know how to manage.

In the case of a child's education, doing their homework is equivalent to the quick method of surgery. They will get a good grade the next day, but there are consequences to not allowing the child to learn, to challenge themselves through trial and error, or to handle failure. Meanwhile, guiding them, challenging them, and letting them try to find their own path may present them with the risk of failure, but in the long run, these will propel them toward awareness and maturity, which will bring them autonomy (It is like a treatment. It is the long path with its risks and consequences, but in the end, for this example, it is much more productive).

Now, not everything is surgery, and not everything is treatment. Not all surgery is preferable, and not all treatment is better. There are times when one procedure is appropriate and times when another is preferable. There are times when surgery and treatment have to be combined to achieve the goal.

When I was little, many years ago, the dentist took out a couple of upper and lower molars so that my teeth could move because they were crowded and protruding. This way, I did not have to use the infamous orthodontic braces in a long, expensive, and annoying treatment that is preferred these days because each tooth deserves to be saved or preserved. This particular case illustrates what we have been discussing: the fast method of removing four molars, which would nowadays be seen as a wild approach, and the slow method of treatment, where the teeth are slowly adjusted until they are perfectly organized.

In the world, there are strong confrontations against the two styles in numerous scenarios, such as with food and the well-known fasting. Food or fast whatever or slow cooking or slow eating or slow whatever. Each one has its own pros and cons and its own fans.

As for losing weight, there are methods: do daily exercises and lose pounds or strengthen muscles or go on a diet. Which one is best?

The general answer is that we must analyze the situation we find ourselves in, ascertain the alternatives, evaluate the pros and cons of each, and then decide what is best or what suits us in our case.

I will leave you with this reflection so that you do not go down a single path without reviewing other possibilities. Study and analyze what suits you and then choose between the fast or slow method. Each has its charm.

Patience, a necessary virtue in the face of great challenges

I recall the story of a friend of a friend: her husband was very impatient and that after the first night on their honeymoon, he got up asking when she could give him a child. Surprised, she told him that she did not even know if she was pregnant, much less when she could give him a child. He asked her to hurry up with that because he wanted to have a child as soon as possible—preferably within six months. She smiled and told him that children need nine months to be born. The furious husband told her not to give silly explanations and cheap apologies, and he left the room in a rage. Of course, the marriage ended that day, and the impatient man had a short life because of his follies and for obvious reasons.

The dictionary defines patience as follows: "the ability to suffer and tolerate misfortunes and adversities and annoying or offensive things with strength, without complaining or rebelling. Calm or tranquility in waiting."

I believe that doctors call the sick "patients" because they need to be patient to bear the pain, examinations, treatment, postoperative procedures, and care provided in the doctor's offices or in the clinics. A friend once had a cough that lasted for two years. Another friend mentioned that he was ill and required three-hour daily therapies for 12 years. Another had a severe pain in one arm for several months and said it was like love pains that do not go away with acetaminophen or ibuprofen. In all cases, persistence, patience, and courage were required to endure the healing process.

I am reminded of that well-known request, "God, give me patience, because if you give me strength, I will kill him." Good thing God grants patience.

Speaking of relationships, there's the other notable phrase: "Love does not end; patience does." I think this is mostly true. Marriages are short-lived because patience runs out very quickly. Time is the key measure in this subject of patience.

It took months and years to build most of what we have in life, but then we forget that it did. How long did our childhood last? Did we take time to learn to read or write? How long does it take to learn how to use the toilet? How long did our adolescence last, including its trials and errors? I ask these questions because we forget that life is built over time. We are not born and become professionals the next day. You do not build a house and a home or furnish or decorate in a day. Oftentimes, it takes months and even years to get the details perfectly.

Another reflection on patience refers to the traffic blockades or jams in the big cities of the world at rush or peak hours, when people go to or leave work. There are traffic jams that last for hours, and that is when one is forced to learn to be patient. In the city where I live, you have to plan to leave an hour and a half in advance to be able to arrive at a business meeting with a little bit of time to spare. Leaving half an hour or 45 minutes in advance is no longer appropriate; you run the risk of arriving too late.

Recently, a friend had to experience some uncomfortable health complications that resulted in severe muscle pain that did not go away with pain relievers, anti-inflammatory drugs, or physical therapy. The pain was permanent, and he could not sleep because of the intense and constant pain. His muscles were contracted, as happens after an operation or some trauma, and being able to stretch them back into their original shape takes weeks and even months. He needed tremendous endurance, plenty of courage, persistence, and patience, in addition to holding out hope that everything will be okay sometime in the future.

It is popular knowledge that "time heals all," and it is true.

Even to loosen a simple rusty nut, you have to wait for the oil to penetrate before it can be turned. Many famous delicious recipes require long and meticulous preparation, and even a simple steak or thick piece of meat requires a good dose of salt and a lot of patience to roast, as a Chilean friend who is an expert in Patagonian roasts taught me.

I am reminded of the patience that I had to have to go up the ladder in a multinational company until I became a manager in the internal area, and then started from scratch in the commercial area until I became a manager again and finally become a top executive and general manager. I was very fast compared with the average person, reaching my goal when I was 37 years old, after 15 long years of working on my career, burning my eyelashes, staying up late, sacrificing weekends, employing a lot of intelligence and strategy. If I spoke to a millennial today, what would they think after listening to me? Would they have the patience?

I graduated as an engineer at 23, and I received my MBA at 29, but I got my PhD at 50. That is a long time, and one wants everything instantly.

Many times, we want problems to be solved overnight or decisions about important business deals to be made within days or weeks, and then we crash into the reality of life and realize that things take months and years of pushing from behind, creating, and searching. How about when there is a labor, commercial, or criminal lawsuit? Some may take more than a lifetime to resolve or clarify, and sometimes, there is not even a solution.

At this point, I am not encouraging anyone to lower their speed or level of perseverance to achieve a goal, but to become aware that it is necessary to combine a certain dose of balance and patience in real life, which could be demanding and even painful. Most of the time, we forget that we have to be patient, and we say to the one above, "God, give me patience, but give it to me now."

−79−

Differences in vision create opportunities or problems

Many conflicts arise owing to differences in vision of the same reality, a frequent issue given the diversity of cultures, training, education, or experiences. I am going to give you some current examples.

Bullfighting. There are people who enjoy a sunny afternoon with a fascinating and elegant bullfight, while other people think that it is a modern version of the Roman circus to mistreat and savagely kill defenseless bulls. Opposite poles that are valid according to each person's view.

In a well-known city, horse-drawn carts were banned and removed, and now people carry the carts by hand, but they no longer mistreat the animals. The poor men who now carry the carts are not as important as the animal abuse. Different views of the same reality. Are both valid?

For their environmental impact, energy or mineral exploration operations are to be suspended to protect and preserve nature. Which comes first or which is more important: industry or ecology? Depending on which side we are on, either could be valid.

Cities exchange fields and mountains with trees for concrete and asphalt. What do we do? Invest in housing and infrastructure or keep nature alive? Infrastructure development or nature and conservation of the planet? Two contrasting viewpoints.

In a modern marriage, the decision to have children is a fundamental topic and a life decision. If you have children, your primary objective is to create a family and raise children, watch them grow up, see them face challenges, accompany them in life, and ultimately be accompanied by them in old age. Meanwhile, we may make the decision to share our lives with our partner and not have children, to enjoy a double income that allows you to roam the world with a light luggage and enjoy a better standard of living. Are both visions valid although they are different and oppose each other?

There are people who create companies without much study and are financially successful. There are others who dedicate their lives to study for their professional career and get their master's degrees and even several doctorates. Although they are very intellectual, their income as employees is far from the millionaire gains in the former example. Which one is the valid path? Everything is about preferences and objectives. Not everything is about money, and not everything is about study. Two valid views.

How about the differences that exist when you are 10 and your older brother is 20? In terms of knowledge and experience, the older brother has a 100% advantage. Over time, however, when the older brother is 80 years old and the younger brother is 70, this difference is not even 15%, and they may have even grown similar in their external appearance. That is life. When I was little, my older brother seemed old or really big and very tall. My brother saw me as a dwarf and as a baby at the same time, and it was valid. Everything is relative, said a famous genius.

In the home, the differences are evident between husband and wife or between the feminine and masculine energies. People view life based on their gender perspective. Even when both partners observe the same event, each one may be seeing something different, despite many years of marriage and living together. This difference in viewpoints generates conflicts, and both sides have to be willing to handle them. They are two different and perfectly valid views, but a common life must be built based on the two visions.

Each of the partners in a company sees and thinks differently in relation to the same event, and that is the great thing about diversity and its richness. Aside from the evident conflict of differences that may emerge in the beginning, they will arrive at a conclusion in the interest of achieving what is best for the organization, without competing to determine who has the best solution. It is better to combine the two visions and make the best of both.

The famous image of the two men positioned at either end of a number on the floor, and one sees the number nine, while the other sees the number six—they both see a different reality because they are at the opposite ends of the number. Like people in front of the same river, but each one is on a different shore, with very different panoramic vision, a perfectly valid and respectable perspective. If the two visions are put together, you have a 360-degree panorama. Magnificent.

Where do we go with these reflections?

Each day, many of us forget the reality of valid differences, and we do not understand why other people think differently. We tend to believe that we are right and they are wrong, when it is very likely that we are all right and there is nothing wrong.

If we are all right, what do we do?

The first thing is to listen carefully to each person's viewpoint, and then the key is to search for the best option among those involved, the one that best rewards the parties or the organization, regardless of who wins. The important thing is that the best solution wins, and in this sense, it is useful to go over the pros and cons of each alternative or vision and together build the one that best suits the parts or the whole, based on the overview of all the alternatives analyzed in an attempt to join forces. Take advantage of the differences instead of making them a reason for confrontation. Build on them. Addition instead of division.

The difficulty is in the distraction of competing to beat others, which often does not lead to a good ending. If there are two suitable options and it is time to move forward, you can choose one option, let us call it A, first. If it does not work, assume the cost of it, and then move to the other option, let us call it B. Do not stop or paralyze actions by not reaching an agreement. If option A works, that is it, and if not, it is time for option B. This is how things work in real life. You have to be practical, assume responsibilities, and take risks.

There are people who look at themselves in the mirror, and for some strange reason, they look cute, as if their features had been fixed with Photoshop or some other graphics editing program, when in fact, they are ugly. It is interesting to take so much pride in oneself, but when it comes to decisions and moving a relationship, an organization, or a nation forward, it is useless to "Photoshop" bad ideas. In this case, it is better to accept quickly that there are better or superior ideas or visions instead of stubbornly staying on a path that has no future, for the sake of pride.

It is better to lose a battle so that we can win the war. Everyone is entitled to their opinion, but the key is to determine which view is best for those involved at a given moment.

In chess, there are times when we sacrifice the queen for a checkmate. There are fights or competitions that are worth losing. It hurts to learn it, but it is wise, if we let the greater good ultimately win.

Ideological bubbles

J ust as economic bubbles are created by people who seriously and credibly establish ideas or thoughts that, although most of the time are correct, sometimes they can be wrong, such as "Buy real estate because the price will always increase" or "Invest in dollars or in shares because they always increase in price in the long term." The same happens with non-economic ideas expressed by ideologically respectable people, which many people follow blindly. However, as time goes on, those affirmations are discovered to be not so true, and people are disappointed.

The point is that you have to believe in something. What do you believe in?

A friend taught me that it is vital to check sources and verify the claims that trustworthy people often make, because they are not all 100% true, and you can end up believing lies through blind trust.

That is why they say the wise and popular phrase, "Create fame, and then go to bed."

Magazines or traditional newspapers publish many statements that are false or have wrong facts because they only show one side of the coin, or because they are influenced by an ideology that only shows one color from the immense range of colors, or one position or vision of the many that exist. Ultimately, these publications promote what their owners want the public to believe, which are usually views that would benefit them, the wealthy and entitled.

I also want to talk about that very common phrase in the news, "A highly reliable source told me." Highly reliable sources are not so reliable because there are hidden interests behind each statement, which are even paid or rewarded by invisible forces that want to lead humanity towards some goal or belief that produces substantial results for the few who manage them. The antidote is the well-known phrase, "Do not swallow whole."

I have a friend who is a specialist in auditing content sent in chat rooms. Often, they return with the information that verifies or shows that some of the news or statements that have been shared are false.

In the political context, false factoids are stated every day, and we are left to determine the actual facts. News could go around for months, some favorable to one side and others favorable to the other, until it is demonstrated that the first statement was false. However, the damage has already been done to someone's image, reputation, or reliability, or to the decisions someone made based on what they were told, or on what they read or heard, and the taste of doubt or the pain of the mistake or its consequences will always remain.

The same thing happens in everyday life at smaller scales, such as within companies, families, friends, or acquaintances. Someone creates a bubble with an idea, a suspicion, or an assumption, and there begins the damage, the mistrust, and even the rupture of friendships or marriages, the disappearance of heads, or the separation of people. All of this for having been involved in a mess initiated by someone with a fixed and malevolent intention to foster division based on the evil or brilliant phrase, depending on how you look at it, "Divide and conquer."

Families and companies have been destroyed by ideological bubbles released by a person who is supposed to be highly reliable. Brothers, spouses, or partners fall out, and because of the doubt generated, the relationships are no longer the same. The deep mistrust precedes the breakup. Even when everything is cleared up, the damage has been done.

Several of you at this moment must be thinking about the times that you have had to witness or suffer what I have just described and the importance that you should have given to the verb "verify." Owing to ideological bubbles, many people have followed the right or wrong leaders in many scenarios of life, as if they were the idealized example of a superhero. Remember musical icons like Elvis, the Rolling Stones, or the Beatles, who influenced even the fashion of their time, most of the time innocently and benignly.

At present, there are musical icons who have a similar influence, and young people imitate and adore them, thanks to the bubbles they generate. The same happens in literary thought, politics, sports, religion, and all social spheres. Right now, the YouTube phenomenon is simply enormous. Thanks to social networks, we see the many followers, which are oftentimes in the millions, delighted with their superhero, until something happens and their ratings go down as if they were a television program. The superhero goes out of circulation or their influence is minimized, either because some newer figure surpassed and replaced them or because they fell out of favor or became obsolete.

The good thing is that everyone enjoys being a follower. The bad thing is that the influence can be harmful when the character we follow leads us to the precipice, to die happy but before our time.

It is important not to go blind and become a fanatic who loses their mind. You have to solidify each action and leadership to evaluate the good, and you have to learn to filter information to prevent emotional or intellectual deceit or abuse.

Let us have fun with one foot on the ground. "Do not swallow whole and always check."

Stay alert

We are all born with natural sensors that warn us about the kindness or hostility of our surroundings, but few of us have an awakened conscience relative to these sensors and how to use it in our favor.

One night when I was sleeping, I started coughing uncontrollably. I got up and told my wife that I felt cold. I put on a sweater and socks, and we added a blanket to the bed. Twenty minutes later, the cough stopped. The next day, the most powerful hailstorm in 100 years fell, and the entire city was blocked, and a state of emergency was declared. My body gave me a warning 12 hours in advance, through its alarms and natural sensors, that a major change in weather would occur and something serious was coming. When it is excessively humid, I start coughing.

Our sensors are a vital part of our body, and we must learn to use them. First, we must recognize that we have them. Several of you at this moment must be remembering your cold or heat or humidity detectors.

The most common sensors are triggered by food. Not everyone can eat everything. There are those that do not tolerate meat, seafood, or even coffee. There are many who cannot drink milk or consume its derivatives. Others do not like avocado. Some cannot even taste beans or lentils. Others cannot eat blackberries. You know what I am talking about. Our body indicates to us what is good or bad through its sensors, and if we are not aware of these signals, we will have a rough time.

The alarm bells go off in the attraction or rejection of human beings as well. There are people whose presence we enjoy very much. We take pleasure in it and even pursue it because it makes us feel good. There are people whose presence causes us discomfort and even an instant stomachache. These are people we do not want to see and with whom we would not like to share even a minute. Exactly the same occurs with food or with heat or cold. There is no problem with the food, neither with the cold nor heat, but not everyone is made for everything.

Our natural sensors resemble those that we see in machines. There are rain or darkness detectors in our cars, motion detectors in bathrooms and corridors of hotels or buildings, indicators of low levels of oil pressure, tire pressure, or gas. These detectors are like our own biological detectors, which may signal to us that we have an empty stomach. Muscle pain and chills may indicate that we have a fever.

There are people who have headaches with certain frequency because it is their sensor for heat, excess of food, bad mood, or hunger. Others feel pain in their knees or bones or joints, which may signal potential rain or cold weather. However, the most powerful signals are those that anticipate events or read energies that are on the way, like when people tell you that they called you with their mind. "Hey, I was thinking about you, and you appeared." What actually happened is that the proximity of the arrival emitted enough signals for the brain to act and place us in the person's thoughts. This is evidence of proximity. When the same event happens without the proximity and we get a call instead, it is obvious that the connection occurred on a superior plane, and we have a real connection to the person who wanted to contact us and who made us think about them through the power of their desire, so that we immediately receive the call. Our thoughts are almost an alarm that says, "So-and-so is going to call you."

We have warning alarms installed in our natural system, but like I said in the beginning, some people do not even know they have them, much less know how to use them. Those of us who have developed a deep perception of our alarms are the type of people who are often told that we are intuitive or that we have a good nose, a good eye, or a good compass.

Check your alarms and sensors. Turn them on and learn to monitor what they indicate to you. You will see how life will positively surprise you through your ability to perceive and anticipate events.

Cranky people and when to win the battle

Have you ever heard of people who consume poison and then want others to die? Have you ever arrived at customs and met a police officer who was spitting fire like a grumpy dragon? How many times have you had to stand in a long line waiting in fear to be served by a character who must have suffered something unpleasant and is determined to make everyone feel pain by delaying actions, arguing with people, and making unnecessary demands? In other words, something happened to that person, and they take it out on others.

We always know that something is bound to happen to us with these types of characters. We stand before them with the same kind of fear we used to feel when we were seven years old and knew that our mother was about to scold us for having done something wrong. In those moments, people remember to ask a higher power for help and beg for a miracle to come out unscathed.

The same happens when the boss arrives in a bad mood or when one comes home to an ill-tempered partner. Another instance is when a teacher delivers the class after an altercation with their wife or child (there will be an exam for sure, and it will be so difficult that everyone will receive a bad grade).

What do we do? During tough times, we can only pray, seek distance, keep quiet, or hide. If we were going to ask or propose something, it is better to do so another time when the tide is out or when the person is in a good mood.

Life is full of all kinds of moments. You have to know when it is and when it is not convenient to execute a task, request, or movement. A friend always waited for someone to enter the boss's office with good news (the boss was very ill-tempered). Once he saw that the boss was happy, he would enter their office to make any request, and of course, the boss would approve it.

It is in times like these when one understands there are battles in which it is better to let the other win or those that we should not get involved in or should let pass. There are games in which the best decision we can make is to postpone or not even play. Sometimes, the best decision is to do nothing. Stay in first base, as they say; do not move.

Doing nothing—not playing, not answering, or not replying—is a strategy that many forget can be used, and it is a brilliant exit, most of the time. One can accept or reject challenges and competitions. In a worst-case scenario, it is better to have a minute of shame or apparent weakness or excessive inactivity than to get caught up in a fight, lose your life, or generate a conflict that affects many.

Companies and people must make decisions regarding what they do or do not comment on through the different means of communication that exist today. In this sense, we must remember that we are not required to provide an answer on every occasion, just as we are not required to answer immediately.

Delaying a response to produce something of good quality is a legal matter, and it is a right that we all have. Unfortunately, many people forget and answer immediately. If someone asks for something, we can answer only to the part that is convenient to us, not answer at all, or provide numerous details that are not even part of the question. What position would you adopt? Depending on the situation or the moment, one of the three is convenient. The important thing is to know that we have every option and do not necessarily have to answer immediately.

A friend taught me a phrase in the Bible, specifically in the New Testament, that wisely depicts what I have described above. I want to give it to you because this reflection is useful in business, companies, and our personal lives when it comes to taking action. I never thought I would find a recommendation applicable to business or strategy in the Bible.

"Behold, I send you out as sheep amidst wolves, so be wise as serpents and innocent as doves."

—83—

The soul's pain in business and life: solutions and antidotes

I am pained by your insults, aloofness, rejections, and surprise outbursts. I am pained by your arrogance, threats, public criticism, invalidation, indifference, ignorance, and mental and psychological torture. I am pained by your impositions and everything that you make me do by force or fear. I am pained by failure, deception, betrayal, abuse, and manipulation. I am depressed, listless, insecure, and bored.

These feelings are silently expressed by people daily and deep within their thoughts, without us even realizing that they are in pain, and they find no relief. It is a constant and intimate pain that destroys or depletes them like in slow cooking or as if they had a disease that consumed them gradually, like infections that slowly kill you.

I make this reflection because most human beings go through such horrible situations many times in their lives, either in the office or in personal life. This type of disposition affects our daily behavior and can significantly damage our response capacity and professional and relational performance.

The question we all ask ourselves is whether there is medication or a painkiller to ease the pain or something that allows us to prevent or cure our agony.

Those of us who already have the advantage of a long life know that these types of maladies are difficult to prevent and take time to heal. There are antidotes and remedies.

The first and easy solution is to run or stay away from or set aside the cause of this difficult condition, like how we treat something that causes us allergy. If you have a seafood allergy, do not eat it. Distance yourself from it.

The second solution is to replace whoever makes you feel bad with someone who makes you feel good (The best way to get over someone is to get under someone, as the saying goes). If you like pasta, you eat it instead of seafood. You substitute seafood so that you do not miss it, and you feel like you have been given a treat.

The third solution is to apply an antidote so that nothing can cause pain, sadness, anger, depression, or fear. This is the key point. We need to be immensely aware that nobody and nothing can make us feel anything. We are the ones who decide what to feel or not to feel; it is a mental decision. One states or declares their feelings.

It may be raining, but we are happy. Even upon the death of a loved one, we can find happiness and celebrate their legacy and departure instead of feeling sad over their absence.

There is always a positive side to everything that happens to us, which we should appreciate, cheer for, and celebrate. When we find ourselves focusing and dwelling on the negative aspect of things, we should immediately look at the other side, the positive, and we will surely realize that there is so much to take advantage of and in our favor to consider.

My father died, but he left me with many life lessons that I apply every day; the same happened with my mother. I celebrate their legacies, and I receive guidance from both in their new capacity as Beings of Light who accompany, advise, and watch over me every minute. It was hard for me to think of them like this because my father and mother were my idols. However, I managed, and now I am convinced of the benefit of always thinking about the positive instead of the negative.

There are many companies and people that I have loved for what I have learned with them and for the pleasant moments, tremendous satisfaction, and experiences that they left me. Many of the lessons were painful, as expected, but they allowed me to grow and become wiser. Each one has made me a better human being.

I have always had bad moments and events as a temporary reference that teaches me something powerful that I have had to learn. Most of them are in my dead file, which is what companies do when past events are no longer valid, and we look for them only for reference.

In short, I have only gratitude for each person and company that I have known and served in life. Meanwhile, I have developed a quick and powerful way to forgive and send bad memories loaded with toxic feelings to the dead file. They serve as simple references to life's lessons that do not carry any weight other than my own story of personal growth.

I invite you to develop your antidotes so that nothing causes you pain beyond a day. After that, you are ready to move forward again with plenty of energy, similar to what cyclists do. From one stage to another, they compete for their resilience, and those who get up as if nothing happened and face the new stage with renewed strength are the ones who take the glory. Salespeople are psychologically beaten by stress and their bosses pushing for results; they receive ungrateful treatment from clients, their bosses, and the people at their companies. Everyone sees them as non-compliant, lazy, and liars. Good salespeople can generate sales despite always having everything stacked against them because they carry immense self-motivation. Their ability to recover from blows is enormous and extremely rapid. That is what they call resilience.

The tough times and experiences of life can knock us down. However, it is up to us to accomplish a speedy recovery that allows us to emerge stronger and behave like champions.

Secrets to success

I remember, as a child, my father giving me the first couple of secrets to success when he was teaching me to float in a pool, "Lie on your back. Relax with your legs extended. *Trust me. You can do it.* It is almost unbelievable, but you will float; you will not sink." I trusted, and I floated.

Trusting ourselves and our ability to accomplish what we propose to ourselves is the beginning or the first secret *to achieving success* in any plan, project, or activity. This secret comes with a key warning: always maintain the nobility and the mindset of an apprentice; otherwise, pride and arrogance can lead to failure.

Following the advice of someone who knows or is an expert in a specific field is the second secret to success. This is hard to do because, in today's world, we do not trust anyone, not even ourselves. I have seen companies and people hire experts only to ignore them later or ask for advice and then do the opposite because they disagree with that person and want to follow their own will.

When we fail, we often seek to blame the system, the environment, the market, the weather, or a third party not to recognize that we are responsible for our own deafness and poor decisions. Success is always accompanied by a good team that surrounds and supports us. It is extremely difficult to succeed without this kind of support.

Another way to phrase these two secrets is *"Believe what the expert says, do it, and trust your ability to execute it"*—two secrets in one.

The third secret to success, derived from the previous one, is to *Observe and execute through the eyes of those ahead of the curve in any subject or discipline*. It is like traveling to the future or going to a new country and observing what they do and how they do it and then copying their best practices. Do you remember what you did in school or college to learn faster? It is the same thing. Abandon your peasant self to move faster and make progress quickly. Adopt the thinking and best practices of those clearly ahead of you. Learn from them. Always reserve time in your day to learn from others and stop believing you know it all. You will see that you will advance much faster either because they have given you an idea or a concept that you did not have or because they have made you think about and helped you confirm that you are on the right path.

Relationships play an important part in success. The rest is composed of knowledge, experience, intelligence, astuteness, discipline, perseverance, quality execution, and even a dash of good luck. This is a topic that does not warrant much discussion.

The fourth secret and the key to success is in the definition that an excellent boss had taught me by example early in my life, and I now encapsulate in my own phrase: *Treat everyone as if they were your clients*. Thus, you will ensure permanent success in whatever you do. This lesson is a 180-degree turn in thought and daily actions. One always seeks the satisfaction and even the delight of their clients. We are willing to perform many tasks and go to significant lengths to keep them happy, enjoy their patronage indefinitely, and gain their loyalty, which is considerably challenging these days.

I will pose some questions for reflection to advance in the understanding of this powerful secret. What if you treat your siblings, partner, children, parents, neighbor, or any relative like your client? Would you treat them the way a client, your best client, deserves to be treated?

What would happen in the company if you treat your boss, co-workers, or employees like your clients? How are you going to treat them? What are you going to do for them? How are you going to satisfy them to the best of your ability?

Has your perspective changed?

I treat everyone as if they were a client (even my detractors or enemies), and I do my best to ensure that the client feels taken care of—this has been my great secret to success in business and personal relationships. Remember, if your client is your priority and you treat them as such, you will always be successful. Notably, anyone can be your client.

The fifth secret to success is to use your *sense of smell to follow the right path*, like a hunting or a tracking dog. It is a perception or intuition exercise or both. You have to exercise this vital quality. We can develop this characteristic similar to how we tone our muscles. Remember, do exercises that allow you to improve your intuition or antenna or perceptive intelligence. This will help you follow the trail like the dog who locates objects with their olfactory ability. I have developed my intuition, which is ten times more powerful than a woman's natural intuition. Interestingly, I managed to achieve this quality through my own will and relentless practice. The person who manages to deepen their intuition will surely be successful. Think about doctors and their famous "clinical eye," and you will understand how crucial it is to have this quality.

The sixth secret is an insistence in considering a traveling companion for the journey that leads to success. *Find a tree that gives you good shade*, as they say, and do not cut it down for firewood. It is tough to achieve success alone. We always need someone to hold our hand and support or help us, even if it is only to give us confidence or moral support. Unlike the expert who is useful and necessary for success, we need people who believe in us—those who recommend, guide, give feedback, accompany, question, and motivate us. We need people who make us reflect or stop us when we run amok and show us what we do not see or do not want to see. If you have not found that tree, go out and look for it because having one or several is crucial.

Finally, whatever you do, be yourself. Focus and learn to love who you are, what you have, and what you do. Perform your tasks with passion. Work hard without wavering, keep it simple or easy, and always maintain a sense of humor despite the challenges, which are usually numerous and frequent on the way to success. Further, try to do something different, unique, and unconventional any time you can.

Law of attraction and success in business and personal life

H uman beings possess a mind that consciously or unconsciously works like a magnet that attracts everything, whether good or bad, as if it were sending a written formal request to the universe and then being granted the request. During a period of low productivity at work, specifically in sales, a friend provided some insight that caught my attention for its brilliance. He said that everything was going wrong for him and that he felt that everything was coming down on him—mostly bad things. He referred to health, but therein lay his moment of mental clarity: *When one has weakened immunity, one catches everything.* Inadvertently, my friend went beyond the simple phrase and the sympathetic and even humorous comparison.

The sublime fact about the phrase is that it is precisely mental weakness and doubt that attract the negative to us. Instead of getting better, everything ends up becoming worse if we do not change our perception. Everything occurs as described by the phrases "money begets money" or "the poor are getting poorer." When someone has confidence or faith, they accomplish what they propose for themselves most of the time, albeit not necessarily the first time around. They ultimately achieve it as a result of their tenacity and their indestructible hope and certainty, although "misfortunes never come alone." Like the religious phrase "faith moves mountains," the law of attraction works mainly in the negative way. In other words, "owing to lack of faith, the mountain is coming upon us."

Therefore, the phrase "when one has weakened immunity, one catches everything" is a discovery that allows us to examine our weaknesses and correct or address them. This will help us build the maximum defenses possible and become immune to all evil or infection, figuratively, in both business and personal life.

In other words, if I strengthen my spirit and thoughts, I will never allow the negative to seep in. Consequently, I will get positive results most of the time, owing to my "mental immune system," which protects me from any bad streak or misfortune. Just as our body has and generates its own defenses against infections and viruses, our mind can do the same so that our mental, vibrational, and spiritual defenses are active and strong. Subsequently, we will generate positive results in our work or personal lives. "Believe in yourself" and "trust yourself" are the direct phrases that support the generation of conscious and subconscious antibodies.

What if I am frequently attacked by negative and fatalistic thoughts? In that case, you have not yet built muscle. Given your mental and spiritual flaccidity, the bad energy chases you repeatedly and infiltrates or invades your being. You need to exercise and strengthen your mental muscles to achieve the strength required to keep you in shape. Winners believe deeply in themselves and that things will work out and become easier despite the typical challenges of everyday life. In the long run, the stars will line up, and positive results will be produced. When I notice that I have had a bad thought, I mentally ERASE or CANCEL what I have said or thought immediately, thus neutralizing its effect on the energy of the universe. I learned this from a highly enlightened and blessed friend. Since I started practicing it, I erase mistakes in my thoughts, words, and deeds, like someone who deletes a poorly written text. I must stress that, according to my friend, erasure must be done immediately or at least within a minute following the moment in which one mentioned or called something bad; otherwise, the request remains in effect on the energy of the universe. Always think that the glass is half full. It sounds trivial, but it is not easy during hard times. If you think that you will not achieve something, it will happen because you are attracting defeat into your life. In business or personal life, there are no flat roads without potholes or obstacles. However, you can reach your destination if you put your mind to it and know how to avoid potholes. The difference is that you do not stagnate if you know that adversity exists and is fleeting and that your projected objective can be met if you attempt to find solutions to problems instead of seeing problems in every solution. Solutions flow when we are open to receiving them. If we block them, they will never appear. Remember that "there is no evil that lasts a hundred years, nor a body that can endure it" and that "the darkest hour is just before the dawn."

Everything changes, and even the darkness can become light in the blink of an eye. I have found myself at a crossroads numerous times, where I do not see the way out, but then everything is resolved almost magically without much effort. The last serious illness I had lasted 12 years. I received daily and partial-service therapies, but ultimately, I was miraculously cured of the incurable from one day to the next. Remember, "if you do not consciously or unconsciously strengthen your defenses (have faith, trust yourself, believe that all good things will come to fruition), then you can become infected with any fatal virus in your environment." I will leave you with my reflection on a positive note: *If I have strong immunity, I will not catch anything.*

To whom can we attribute success or failure?

We will always find people who claim other people's successes as their own and attribute their failures to another person's lack of action or control. In short, they are never guilty or responsible for anything bad, but they are the irrefutable authors of everything good. Has this ever happened to you? Have you met a person like the one I have described?

We become mature when we can responsibly distinguish the authors of something good—generally the result of many people involved and not only the last or first person. We mature even more when we have the courage to recognize that failures result from our errors in action and omissions, as well as lack of vision or control.

However, do not be surprised if you find people in their 40s or 50s doing what I described in the first paragraph. There are almost eternal adolescents. Regardless of their age, you have to learn to handle them as such.

Another similar problem occurs when society, colleagues, or family end up convincing us that they are superheroes. This happens considerably often, and it is extremely serious because we come to believe that it is legitimately true. Even if it may well be, does it happen always? Did our ego grow? Or is it true that we are extraordinary? The key is in the facts and performance that certify or support our accomplishments.

There is also the opposite case where the family or society does not believe in someone because they see them as ordinary and even less than ordinary as if they were "defective." They do not believe that that person can achieve or has achieved something important. Those are the times when one has to leave to succeed away from them and then return because "no one is a prophet in their own land."

The latter hits the ego extremely hard and lowers self-esteem. If we are strong and courageous, we will look for a setting where we are valued and, ultimately, we find the success that initially eluded us. History shows how necessary it is to persevere until we succeed in standing out or achieving what we believe we can.

The key in life is the end result, as posed by the old physics formula, $W = F \times D$.

Work is equal to the force multiplied by the distance traveled. If I exert tremendous force but I travel zero distance, work is zero (great effort and zero results imply that work is zero). Conversely, if I exert a small force but travel a long distance, work is significant.

The key is how much I have advanced or achieved. In this sense, "skill is better than strength." This is like when one tries to open a jar with considerable effort, but the lid does not move one millimeter. However, someone else comes along with a technique and opens it in a second without much effort, a notable and frequent condition of everyday life.

In today's world, no one can complete the creation of a new product or service alone. We are forced to work with others, and we have to integrate pieces of knowledge, programming, or equipment to produce something new. Aiming to create everything from scratch, as was done in the past, is impossible in terms of time and money, let alone in terms of common sense. Companies are managed by managers who are integrated, and each one is responsible for their portion of the business. The "white feather" bosses who did, knew, controlled, and were accountable for everything are like business dinosaurs or organizations in a world where no one can say they know it all—an attribute that we cannot even assign to the sage of our time, Google.

Currently, we are witnesses to an unstoppable phenomenon: the level and quality of education that sets people apart, like when a person travels and spends time to understand the culture and customs of another country with better or different conditions compared with their country of origin. In many settings, the frequent and profound traveler ends up being a practical and wise person—someone who understands who they are and where they stand and how they can make the most of their knowledge to be ultimately above average in their life.

People who study at the best universities acquire knowledge far ahead of the rest, and it gives them a vision that makes it easier for them to, in a certain way, "consume the world," unlike the prospects of studying at a low-quality university in a small village of a developing country.

Of course, sooner or later, a talented person will end up scaling heights. However, if that talented person had the opportunity to study at one of the ten best universities in the world or take long trips to the most developed countries, they would surely have a much brighter future.

There is no problem with "consuming the world" when one has the legitimate and actual capability and merit. It will inspire envy or admiration, but it will be the unstoppable and irrefutable truth.

Where do you place yourself in all these reflections?

Where a captain rules, a sailor has no sway

The title allows many of us to think about our business and personal life. My wife says that I may be a top executive at work but that, at home, I am hardly a messenger with some privileges typical of my role as a husband and father. How does it work for you?

Now, there are men of strong character who impose themselves during the courtship stage when they have not yet had children. At this time, girls with strategic integrity accept the leadership of their honorable "alpha male," who, as time and events pass, will stop being so macho to be more like the letter zeta in the Greek alphabet or, better yet, the letter kappa, which is more representative and sonorous.

A highly intelligent boss whom I had the honor of having and with whom I maintain a close-knit friendship used to say a notable phrase that demonstrates what happens when one competes to beat the person in charge: "hierarchy kills poker." We may have the best argument and solid logic, like someone with aces in poker. However, although the boss has listened to us for a few minutes, they may make a decision that goes in another direction because they are the boss. Whether they make good or bad decisions, the boss is in command and signs off on the roads on which we shall travel.

This fact deserves the utmost respect, and it is up to us to see how we try or manage to sell our ideas to the boss. In the end, it will be like when we tell our spouse about the wonderful walk we want to take on a Sunday, and after listening, they say they feel tired and want to sleep, which terminates our plans. We will then understand why "hierarchy kills poker."

In my long business life, I have seen many cases of naïve people who were fired or moved to a different department, reporting line, or city for repeatedly going against their bosses and stoking internal revolutions in favor of lost causes contrary to their bosses' guidelines. Backed by logic and facts, they believe they have a better alternative than the one proposed by the boss are bold enough to indicate that they would operate differently if they were the boss.

This happens often, and we all know that many times, these people are right; however, they are not in charge. Consequently, they have no alternative other than to abide by the guidelines if the boss does not buy their well-founded arguments and ideas and decides to do something different. As the popular saying goes, "the boss is not always right but is always the boss," which is true.

There are people who enter organizations thinking that they can do as they please. They are convinced that if they manage to demonstrate that a plan or project has all the rationale as well as professional and financial support, then it will be approved and implemented. Subsequently, they collide against the cultural and hierarchical or political wall of the company, which does not operate according to this logic, much less with common sense. Everything is done according to the method of the boss or the board leading the organization. The person ends up being frustrated. Of course, I am assuming that the person presents something worthwhile and well-founded. Otherwise, they would not get anywhere.

When we join an organization, we have to learn to perceive what the organization likes and dislikes and how to push an idea forward. Only after this should we present a project to be developed. One cannot enter an organization assuming that the company and its bosses will behave the way we want them to and approve our ideas just because it is what we want. One has to adapt to the organization, and if we are incompatible with or do not like it, we must find another organization where we fit in better. Not every organization is for every person, and not every person is for every organization. It is easy to say this, but it is hard to convince people that they suffer and make others suffer by being in the wrong place.

The problem also arises when the boundaries of each position's responsibilities are not clearly defined in the company. In such a situation, neither the bosses nor the personnel know what they can and cannot do, or people are stubborn and insist on what they should not do or asking what cannot be granted.

What can we do before this overwhelming reality, aside from being aware of and understand it? My recommendation is to accept it without resistance so that it does not hurt. The world has an order, and we have to respect it regardless of whether we like it. My other recommendation is to work intelligently and take the time to learn and prepare a strategy to sell your ideas to your boss. The latter is a process worth working on. Some people become experts in achieving their goals by operating intelligently.

I will provide a couple of simple examples. A friend had a high-strung boss who would become furious when someone gave him bad news, when he lost a business, or when he discovered a mistake. His bad temper would last all day. If someone came up to him to ask for something or for approval, he would scold them and deny the request almost 100% of the time. My friend discovered that the anxious, ill-tempered boss was extremely susceptible to good news and that the way to get anywhere with him was to walk into his office minutes after he had just been notified that he had scored a deal or received excellent news. At that point, he would approve whatever was placed in front of him without question. Another friend discovered that his boss always decided on the opposite of what anyone proposed, which is why he proposed the opposite of the idea for which he really wanted to get approval.

Anything is possible. You have to be patient, examine the situation, plan a strategy, and then execute wisely to win. Test this at home. Apply the same strategy that your spouse uses on you when they want to make something happen.

Sow the wind and reap the whirlwind

Life carries its charm with its natural laws, such as cause and effect or action and reaction. "Every cause has its effect; every effect has its cause." People forget that when they "sow the wind," they "reap the whirlwind." They spend their time creating waves that then return and drown them, like a boomerang effect.

Generally, the following famous phrases apply in life: "with whatever scale you measure, it will be measured to you" and "the wheels of justice grind slow but grind fine, and if human beings do not apply it, Divine Majesty will." Notably, one thinks that this will happen in the next life. However, in reality, it happens in this life and sooner than we think. People do not realize the damage they cause with their actions, attitude, or words, which "harm, injure, or kill," and then they wonder why others attack them, close their doors, and block, reject, or beat them. The typical phrase is "what did I do to deserve this treatment or this situation?" Honestly, many do not realize the harm they have caused because it is in their nature to be bad or evil. This is why these people are referred to as the "cursed ones" because they seem to be possessed by a pattern of evil.

In families, organizations, and companies, we find the infamous "cursed ones" who turn out to be a nightmare for everyone. They are so evil that they end up taking over the minds and spirits of many people, who serve them as informant puppets and useful idiots to consolidate their permanence and dominance and ensure a shield of protection.

I imagine that you remember past events with the "cursed ones" you have had to deal with or that you are feeling the pain in your skin that comes from knowing that you have lived or are currently suffering from the experience.

A friend told me about a character at the company where he currently works. It was a senior international executive who had "possessed" the top corporate managers, all of whom saw him as the eighth wonder, like a lover who sees only beauty and no imperfections in their partner. However, this executive created problems everywhere, withheld key decisions, complicated every step for many people, and had the organization on its knees, as it continually lost businesses and opportunities while the traditional clients were totally dissatisfied. The executive created the illusion that everyone else was guilty and that he was the savior, the only one who worked and produced results. He took advantage of the fact that the top managers rarely visited the countries, and they only listened to what the executive communicated to them. However, when they decided to visit and speak with the clients, suppliers, and employees directly, they realized the terrible reality and the lies that the executive had invented for years, and his termination was immediate. The company changed over time and managed to recover. Today, it is operating at an incredible rate, given its evident growth and the satisfaction of its clients, suppliers, and employees. The executive who caused the damage has not found a job in three years and has already used up all his savings. He is desperate and does not understand why he is in his current situation.

As we may surmise from the aforementioned real-life case, without mentioning names to avoid problems, the solution always comes, whether alone or with reinforcements. This is illustrated by the opening phrase of this written reflection, "sow the wind and reap the whirlwind," and the subsequent notable phrase, "with whatever scale you measure, it will be measured to you." There is an automatic reaction to evil, although it may take some time to occur.

Notably, there are other famous expressions that refer to the boomerang effect: "raise ravens, and they will pluck out your eyes" and "there is no tighter wedge than the one made from the same wood." They relate to treating others well and always doing the right thing because the world is round, and life takes many turns. Sooner or later, the equation flips, and we end up in the hands of those who were once our collaborators, apprentices, or colleagues. At a given moment, they become a key client, a star supplier, our bosses, or the people who will vouch for us either as a reference or as caregivers when we get old.

What goes up must come down over time. The important thing is not to burn bridges so that we do not fall victim to the revenge that someone has been plotting for years against us when we are down. Today, we are strong, but one day, we will present weaknesses, and we will then be vulnerable and defenseless.

If we leave behind affection, admiration, and respect in our lifetime, we will most likely receive the same from others in moments of weakness or when we are old. Everything comes back, the bad and the good. Let us sow goodness to reap goodness and sow support to reap support so that when we fall, someone will come along and lift up rather than walk all over us or leave us lying on the ground. Remember, "everyone makes firewood of a fallen tree."

In any case, notable remedies can be found among popular proverbs, and they are useful when one is attacked from the front or the back: "foolish words fall on deaf ears," and inexorably, "the calm that comes after the storm." "You break it, you buy it" is another well-known saying and which is fulfilled sooner rather than later.

Think about the people around you and the experiences you have had. You have certainly seen how some students are grateful to their teachers while others attack or mistreat them, although they are good teachers who have done their best to pass on their knowledge and experience.

I am sure you remember a story you have heard or experienced with people who have intentionally caused harm, and over time, you have seen how that evil was overwhelmingly returned to them.

-89-

Response time to winning acts and actions

A slow response time to whatever is happening around us can be expensive or deadly. In one tiny second of oversight, we can lose everything—opportunities, business, and even life. How is your alertness? How many times have you suffered because you did not react on time? A quick and decisive reaction can save lives or win opportunities. Businesses can be lost in a second.

I have saved myself many times by mistakenly taking a different path other than the marked or established path or not showing up to a scheduled appointment. However, these are causalities (not coincidences) of life and are not frequent or conscious. Many events in life happen because they are inevitable. There is a kind of programming for them. Remember, *life for winners is a game full of interesting and attractive challenges, but life for losers is a continuous fight against adversity.* Which of the two shores are you on? How many times have you heard the phrase "change or they will change you"? Have they changed you by not changing? Have you seen people who have been changed by not changing?

How are we affected by our surroundings, especially by what we have no control over? We cannot prevent rains or storms, earthquakes, floods, fires, or an attack by an evildoer. Nevertheless, how we react to whatever happens to us is the key to our success or the trigger for failure. We alter our destiny or confirm it based on the way we behave toward those around us. In conclusion, *we cannot prevent what happens to us, but we can alter the result through our reaction.*

A relative once told me when we met, "I see that you have gotten fat." I replied, "Thanks for the compliment. I feel wonderful like this." I transformed the negative sentiment they wanted to evoke into strength and pride, avoiding any controversy by disarming my enemy with my unusual position.

I remember once when a vice president of sales challenged me to make a fool of myself in front of his team, and I became famous for the answer that I gave him. He said, "Valderrama, if you are so macho, answer this question." I listened and said, "Who told you I was macho? I am just a normal man. Have a good afternoon." I did not play his game. They all burst out laughing.

Some people think that people and organizations have to adapt to them. Usually, the opposite occurs, like the person who enters a room of about 100 people and asks aloud for the smokers to raise their hand. When nobody raises their hand, they immediately tell everyone to get out because they are going to smoke. Another instance would be when a person enters the highway in the wrong direction and has the audacity to say, "There are about 30 cars going the wrong way."

Attitude toward others or events is one of the keys to one person's failure and another person's success. I invite you to view all problems as opportunities and challenges in a positive way and not to spend a minute lamenting or crying over spilled milk. For each case, study a solution and decide quickly. Try to adapt to every environment as quickly as possible and find a way to survive and build favorable conditions in that new environment. See opportunities where others see difficulties and limitations.

The important thing in life is to make decisions and act intelligently as soon as possible by maintaining a permanent state of alertness when on a mission or facing a risky situation.

A good friend of mine often says this wise phrase: *Do you know what a problem is? It is the consequence of not having made a timely decision.*

The importance of having big ears

A friend once said that he would like to work with people with big ears like the little elephant named Dumbo. There is a significant reflection in this statement.

Dumbos are much needed in companies and personal life because most inconveniences or problems arise owing to many people having tiny ears. They are almost deaf without being physically deaf. As the popular adage goes, "There is none so deaf as those who will not hear." Meanwhile, the famous Carl Jung said, "The true leader is always led," which implies that a leader must have big ears.

Many conflicts in interpersonal relationships occur because people do not want to listen to others, which means listening carefully to understand what others feel or think and then doing something positive about it. Generally, we do not let the other person conclude the idea before questioning or opposing it; we forget that **there are**

thousands of valid positions relative to the same situation. I will offer a brief, simple example.

One may invite seven different people to look through a large window and observe the way the rain falls during a storm, and we may be surprised to hear the following answers to the only question: What do you feel when you see the rain? One responds, "Rain inspires me to paint." Another says, "Rain makes me angry because I cannot go out." Further, one replies, "I would like to dance under the rain." Another answers, "Every time I see rain, I get sad." Moreover, one says, "Watching the rain makes me sleepy." Another states, "Storms scare me." The last one responds, "I am so glad to see that the plants and animals will receive the water they so much need." Although rain is the same inevitable natural phenomenon for all seven people, each has their own interpretation of it, and they think and act accordingly. I conclude my observation by noting that we generate our own feelings and attitude toward a situation or an event, such as the rain. In other words, the rain is not responsible for our good or bad thoughts or feelings. Rain is just rain.

The same happens to us any time we face a situation or an event, as well as someone's comments, criticism, or opinion. *Our reaction is ours, and we are the owners and generators of what we feel and how we react.* Once we understand this, we see that we must let events and comments or conversations flow. We must **take a second to accept that the fact or the event is something that we cannot change** or that whatever was said or heard is merely a phrase or an idea, such as the rain in the previous example. Subsequently, **we must define how we want to interpret it, what we want to feel, and what we should do**

about it. Without a doubt, we will see that it is up to us to create drama or take careful notes so that later, we can analyze, take action, or be grateful because it adds value or let it slide by assigning zero value to what happened or what we received.

With the simple exercise that I have indicated above, we can symbolically expand the size of our ears and our ability to react to daily situations; we can avoid taking events personally or getting caught up in a conflict or a war of pride and senseless egos. We will be giving the right value or the right amount of attention to life situations, and we will not be affected by what does not serve or apply to us.

Having big ears allows us to understand the facts without affecting or attributing feelings. Big ears help filter the garbage in the face of any event. They ensure that we concentrate on the essential or substance of whatever is happening and thereby give it the value it deserves and take the appropriate action.

When you have big ears, you listen to those at the bottom, the top, the back, in the front, and on the side. In a company, you listen to all the players involved, the employees, bosses, suppliers, clients, community, shareholders, and even the competition. After listening to them, you will have a better perspective and vision that will undoubtedly allow you to take appropriate actions and make better decisions. In turn, everyone will feel that their position or perspective has been considered. This is important not to generate the idea that we live in tyranny or a deaf world.

We can say that the method of growing our ears is not infallible and that it takes a little more time. However, it is a considerably effective way to get ahead with greater success in personal life and organizations.

People often make decisions assuming that the world is in their hands, bringing them serious problems. If you listen to others, you may avoid negatively affecting areas or people whose involvement may help you find a better way to execute a given task so that the majority wins in some fair proportion or so that the impact, if any, is minimized. In companies, bosses tend to believe that their title gives them the infinite power to do whatever they see fit without considering the other people involved. Over time, they end up crashing into reality when they have to face the conflicts generated by their decisions or actions.

I have seen many average and important bosses fail because they do not exercise their listening skills. In a world as interconnected as ours today, it is almost impossible not to harm someone if we keep assuming that we are the owners of truth and absolute power. Worst of all, sometimes we not only affect others but also harm ourselves or, in the case of organizations, the company where we work.

Therefore, **I invite you** to consider **initiating the process of enlarging your ears as soon as possible.**

91

The company we keep is key to our success

The company you keep in your private life, at work, in society, or in a group is the key to your success. Surround yourself with people equal or better than you, and you will succeed. It is as simple as that. Think about your partner. Are they better than you? Do they add value? Do they complement you? Do they guide or advise you? Do they support you during tough times? Do they reassure you or give you peace? Do they teach you and help you understand? Do they encourage you to reflect? Do they challenge you to grow? Do they enlighten you? Do they warn you of risks? Do they help you solve problems? Do they perform some tasks for you?

The reflection applies equally to your partners in an organization, collaborators, co-workers, or team if you are the boss at a company. You have to surround yourself with people who are better than you or complement you—they should be better than you in areas in which you need improvement. Throughout my life, I have seen and had the opportunity to experience firsthand the benefits **of being around people who are my equals or better than me for my success.** There is no doubt about it. Curiously, the opposite occurs more often—people surround themselves with mediocre people so that they stand out among them. I have chosen to surround myself with people who are my equals or better than me in my life, and the professional, business, and personal results, among others, have been extraordinary. The success is evident.

Meanwhile, I have sometimes seen those who surround themselves with mediocre people shine. Although they succeed and are extremely good, they do not leave room for the people with less rank to grow. When the top performers are not there, everything collapses because there is no one with the level or the appropriate experience to replace the leader or the head. When we surround ourselves with people who are our equals or better than us in the present or our future projection, anyone can assume the role of the second-in-command or leadership because they will have the skills. This, in turn, allows growth and promotion because there is enough strength, dexterity, intelligence, and ability throughout the team.

I have been in several multinational companies that carefully hire professionals who are starting, ensuring that their future projection is analyzed and that they can become general managers. The quality of the personnel in these companies is impressive, and they are part of prestigious and well-established companies.

As for couples or business partners, the concept is vital and can make a big difference in the results. In the case of a team with many people, the results can be amazing if the simple criterion that I have recommended is applied. It is a good rule in our everyday lives. We all know and understand the consequences that bad friends have on people. Sooner or later, these people get mixed up in problems and become affected by bad influences or references. It is hard to verbalize and admit, but someone has to point out the reality, although others may disagree.

One sees the examples that I have mentioned in all of life's scenarios. I could reflect some more and illustrate many examples, but I think the idea is considerably clear.

"Surround yourself with people who are equal or better than you, and you will succeed."

92

How to avoid mental damage or scars

The words and attitudes expressed by some people are as dangerous as daggers that plunge into the heart. Meanwhile, good attitude and words of encouragement or recognition strengthen people and turn them into superheroes.

Unfortunately, people mostly express destructive attitudes and words that often cause almost irreparable damage—they significantly affect one's self-esteem and confidence to achieve goals or objectives or perform tasks. The weakness generated almost instantly belittles the person and leaves them paralyzed or senseless. If the person who receives the offense is not strong enough to avoid the impact (resilience), the damage can be serious, and the mental scar could be large.

I will provide a few examples of the comments that people make: You are incapable. You are inept. You are incompetent. An elementary school boy can do a better job. You lack initiative. You need to be pushed. You are not proactive. You are slow. You lack intelligence. These are devastating words to hear. People associate any despicable qualifier with you. In addition to being a modern form of torture, they end up worsening the condition of those already dejected.

Fighting couples make comments that disqualify the other's sexual performance, love, actions, or daily tasks, and these comments are more dangerous and devastating than a magnitude 10 earthquake. The reason is simple. The opinion of a loved one has 500 times the power of a comment or attitude expressed by a standard acquaintance because of the intimacy and their depth of knowledge about us. Just as a loved one can make us feel very loved and cared for, mishandled criticism can demotivate us and push us straight into a dark abyss with no easy way of getting out.

Conversely, one can achieve wonders with people by expressing the right words and attitudes: I am sure you can do it. I trust your ability. You have my support. You are wonderful. You are doing great. One can use challenging but inverse motivations: Do you think you can demonstrate this? I think that you may be up for this challenge. Are you? The person will surely say that they will show you that they are capable, and they certainly are, and they may even excel at it. This type of stimulus generates challenges and self-confidence, and people embark on a journey to seek their fulfillment.

An antidote to destructive words is to improve our capacity for resistance (resilience). No one can make us feel something we do not want to feel, which is easier said than done when we are being offended. However, we can achieve it if we practice, and there are ways to divert the negativity so that we are not affected. Let us suppose that a mean girl meets another girl whom she envies and says, "I see that you have put on weight." An answer that disconcerts the aggressor would be, "Thanks for the compliment. I feel good the way I am. Nice to see you."

A colleague once challenged me in front of a considerable number of people, saying, "If you are as good as they say you are, answer this question." I simply answered, "Who told you I was any good?" Everyone laughed. "Have a good day, gentlemen," I said and left. I did not play their game.

The response to an attack is in our hands; however, it takes practice not to get caught up in a fight and to disarm the opponent in surprising elegance. Nobody and nothing can make me feel happy or unhappy—only I can decide that. Disarming the enemy with intelligence requires some practice, but the point is to show them that their aggression did not affect you or cause you discomfort or pain. They will be perplexed by our immunity. The famous expression "foolish words fall on deaf ears" is so true.

In any case, I invite you to use words that add value and make others feel good, and in case of aggression, to be courteously immutable and even express gratitude as if they had praised us. Ultimately, remember the phrase, *Kill them with kindness.* Try it, and you will see incredible results.

93

Doing the right thing in the right place at the right time with the right people

"Doing the right thing in the right place at the right time with the right people."

How easy it is to say and write, but how hard it is to have that coherence in the moment of truth.

I will give you an example of what usually happens. I have attended many wakes, and after greeting the bereaved relatives of the deceased, the gathering outside the room turns into several conversations between people who had not seen each other for a long time and take advantage of the moment to catch up on life stories and relive dramas, until they reach the funny moments that everyone remembers and laughs about, a conversation meant for another occasion. The truth is that I have heard some good jokes at wakes, and I have felt embarrassed, which is why I have had to move away from those who confuse the place, the situation, or the moment. I have also attended wakes where there were people who took advantage of the encounter to start talking about business with me.

One could say that reckless or unscrupulous people exist, but the problem is that they are growing in number given the absence of good training in homes or schools. Consequently, people are raised and develop wildly or naturally without boundaries or respect, like a person who learns to drive a car with the help of a friend and then gets their license through influences but has never studied the traffic signs or rules and laws. They then violate or break laws continuously, apart from their enormous and bold ignorance.

Thus, what do we do with our sense of humor, which takes advantage of every opportunity or tense moment to be inspired and turn a bad moment into something pleasant?

Good point!

A good sense of humor is welcome as long as we do not harm, violate, or offend the rules of decency or fine behavior. Good humor plays with that boundary, and the more refined it is, the more it manages to entertain without annoying anyone. Therein lies ingenuity and the difference between bad taste, recklessness, and audacity. Of course, you have to know when and where good humor is welcome. We all know that there are times when a joke can backfire and result in a wake-up call instead of a laugh. As time goes on, many of us lose our notions of good behavior and good manners, and we often fall into reckless or rude behavior with disproportionate, inappropriate, or offensive jokes because we want to please everyone. We then end up having to apologize to the audience or leaving a bad image if we do not reverse the mistake. Sometimes we make mistakes and do not even realize that we have committed an infraction, which is even worse. In other words, we violate the rules and offend, but we are oblivious to it. What do we do in these cases?

If no one helps us by calling our attention to our mistakes, we are lost, and we will go down in history as being rude and shameless. If instead someone helps us by telling us that we are wrong, we must accept their indication without discussion and immediately see if we can blush and offer an apology to minimize the impact and bad image and repair the mistake as much as possible.

A more notable and current case is the chats, where people are reckless and forget their setting, and end up writing and introducing topics or making comments that attract attention, start arguments or serious controversies, or compel some people to withdraw from the chat on bad terms.

In any situation, it is best to think for two seconds before acting, answering, writing, or saying something. It is something like "Think before you act instead of acting before you think."

I will give you four questions that will always help you avoid making mistakes or failure in the future:
Is it okay for me to say or do this?
Am I in the right place?
Is it the right time?
Am I with the right people?

If the answer is YES to all the questions, proceed. If you answer NO to any of the questions, please refrain.

I could give more examples of all kinds, but "to a good listener, few words are enough," as the saying goes. Therefore, it is key to *"do the right thing in the right place at the right time with the right people."*

Simple, right?

The key is to make a fine closure
and not to leave loose ends

The best example lies in the seven basic musical notes on the traditional scale: Do Re Mi Fa So La Ti. If we sing them one after the other, when we reach Ti, we feel as though we need closure, and we get somewhat anxious and want to place another Do at the end: Do Re Mi Fa Sol La Ti... Do.

The same thing happens with dinners. In the end, coffee or liquor is required to cap off the meal and provide a brief sense of completion, also allowing to conclude the conversation and say goodbye.

In Catholic churches, the priest gives their blessing to those in attendance in the name of the Holy Trinity at the end of mass. No one leaves without the priest's blessing. You have to have a closing for the ceremony.

Closure is extremely important. To be done properly, it must be polished, refined, elegant, and brief but firm simultaneously. The most famous example can be found in movies and real life when couples kiss in reconciliation or to say goodbye—fine, elegant, conclusive, and brief but with depth and feeling.

Songs always have closure, and when artists do not plan or execute them properly, we are left with the feeling that they did not finish or that they owe us something. Among other things, the closure must be perfect so that the group or orchestra ends simultaneously and generates that feeling of joy over the performance and immediately motivates the audience's ovation. Every closure must cue the signal a few seconds before indicating that the end is coming or is going to happen. Plays and operas always have a rehearsed ending to leave emotions and sensations or feelings high but with a sense of completion that wins the well-deserved applause of the audience. Speeches or presentations must come to an end that leaves the audience with a clear idea of what it is about and the intended message and, of course, a brief, firm conclusion that unmistakably signals the end and the unanimous, synchronized applause of the audience.

I have attended many religious sermons, and unfortunately, many of them lack that wonderful closure that you now see is essential. Sadly, there are ministers, pastors, or priests who have not learned how to close their sermons properly.

Although there are fewer bullfights, out of people's growing respect for the life and treatment of animals, I remember that my father took me to one once. I will never forget that although the bullfighter can execute many great scenes or wonderful, elegant, or risky passes, if they miss on their final lunge, the show is spoiled. Again, the ending has to be excellent.

At the end of an excellent performance in the bedroom, ladies often complain about men's carelessness in providing an affectionate and loving end that is required in such times, given the different speeds at which moods drop according to gender differences. Here, again, the finish must be spectacular and remarkable, for everyone's sake.

I could continue to call your attention with more examples and reflections on the brief, deep, and intense episode that I have called "the closure," which is usually the conclusion that punctuates the end of a great performance, meeting, or event. Owing to its importance, we must be extremely careful about planning and executing it so that we can give it the memory it deserves and receive the ovation we deserve.

In short, *every closure must be spectacular and remarkable.*

It is smart to use the current in our favor

*I*t is common sense to swim with the current. However, few people practice this in settings other than a river.

There are some occasions in which it is convenient to swim against the current, although the wear and tear are noticeable. It all depends on the objective you want to achieve. If you go in a boat with an outboard motor, you can go wherever you like, in favor or against the current. Going against the current requires a powerful motor, and if you do not have it, the best thing is to go with the current.

If swimming with the current leads us to a waterfall from which we will fall, it would be wise to see if we need to walk upstream and then swim with the current to cross the river diagonally. If it is not possible to walk upstream, we must exert strength to swim against the current and manage the crossing before we fall down the waterfall. This is a complex, risky, and extreme situation if done without the aid of a motor. If there is no waterfall in sight, the best thing is to let yourself be carried away by the current and cross diagonally to get to the other side, and then walk up the river if you want to return.

Regardless of the goal, it is best to think and make a plan that harnesses the current as much as possible. It is always better to flow. A typical example is when one is on a sailboat at sea or in a lagoon, and the wind is blowing. If you set the sails correctly and handle the rudder properly, you can go wherever you need to go, not necessarily in the direction that the wind is blowing. This is smart. Curious, is it not?

In other words, *ingenuity allows us to use the headwind to our advantage.* Of course, we must perceive where the wind is blowing before we design a plan to take advantage of this flow to help us get to where we want to go. The same happens in the martial art called Aikido, where we use the opponent's strength in our favor. The stronger the attacker is, the more force is returned to them. It is a noble martial art because it neutralizes the opponent without harming them, maintaining total self-control in an atmosphere of peace and respect.

When airplanes take off or land, the headwind or the wind blowing against the plane must be used. Aviation was born from the ingenious use of this principle, the headwind. A classic example is the kite that flies when there is a headwind.

Have you ever heard of people who follow their hunches? They have an antenna, or rather, an acute perception of the messages of the universe, which is nothing other than energy. People who have this gift or the ability to be led by hunches are only going with the flow. They follow the energy pulses that tell them if something they are going to do is the right thing or if they should avoid it. They follow a kind of radar that alerts them whether the path is the correct one to take with a simple yes or no. Here, too, we have a clear example of what it means to take advantage of the current in our favor. Of course, many people do not have or have not developed this gift of hunches or do not believe in it and often collide against the world with their decisions because they do not go with the flow or use the current in their favor.

The current can also be a light in the dark, the light at the end of the tunnel, the dawn, a lit candle in the middle of a dark night, a light bulb in a dark room, a started engine or a car, the red or green light of a traffic light, or a flashing yellow light. The current is also what delays us and makes us late for a flight. We miss our flight, and then we see on the news that we were saved from an air disaster and death. The current is also the opportunity that presents us to a new job, friend, or business.

In short, intelligence is to know what we need from the current or the flow, the force or intuition to achieve our objective and, consequently, to become more alert or awake so that we may identify it and use it to our advantage.

The "Let Them Be" method for people development

*T*he best method to develop our children or our collaborators continues *to be setting a good example, providing close guidance as needed, and letting them flourish within a framework of self-control and empowerment, seeking to treat them as the responsible adults that we want them to be or become.* I call this method of management and development, Let Them Be—a mnemonic taken from the famous Beatles song but adapted to the plural.

When we treat our children or collaborators as adults from the beginning and encourage them to grow by challenging them and telling them that we trust they can achieve the great feats that we envision for them, the result is immediate. It astounds many—even the children or collaborators who did not know that they could achieve so many good things. Just saying that they can count on our support and total trust and that we support them in everything, even when they make mistakes, already creates a condition that allows them to obtain incredible results. Of course, we have to be willing to allow them to fail so that they learn, which comes at a cost but brings unparalleled growth and maturity in the long run. I have applied this method numerous times with many professionals who have become CEOs and presidents of organizations. As I said, you will see the same result in your children if you apply the method.

Of course, *everything starts with having good people who want and are willing to develop and make progress rapidly to get ahead.* We must also be careful to provide an experiential example of how to behave in our approach to solving problems and overcoming challenges and our attitude toward difficulties.

People who want to grow are willing to absorb all the guidance given to them like a sponge. Without a doubt, the fastest method is to let them copy all the experience that they can regarding our performance in senior management positions or life in general, in the case of employees or children.

Further, notably, a good teacher can guide more adequately when the student makes mistakes than when they perform the tasks well. The best teaching opportunity is when you help resolve a painful mistake or failure.

People often treat their children and employees like kids or teenagers. This is a serious mistake that slows their mental development. It also makes them insecure when everything has to be consulted with their parents or their bosses, who are the only ones who know what to do and what to decide at any time, apart from generating a harmful dependence. Responsibility always falls on the boss or the parent who never empowered and never trusted the person to learn to take their own controlled risks and assume the mistakes of their decisions and their actions.

The Let Them Be method facilitates and accelerates the development process and helps achieve outstanding results. However, we need the courage to trust and be willing to teach/learn together to view trial and error as something natural to the growth/delegation curve. It involves letting go of or managing fears.

I have applied this method for many years, and I have been successful in 99% of the cases. Those who have not applied it, I encourage you to do it at least once to see the power of its results. Let them be!

Life is like a river channel

One believes that life and its events occur in a straight line that takes us directly from one point to another by the shortest distance or that life goes like circles, triangles, squares, or parabolic or hyperbolic curves. The truth is that little of that exists because they are merely models that help us interpret our surroundings, only giving us a general idea. However, *real life is like a river channel that winds in different directions like a snake in motion*. It has different widths, currents or turbulences, and inclinations, with waterfalls or jumps, rapids or lagoons, backwaters, and quiet paths. It has different depths, temperatures, densities, shades, or colors, and, of course, it is considerably far from any imaginary standard.

Life is a daily and even hourly challenge. Real life is full of surprises and winding roads. Life teaches us every minute that there is not one single situation that does not change and that every situation, regardless of how good or difficult it may be, will not last forever. At one moment, we are celebrating a triumph, and at the next, we are crying about a defeat. Life has various aspects that alternate randomly. It can be salty, sweet, sour, bitter, or spicy, to mention the most traditional or frequent flavors. Anything is possible. Everything changes and nothing is sustained or eternal.

In any case, it is amazing how people do not reflect on this and believe that life is a constant straight line. They spend their days believing that their life is flat. They still naively think that they are going to get everything they want the way they want it. However, the reality is that one navigates through life as it unfolds amidst many variables that alter or undermine one's path to set goals.

In each situation, we have to be skillful, brave, fast, and ingenious enough to turn the conditions in our favor successfully while moving toward our purposes, dreams, and plans. Life challenges us every second, every minute, every hour, and every day. You have to keep all your senses open to detect variations or anticipate anything you can. Therefore, you have to adapt and be flexible to react intelligently to each challenge. Nevertheless, there are surprising situations that we cannot overcome and force us to back down or find other ways or routes to continue on the path to our goal.

Of course, there may be surprises that speed up, aid, or facilitate the process. We must not forget that it will always be possible to find traps, deception, barriers, and friends or enemies that will make our journey more challenging. We will always find people who will give us a hand and those who will take their hand away.

This is what life is like. Everything changes, and this should give us joy.

Life is like a river channel that we have to be willing to navigate as it flows along through each section. Most of the time, we have to let ourselves get carried by the current, applying the greatest intuition and intelligence to get ahead. We must be aware that every minute, every hour, or every day brings different challenges and surprises that we have to know how to avoid or take advantage of in the best possible manner.

We must be grateful for everything that happens and live life as it presents itself, which may not be exactly the way we want it to or according to plan. Life unfolds as it happens. We have no other alternative at the moment. *Every event that happens, regardless of how good or serious it may be, is only an opportunity for reflection and learning.* Therefore, once a stage is over, we must continue along the path without getting left behind because those events are already history.

Let us seize opportunities and transform problems and challenges into opportunities.

98

Crucial decisions always bring risk and deep reflection

E very transcendental decision in our lives presents its consequences and risks. Therefore, it is convenient to analyze the pros and cons thoroughly before we have the courage to assume them, which is undoubtedly an additional factor to taking the next step forward or backward.

I am referring to decisions such as marriage, divorce, changing companies, finding and establishing a good partnership, breaking up a partnership, deciding where to live, leaving the country, firing an employee, closing a business, selling a business, having a child, leaving home, returning to one's country, working toward a career, authorizing a high-risk surgery, or distancing from a loved one. What if I make a mistake? It is a scary thought.

Each of these transcendental or crucial events merits a prior, detailed, step-by-step plan, relative to the previous stages, to manage the definitive moment when we make the decision, which then requires a systematic management of the consequences. All stages are important—before, during, and after the crucial moment.

In most cases, the previous stage and moment zero, which is when the action is executed, generate anxiety and tension or emotional weight. We must know how to carry and manage them to maintain balance. When the event has occurred, you have to fill yourself with strength, willpower, and enthusiasm to manage the new path in your personal or business life because you either closed an old chapter or started a new one. In all cases, starting or finishing requires a certain degree of courage.

Meanwhile, every time we face a crucial decision, it is clear that we are going to have a unique experience, which is like learning to live again, as each challenge is a different world full of surprises and new emotions.

Every time we face a crucial decision, it is natural to get nervous days before. Once the decision is made, we may struggle to sleep for days before executing it. When the climax or moment of truth arrives, our nerves rise to the crest, which is normal, and only after a while does one wake up from a kind of temporary anesthesia to realize that the challenge is over and that it has been met. We are now in the post-decision phase. Each moment used to plan, make, and execute a vital decision is unique and unrepeatable, and each one generates its own tensions as well as fear of the unknown. It is normal. In any case, the key is what happens after the decision is executed, which must be planned well in advance, as this step generally requires greater caution than the previous one, given that it will last a long time.

Crucial decisions require the mettle to handle the initial nerves and the courage to face and manage the consequences of the impact of the result. However, they must be made so that one does not stagnate and can turn specific life situations around.

99

Count on me to dance to any rhythm

I dance to any music" is a well-known saying.

A Colombian friend, who had been a human resources manager at a multinational company for many years, told me that he had brought rock bands to the company's Christmas party when there was an Englishman as general manager. When a Spaniard took over, he brought Tunas. A Mexican arrived as general manager, and he would bring in mariachi. For the last one, a Colombian from a region called Boyacá, he brought typical music from that area: the *carranga*. Each manager lasted in their position for between four and six years, while my friend said that he lasted 20 years in his position because he did his job well and, above all, pleased the managers according to their tastes.

Another friend had worked 35 years for a strict multinational company famous for firing many people every year, and he always performed well. I asked him the reason for his successful permanence. In his extremely brief answer, he gave me his magic formula, "Every time they announce a change in guidelines or strategies, I offer to be part of the team that leads them."

The speed in which one adapts or reacts to new conditions or extreme changes is the first key factor to successful survival. The second is the willingness to adapt to or read and understand new conditions, which is not easy for many people.

We have all heard the stories of people who have survived shipwrecks or a plane crash in a jungle or snow-filled mountains or those who emerged alive from a desert, who were saved from an earthquake, a fire, or an accident. These are not merely coincidences or good luck. They are the intelligent application of one's adaptability, which may generate surprising or unpredictable conditions. In this case, willpower and speed, apart from ingenuity or creativity, are vital.

Let us use the example of the frequent traveler who flies from America to the Far East and, in less than 24 hours, finds themselves in a different time zone, climate, and culture, with different customs, rules, laws, foods, and people. What do they have to do if they want to survive in these new conditions abroad? They need to adapt as soon as possible and enjoy the change. Does it make sense? Of course, we may decide not to adapt, but it will cost us, or it will hurt because something will not get accomplished or will not turn out the way we like. We could also end up committing some infraction and will have to suffer the consequences. The world is not made to our own image. In other words, the world does not adapt to us; we are the ones who must adapt to the world. In any case, the decision and choice are in our hands, and we are free to do as we please. I will leave you with the reflection.

If there is a fire on the 50th floor of a building and you are on that floor, you can choose to sit still and do nothing, or you can think fast and calmly look for an option to save yourself. You can pass out and burn, or you may be fortunate enough to have someone else throw you over their shoulder and save you. Which option do you prefer? Are you interested in getting out alive?

The problem is that the universe plays music or a rhythm for us to dance, and we are so distracted that we do not hear it, or if we hear it, we remain seated and do not dance. We then ask ourselves, "what is happening to us?" Why does everything go wrong for me?

I remember that when inviting my parents to go out for a walk or dinner, they never hesitated to say yes. If they had to change their plans, they would do it in minutes. Packing suitcases was not an inconvenience to them because they did it in less than an hour. They were like the Boy Scouts—"always ready." They had tremendous adaptability because they had permanent willpower and speed. How long does it take you to get ready to go out on an instant invitation?

Whatever happens, one has to dance to the rhythm of the music that life plays. If we can adapt quickly to new music or new rhythms and dance, the universe will be in our favor. Make no mistake about that.

That is why I dance to any rhythm. Count on me.

What is rightfully ours eventually comes to us

The title is short and substantial in its content and wisdom. Many people spend their time fighting to achieve their dreams. When we analyze the history of their lives, we are surprised to find that only a few of those people achieve their dream and that a good portion endure only mental wear. Other people go through life without even trying, and opportunities are effortlessly given to them one after the other. Why does the universe seem to support some and abandon others? Life is like that.

When you are on the right track, every step is made easy. When one is on the wrong path, every step becomes difficult. It is a law of life that we are not often aware of or do not perceive exists. The universe gives us daily clues, but we do not pay attention to the wise orientation we receive, and we decide to go the other way as if we want to do the contrary.

What is meant for us appears or comes to us, whether it is an opportunity or a person. What is not meant for us never comes or escapes, regardless of how much we desperately and persistently search for it. When we encounter difficulties instead of opportunities, we must verify whether they are normal challenges posed by life to teach us something that we need to learn for the next chapter. In any case, if a door closes, it is because we must look for another until we find the one that opens to continue our journey.

Although many may not believe so, these are the laws of the universe, and there is nothing we can do but accept them. When we feel that we are in the wrong place or that we are with the wrong person, the universe is teaching us something. If we do not learn, it continues to test us on the same lesson until we do. The bad thing is that every time it tests us, it does so with greater intensity if we do not accept and learn the lesson so that we can move on to the next level. Once we have learned, the tests are over, and the path continues with new options for us. The great events of my life—the bad, the regular, the good, or the extraordinary (and I have lived enough to have had a few)—happened without my having planned or searched for them. They just happened. A considerable number of my failures or errors occurred when I tried to do things my own way, disobeying what the universe or life has set forth or indicated to me. I have made mistakes because I was stubborn or did not know how to read what destiny had set forth for me. Destiny sends us signals that we ignore, and those signals are extremely simple, such as "it is not there" or "it is over here." It is simple, but one is often blind or deaf to the signals. Has that not happened to you?

The correct route most of the time is right in front of us, but it is the one that we discard first to find another on which we shall later crash against destiny. Similar to when we are traveling, sometimes the best restaurant for dinner is in the hotel where we are staying, yet we go out to find a different restaurant in the area or one that is far away. Has that not happened to you? I got my first job came when I openly said I wanted to work, and someone heard and helped me, opening doors for me. I got my second job when I sent my resume to a major multinational company, without trying anything except my luck, as I had already submitted my final thesis but had not graduated. There was no rush. I was chosen from among 100 candidates. What is rightfully yours comes to you. The woman of my dreams showed up to a meeting or party that I had no idea I was going to end up attending. My presence was accidental and unusual, and I met her there. My first business venture arose from an idea discussed in a cafeteria with a colleague with whom I had never even studied a subject in college.

Everything I have in terms of jobs occurred because someone contacted me to propose a project or an idea, and I accepted the challenge. Certainly, they have not been simple, painless, or effortless tasks but have been wonderful and extremely productive experiences. I never devised a plan in search of them. They came to me as a consequence of having performed well previously and having been referred years later. Gradually, my current life was put together as a result of the seeds that I had sown throughout my life journey. My activity seems to have grown and risen many times based on my past deeds. I never planned to have what I have or do what I do today. I never even dreamed or wanted it.

I want to encourage you to reflect on your own lives based on the reflection that I have made here of my own life. I want you to verify if you have accomplished everything that you have proposed to yourself and how much of your life has simply been happening. I want you to ask yourself if you have been able to swim successfully with the current in your favor. Conversely, have you gone from one roadblock to another or in circles? It is not easy to accept what life offers us and the way it gives it to us. Many times, our desire to force things causes the options that are meant for us to be wasted, and we enter a complex maze that lengthens the road or sometimes leads us to a dead end. Of course, some people know how to interpret the routes indicated by life, and they achieve success repeatedly, but this does not happen that often. Do not worry.

Let go or learn to let go of what is not meant for you or you do not need. Accept life as it is. Soon, and almost magically, you will be surprised by the change that will happen to you because "what is rightfully ours comes to us, and it comes when it is rightfully ours."

Learn to say No so that it sounds sweet to the ear

H ave you seen or experienced the reactions of a person when you say NO to something they need, want, or look forward to?

What happens if your NO cuts the trajectory of a relationship, life, a friendship, or a partnership with a company or a person? *The first recommendation is to lose your fear and have the courage to say NO and assume the consequences.* It is better to say NO than to look bad or accept a commitment that we cannot fulfill or accept something that will make us feel bad for a long time. *It is better to ask a question than to have to clean up after the mistake*, as they say. In any case, you have to know how to say NO, and I have provided orientation and reflections below.

A typical way of saying NO is to do it but to give alternative solutions with ideas, people, or options that do not involve us if we know them or know that they exist. Indicate or recommend others who can fulfill what is being asked of us. *Another typical response is to buy a second opportunity to return with a definitive NO* by saying something like, "I do not think so, but let me see, and I will get back to you with a definitive answer in two days." *The best way, however, is to say NO directly and clearly, without explanations and without being blackmailed.*

You have to say it clearly: I do not feel like it. I do not like it. I do not do that type of task. I cannot do it. I do not want to. I do not have it. Do not count on me. I do not know how to do it. I am satisfied. I am full. I feel somewhat unwell. You may also just say "NO" without a menacing look. It is better to have a sweet look that says, "it was not me" or "I am sorry." People will pressure us and try to make us feel bad (blackmail) by saying the following: "We need you. Do not do that to us. We know you can. You are the only person we have. You are our savior. An offer like this cannot be rejected. We are offended by your answer. Give us an explanation; a No is not a valid answer. We thought you were a better person. We did not expect such an answer from you. You have let us down. We believed in you." They might even send emissaries to press you from all directions. Faced with this kind of pressure, the strategy is to remain silent and not respond or provide any explanations.

How do we say NO in a way that sounds pleasant to the listener so that they ask you to repeat it, or they naturally understand it without taking offense or feeling aggression?

We are going to reflect on this in this short chapter. Although we will provide some basic guidelines, it is up to the reader to create new options or scenarios appropriate to each experience or situation, given the ingenuity that we must have for each specific event or relationship being handled. When a favor is asked, the typical response may be, "I am unable to help you" or "do not count on me because…" The ellipsis can be filled with an elegant and friendly but firm answer, according to each case. However, it is not a good idea to provide a reason for it. *I advise you to give your answer and not give further explanations. Remain silent after answering (take advantage of the right to remain silent). If you want to provide a reason, the examples should* clearly demonstrate the involuntary impairment: I have invested all my money, and I have no cash, sorry. I will never be a guarantor again because it gives me uncontrollable and serious panic attacks; I am sorry. I am not feeling well, and I am not in a position to help anyone at this time. I cannot do it; I am sorry. I am not at my best, and I do not want to talk about this (then give them a nervous look and withdraw eye contact by looking down). It does not suit me right now, sorry. I no longer do that work, sorry. My schedule is full of projects and commitments. My agenda is booked for the next six months, sorry. I have no resources, sorry. I do not eat that. Sorry. I just ate… I am full… Thank you… I am sorry. Although I understand what you ask of me, I think differently. I am sorry.

Sometimes, it is best not to respond, and if you are asked to respond, it is best to say with a firm but kind look, "I'm sorry. I have no answer to give you," and then remain silent. A good response that everyone welcomes is, *"I appreciate you very much. It is a real pity, but I have to decline your request. I am sorry."* If they ask for a reason, respond with silence and tenderly look down or say, "Please allow me to reserve my reasons in privacy or my right to privacy." They can only interrogate you as much as you allow them to. Remember that you are in control and that you can answer with a simple "no, I am sorry" or "no, thank you" and end things there. Abstain from giving more answers. *People will always try to corner us so that we can provide explanations or to make us feel bad, and therein lies the problem. We should not play this game.* Of course, if one does not have the obligation to answer a question, a request, or an invitation, the best recommendation is not to answer. *The best answer is silence. Say, "I decline" or "I pass," like in card games.*

Regardless of how beautiful the refusal sounds, some people will react aggressively or with threats and abandonment. If they leave us after we have provided one of the aforementioned responses, the relationship clearly does not deserve our attention, and we do not lose. Conversely, we win by freeing ourselves of the people who do not suit us. It is a good chance to shout out "Freedom!" If you feel like you need more information or guidance on this topic for a particular case, I am afraid I have to decline. I cannot provide more comments because I have run out of space. I am very sorry. Please forgive me.

Reflections on working at home and the benefits of COVID-19

These days, many of us have had the opportunity to experience what it means to be locked up in an apartment or a house and to go out only for vital matters that cannot be handled at home. We have been given a tremendous opportunity to encounter ourselves deep within and with a good dose of reflection on the value of life, managing distance, and the importance of good hygiene and cleaning protocols when we receive something from outside or simply when someone enters our home from outside.

Our notion of time and space, the value of our planet, people, animals, and things, and the way we manage distances have changed dramatically. I am thoroughly enjoying managing meeting schedules because everything is conducted on time, from beginning to end. This order applies even to gatherings between friends and family. Regarding gatherings among family and friends, they have increased in frequency, and we have managed to see each other and share a good dinner or good wine often, which, in the immediate past, was almost impossible for us to do.

In the beginning, we all occupied ourselves with work owing to the effort of understanding and learning how to accommodate our daily tasks given the new environment that placed us within our house or apartment. Gradually, things have been returning to what we perceived to be normal.

We have also found a significant number of new activities and responsibilities within our home, which have forced us to learn to manage spaces and time in a different way. We do not have to invest time in commuting to work. In the long run, we have been given a good amount of time in our lives—time that we did not have before. That is where we win.

There is greater coexistence and interaction with the people who live with us, in duration or detail. We are learning significant lessons that serve to tighten our intimate bonds and thus pleasantly discover opportunities to deepen relationships that we had not experienced before, and even change our appreciation and definitions in this respect, for better or worse.

A wonderful thing to observe is that each place in our house or apartment may serve multiple purposes at one time and specialized purposes at another such that life leads us to have experiences other than the traditional ones of the past. New and multiple purposes are found for the bedrooms, the study, the dining room, the living room, the terrace, the balcony, or the patio, depending on the layout of our home.

The striking thing about this magical moment is that for the first time, we have everything in one place (all-in-one): the office, the house, the place for fun and entertainment, the gym, the park, the movies, the restaurant, the place of rest, the school, the university, the laundry, the church, and even the vacation spot.

It is also significant to see the incredible teamwork taking place, as we have never seen before, despite the distance and the fact that everyone is in their own homes. There is no alternative. We work as a team, and each one contributes and helps; otherwise, we may not succeed in the challenges that the situation we are experiencing brings to us on a daily basis.

Teamwork is seen not only in the office but the home, school, or college as well. This is a time when we are living the famous game of "everyone contributes." I am extremely pleased by the fact that all of us are having to perform many trades and tasks that we did not perform previously or delegated to other people. Today, we have to work as cleaners, cooks, gardeners, plumbers, electricians, nannies, teachers, hairdressers, manicurists, counselors, psychologists, or anything as needed.

When we come out of this incredible situation that we are experiencing owing to COVID-19, we will have learned many aspects. We will have realized how vulnerable we are, the importance of solidarity and patience, the value of respect and discipline, the wisdom in keeping distance, the role of technology, and the essential nature of human beings regardless of race, social class, citizenship, or employer. A pandemic such as COVID-19 forces us to change our lives and protect ourselves. No country has shown sufficient capacity to face this health tsunami and emerge unscathed. It is clear that creativity has no limits. Amidst all the restrictions, there have been people, companies, and countries that have managed to find positive options to emerge victorious from this crisis and are setting an example.

In short, the challenge for each of us is to turn constraints and crises into opportunities. We need to accept the new life; we have to face and perceive it with positivity and plenty of enthusiasm. Based on the new rules of the game and taking away our fear of change, let us stop doing what we have been doing. Let us move quickly onto the scene and attend to the new market and life conditions. Let us adapt as soon as possible to the new world that demands new behaviors, ideas, actions, processes, allies, and solutions that are starkly different from those we mastered or knew before the COVID-19 pandemic.

We do not deny that COVID-19 has brought problems, limitations, conflicts, pain, discomfort, bankruptcies, losses, and even deaths to numerous people and their relatives, organizations, clients or suppliers, and countries. Despite all the bad things, we must thank this notorious pandemic for all that it is teaching us and making us restructure as people, organizations, or countries. After this health and economic tsunami, we will all be wiser, stronger, and much more cautious. This is a moment in our lives when we have to reinvent ourselves as human beings, parents, children, friends, partners, employees, co-workers, students, people of faith, entrepreneurs, educators, citizens, a country, and a society.

This is a time that we will always remember because it has made us reflect and realize what is really important (and what is not); it has made us learn to value what we have: family, planet Earth, love, work, health, and life.

Willpower moves mountains

For some strange reason, people often forget that they have at their disposal the most powerful force that allows them to achieve what they set out to do, leading them to success: willpower.

What happens when we do not move forward or achieve what we want, and we feel that we have made every effort possible and have been judicious in persevering with discipline? Are we obsessed with the impossible? Have we chosen the wrong path? Have we asked for all possible help, and have we got all the allies or experts we need, or did we want to get ahead alone? Is just having dreams, desire, and enthusiasm not enough? If faith also moves mountains and I have faith, why am I not achieving what I propose to myself or what I desire? Where is the flaw in our life projects? How can I make them a reality?

When you look at people who have been successful in their professional or artistic lives or in business, sports, athletics, religion, or social circles, do you find any elements in common? Undoubtedly, the common factor is the willpower that shields and guides them against the path full of thorns, such as mistakes, pressures, disappointments, deceptions, restrictions, ingratitude, destructive criticism, stress, mistrust, mockery, unfair competition, abandonment, mistreatment, offenses, envy, obstacles, delays, or unpleasant surprises. It is usual to have headwind and rebuffs in response. If there is no willpower, stamina runs out, just as when a car runs out of gas and only gets to a certain point. Willpower gives us the push we need so that we do not lose heart in the face of adversity.

On the way to achieving our dreams, we will find unpaved roads, precipices, steep ascents, and high-risk descents. There will be diversions, roadblocks, dangerous potholes, huge stones, fallen bridges, floods, storms, fires, stalled or stranded cars, speed limits, authorities requesting documents, traffic lights, road construction and repairs, accidents, blocks or traffic jams, curves, straight sections, traffic distributors, checkpoints, shoulders, and speed bumps. If we know beforehand of the many difficulties and dangers we will face, we may have doubts about starting the journey. However, that is how life is made. Not every road is a six-lane highway in each direction, and our cars are not Ferraris or the like. The observation I want to make is that willpower must be helped so that we are not left with only strength and do not move forward.

You have to have the flexibility to adjust the proposed goals and understand the best approach to the path that we have established in our minds. A friend always dreamed of working abroad and achieved it, not exactly by working overseas but by working with foreigners. He always ended up working with foreign companies without going abroad. In other words, you have to know how to use your willpower and apply it to the right objective (where and when it is necessary) to avoid wasting your efforts.

Another way to support willpower is to go from dreams to execution. In other words, take action—do it. *You have to overcome your fear of failure and fear of what others will say.* Through action, verify the response you get. *Only by taking action will we find the answer and the appropriate orientation to correct our journey toward the goal.* When the response to an action is positive, we are doing well. When it is negative, we may have to be patient and try again later, or we may have to find an alternative route or a temporary diversion because the direct road is blocked. Of course, it can also be a sign that we

must pursue another objective. The key here is to understand these signs to avoid being worn out by blockages or roadblocks that are impossible to overcome directly. A famous friend studied veterinary medicine, graduated as a veterinarian, and then specialized in the US. On his return, he gave his father his diplomas and went to the mountains to compose *Carranguera* songs. Today, he is a famous icon and is known as the father of *Carranguera* music.

If I go down a road and find an obstruction that does not allow me to pass, I go back a bit and look for an alternate road to avoid the obstruction. It will probably take me more time, or the path will undoubtedly be longer. However, it is better than sitting still trying to figure out the impossible on my own. *Remember that execution, action, and doing are key to putting willpower into effect.* Curiously, *sometimes we have to back up a bit to move forward,* like in the example of the blocked road. Here, the urban saying, "never take a step back, not even to gain momentum," is not valid or makes no sense. From a practical perspective, it does not apply. Cars have four or five forward gears and one reverse gear. Without the reverse gear, you will need a long road without parked cars to be able to park. Using the reverse gear, you can park in a tight space in the middle of other parked cars. Reversing is vital in many of life's scenarios so that we may move forward toward the objective. Incredible, right?

A friend wanted to become a big boss and realized that if he persisted in that goal, it would take him 15 years or more because of the long line of internal candidates to high positions, given the long permanence of the main leaders. He decided to change companies and quickly achieved his goal of being a great boss. The dream was achievable, but he was either in the wrong place or down a rough road.

This leads us to another way we can put our willpower into effect: we must be able to adapt to the facts as they arise. No plan is static. The dynamism of every day or of the moment demands that we adapt our pace to the circumstances. If I am walking and heavy rain begins to fall, I must adjust my plan instead of moving forward like a robot despite the risk posed by the storm. Willpower is the engine that moves us, but we have to apply some common sense for the effort to be effective. Another way to make willpower effective is to keep in mind that we need support and guidance from other people to continue moving toward our goal. It will be extremely difficult or even impossible on our own. Playing the brave knight is not only reckless but also a sure path to failure. There are only rare exceptions.

Willpower is the engine that allows us to trust that we can turn dreams and plans into reality. It is the famous "believe in your dreams" or "believe that you can." It is also the engine that allows us to do what many thought was impossible owing to the number of obstacles. Willpower allows us to visualize several steps ahead because it forces us to think big in our accomplishments and our timeline. Willpower encourages perseverance and gives us the resilience to jump over obstacles and find new ways out of problems and limitations. Willpower is what motivates us to act intelligently, looking for help or a new path without despairing, even if we have tried hundreds of times.

Anything is possible if you have the willpower to do it and if you have faith in yourself.

Unblocking life is key to its smooth flow

Have you noticed that to many people, it seems as if the universe or destiny has led them to a dead end? Nothing moves, and even if it does, it is to the opposite side. Does it seem as though they have been hit by the seven plagues?

There is a way to unblock these situations and provide results quickly and almost miraculously. What is happening to us? What produced this bad streak? How did I get to this dead end? It is as if we fall into a form of blockage, where everything seems to go wrong when certain rules or laws of nature or the universe have been violated. Therefore, it is necessary to verify the state of six considerably frequent scenarios and correct or change our position in each regard.

The first and most frequent scenario is when one interferes in the lives of others with actions that seek to change the events that the other person has to experience or that will allow them to learn from life. Interrupting another person's natural cycle is a serious matter that immediately creates a blockage for whoever does it. Remember, everything we do comes back to us for better or worse. If no one has asked us for help or has called on us to intervene and if we are not the experts who can solve the problem, the intervention is dangerously returned to us for interrupting the learning or life cycle of another person. We must avoid intervening in the lives of others, or we will paralyze our own energy and the energy of those around us. When one stops intervening, the magic that unblocks blockages and drama appears.

The second scenario, which is also frequent, is when one does not accept reality as it is or as it presents itself, whether they are situations, events, or people. Consequently, we generate dissatisfaction or discomfort because things are not as we wish or want them. The reality is that things are as they are and what happens is as it should happen, nothing more or less. There is no reason for them to bend to our will. When we insistently seek to enforce our will, we crash, and the universe returns a harsh answer to make us reflect until we recognize, learn, and respect the reality. We must learn to accept with sincerity and not out of conformity. Accepting reality and not arguing over it unblocks obstructions and causes everything to flow.

In the third scenario, there is appreciation or gratitude. People live their lives dissatisfied with what they have or with whom they are, and this causes blockage. When we learn to value what we have, even if it is little, the dissatisfaction, discomfort, and agony disappear. The universe sees that we have learned a fundamental lesson, and happiness appears. We must pay sincere gratitude to unblock obstructions.

The fourth scenario refers to the forgiveness that we must ask for or give to erase the errors on the board of life. If we do not erase the errors on the board, we will get dirty, which undoubtedly blocks the flow of energy. Pending forgiveness is like dirt in our life history, which blocks flow consequently.

The fifth is learning to wish others the best, regardless of how we get along with them. Remember that life is like a boomerang, where everything we throw in the air comes back to us if it does not hit the target. We should even wish our worst enemy well. By the law of correspondence, wishing bad on another person is wishing bad on ourselves, and then we block ourselves. It is what is called a self-goal in sports.

The sixth scenario is learning to detach from things, people, or negative experiences, and in this sense, it is knowing how to let go. When one lets go of attachments in our life or thoughts, magic appears and makes everything around to flourish. Nothing new comes to us if we do not let go of the old; when we generate the vacuum effect, the universe immediately fills that void.

In short, *our life magically flourishes when we accept and appreciate who we are and what we have and the reality with everyone else involved, when we exercise forgiveness, when we wish the best to those we do not get along with, when we learn to let go or detach ourselves, and when we avoid nosing into other people's lives.*

Analyze your current situation and see which of the six scenarios you are violating and change the way you act or think so that the magic quickly appears and unblocks energies for your life to flourish and flow as you need it.

You change, everything changes

The world and the universe are as they are. Period.

We can do little against the movement of the planets, stars, or galaxies. We can do nothing to stop the waves of the sea or avoid dawn or dusk. What can we do to avoid a tsunami? What can we do to stop an earthquake? If a hurricane comes, what can we do? If a volcano erupts, what can we do? What can we do if it starts to rain with lightning and thunder?

I could continue to reflect on the little to no capacity we have to change what is happening around us. What can we do if we detect that some external natural phenomenon may affect us— run, protect ourselves, or pray?

Life is not as challenging as having to handle the impact of the aforementioned natural phenomena. Everyday life is far simpler.

What happens around us is less serious and less powerful than the forces of nature or the universe. However, there is little we can do to change the world outside or around us.

People, institutions, governments, and laws are as they are; we are mere mortals who have little to no capacity to change the world around us. Many people in this world are convinced and believe that they can change their surroundings, and they suffer as they see and experience that they can do little or nothing to change them.

How do I change my partner's ways when they have habits I do not like? How do I convince my friends that they should think like those in my political party? Why are some acquaintances not fans of my soccer team like me? Why do vegans exist if meat is so tasty? Why do people exercise so much if it is better to watch movies or play video games? Each person has a world different from mine, and it mortifies me to know that they do not like the same things that I do. Can I change them to be like me, or how I would like them to be?

The following key question arises: Given this panorama, what can we do to avoid the pain of being unable to accept what we cannot change and dedicate ourselves to living happily?

The answer is simple: Accept the world as it is and devote yourself to living your life the best you can with what you have at your disposal. Enjoy who you are and what you have and improve your thoughts by feeling content with your experiences, regardless of whether they are bad, regular, or good. The change you have to make is internal—in your mind, beliefs, and heart. Learn to love life as it is, with all its flavors.

Beliefs are not laws. They are topics you learned directly from the culture in which you were raised or educated, but they are not laws. The proof is that other people from other cultures believe and think differently on the same matter, which confirms that it is not a law but a belief, and it can be modified at will. Laws never change, like the law of gravity on earth. Gravity is the same, whether we are in China, the United States, or Colombia, and regardless of who measures it.

The only thing safe and within our reach is ourselves. Therefore, it is highly likely that we can modify and control our own being. We have no control over our surroundings and other human beings.

If we change the way we think and act or modify beliefs, the outer world looks different and almost begins to flourish and shine positively. In short, it is our decision to continue doing the same or make a fundamental change within ourselves.

The best, almost miraculous advice to end your pain, conflict, or frustration and begin to feel happiness is "you change, and everything will change" or simply put, "you change, everything changes."

The key to success is in your reaction and action to whatever happens

Driving a car is something relatively demanding but simple once we know how to do it. When you have several years of driving experience, you realize that knowing how to drive well is not enough; it is vital to know how to react well to what happens on the street or the highway. From one moment to the next, an animal can cross a road. The car next to us may hit us because the driver fell asleep or because someone else inside the car moves the steering wheel. The car in front of us may stop unexpectedly. The car passing us is closing in extremely fast, and we run the risk of crashing. We can get a flat tire. The car's brakes may fail. Driving a car on the road successfully depends on our reaction and action to whatever happens at each moment of the journey to the destination.

Every day in our lives and in every scenario, at a given moment, events that alter or influence our expectations take place. For example, a friend's daughter was going to get married, and her grandfather died the night before. Does she get married or attend the funeral? A person has some savings and plans to go on vacation. However, they receive a notification of a hefty fine for an error in their income tax statement, which must be paid immediately, or the penalty amount will be doubled. Do they pay their taxes or leave on vacation?

Did you ever wake up to take an early shower only to find that the water is not coming out or that the boiler is not working? As you were working on your home computer, did the power go off along with the internet? As you were going out to run an urgent or important errand, did it begin to rain heavily? Did you go to the bank and find a long teller line because the system was down? Of course, these are not frequent situations, but *the idea here is not what happens but our reaction and action to whatever happens.*

What happens if a very important client sends a letter notifying that they are going to cancel the contract? What happens if a person gets called in by their boss and is told that it is their last day at the company owing to downsizing? What happens if we reach our house and find that the door lock has been broken and that everything has been stolen because thieves had broken in? What if we park our car in a public parking lot and upon return, we find that another car hit one of the doors and left it badly damaged? What do we do when we have an important work commitment, and we are informed about a direct family member who has lost consciousness and is being taken to the hospital?

In all these cases and examples, as well as in other situations that you may have thought of while reading the questions, our reaction and action to whatever happens are key for a successful outcome, regardless of how complex it may seem.

Life is what it is. Although there are people who still believe that they have total control of their lives and can do whatever they want with it, the universe shows us every minute that this is not necessarily the case and that life is not always logical to our understanding. Life is meant to be lived and enjoyed with everything it brings, and it will amaze us every day.

We can react in many ways to whatever happens. We can stay still, get nervous, lose our composure, block ourselves, cry, laugh, scream, have a bad mood, freeze, run away, become depressed, rejoice, think, take action, ask for help, analyze, scold and blame others, deny, and much more. Ultimately, success in facing each challenge in life will be based on what we do about what happens. It is in our hands, and it is our decision, and that is a power we can and must exercise.

That is why I will remind you, "The key to success in life is in your reaction and action to whatever happens."

Change always teaches us
something new

We do what we like. We feel pleased when we like where we are, when we try out or use something we enjoy, when we go where we want, when we spend time with someone we are fond of, when we work with someone in the organization that we like, or when we stay in a country or place that we like. What if we try to change or are forced to change one of the situations I have just described?

Contrary to what one may believe, a change in any scenario opens the door to new experiences that were blocked because we did not want to change or were afraid of change. By removing the blockage, the universe rewards us with the arrival of new experiences that result in new lessons and growth.

In terms of energy, we generate a void signal, and every void tends to get filled.

You have to learn to let go (people, situations, tasks, objects, things, organizations, tastes, bad memories, etc.). You have to have the courage to accept the challenge of change. Paralyzing fears must be overcome. Every change involves a risk of losing some of the stability, comfort, tranquility, security, or confidence that we have. However, change also brings new experiences, lessons, people, scenarios, rules, flavors, emotions, restrictions, allowances, challenges, discomforts or sensations, and facilities or advantages.

Let us say that you lose and win with any change, but that is what it is all about. A friend used to say that there are only three sure things in life: death, change, and taxes. If we know that everything changes or can change, why do we refuse to accept that reality? Is it out of fear or comfort? On many occasions, the change will suit us because we are rejuvenated with the new experience; it unblocks energies and forces us to move forward by letting energy flow freely.

Some people may not feel well and may suffer where they are, with whom they are, or how they are, and all they have to do is change so that their situation can immediately and almost magically evolve into a better one, ending their anguish. It is like being at the front of your house when it is extremely cold or snowing, and you open the door to find a pleasant environment because of the heating or a more bearable temperature inside. Sometimes, the change is extremely simple, and it is in our hands or our willpower to apply a slight turn to find ourselves in a different condition.

I will provide an example of this instantaneous simplicity. If there is a light that dazzles you or bothers your eyes, you can close your eyes, stop looking at the light, put on some sunglasses, cover your eyes with your hands, or merely look away—a natural defense against a light that bothers us. Why do we not do the same when we experience an uncomfortable situation? If something bothers you in life, focus your attention away, move to another place—move and do not suffer. Change is for us to enjoy or at least experience.

I always see a change from a positive perspective, even if it has occurred by force or obligation. I always think that if some change comes, it is because I need to learn something new or live a new experience. The universe knows that, which is why it sends a change in my direction.

In life, we have to decide whether to open and pass through the door of change, end our suffering, or remain happily stagnant. We decide before we can enjoy the new environment and the new life that awaits us.

Fine quality, popular wisdom for life

When I did not know about popular wisdom, I thought that my problems in life were punishments. Eventually, I understood them as challenges or, better yet, opportunities for improvement or growth or learning. There is always more than one way of looking at events. There are many, in fact: some positive and others negative. You can choose the ones that hit you emotionally or depress you or the ones that excite you and motivate you to get ahead and enjoy life, regardless of the consequences. What we experience within ourselves is our choice.

The mistakes we have made throughout our lives are lessons that have a simple reason: if we had already learned the lesson, we most likely would have avoided falling into the error, at least the second time around, and if not, the third or fourth time, when we have already understood and will not likely make the same mistake again. Thus, do not feel bad about failing or making a mistake. We can burn a finger putting out a flame once, twice, or thrice in our life. However, once we learn that fire burns, we are not likely to expose ourselves willingly to a burning candle. Although we may take time to learn, we ultimately do. Thus, we came to this life to learn and are allowed mistakes in becoming experts or teachers. Nobody is born a master. As apprentices, we have the right to make mistakes and correct ourselves. We are always in the trial-and-error phase until we become experts.

According to popular wisdom, if you cannot make public something you plan to do for all the others to applaud or congratulate you, then it is probably not the right thing to do, and it would be better for you to abstain. This is a maxim of ethics summarized in a single sentence: "If you cannot publish it so that people can congratulate you, do not do it." Always choose to tell the truth. If you choose to lie, try not to harm others. Finally, if you choose to lie constantly along your path, you must understand that you will be harming, hurting, abusing, and confusing someone or diverting the course of things to the wrong scenario. If you harm someone as the ultimate consequence of lying, which itself is wrong, then you will be committing a double evil. Professional liars pretend that lies are true and make the truth look like a lie to gain an undue advantage over others, usually causing them serious or almost irrecoverable damage. The best thing would be to tell the truth always and act with it as your support and compass.

Everything in the universe is energy that surrounds us at the microscopic or macroscopic, planetary, and astrological levels. Nothing is destroyed. Everything is transformed. There are no endings or terminations; there are simply changes in state. Different employment, for example, is a change in state, a transformation, a growth, not necessarily the termination of a link with a company. The death of a seed is a transformation that gives life to a plant, and that is how it is with everything.

Over time, one realizes that if we do not know much about a subject, it is better to learn by listening rather than speaking. In short, it is wise to know when to remain silent and when to speak up. Many unfortunate times and mistakes in life result from having spoken out of turn or having said the wrong thing. Have you never gotten in trouble for opening your mouth?

Respect for others is a fundamental principle of community life in a civilized society, which implies respecting properties, ideas, rights, spaces, and timings. In this sense, the old saying applies: "If it is not yours, do not take it." This type of principle, however, seems to have been eradicated in several Latin American countries, where any carelessness is used by thieves to rob us. This generates a series of preventions and precautions and even laws and police actions that delay and further complicate progress, given that everything is based on mistrust instead of trust. In a civilization based on community culture, best practices, and strong trust, no one will dare take a box that has been left in front of your door or the small decorative table you ordered for your living room. The truth is, and I have seen it several times, the box can remain in the same place for days without the risk of someone taking or stealing it.

We all have one or more skills that we are good at or are clearly better than average. We must take advantage of or improve these skills or qualities and concentrate on doing our best. We could try to do something in areas in which we do not have the appropriate skills or qualities, but we will hardly excel, or it will take excessive work orthem. We will then be admired. Popular wisdom says that a fish will struggle trying to learn to fly, and a bird will struggle trying to learn how to swim underwater. Let us carefully analyze what we are good at and what we are not good at to determine on what we should invest our time. This is a simple and clear concept that many people overlook, and they end up suffering the consequences.

time to reach a good level. We all have talents. It is only a matter of discovering which ones are ours and concentrating our efforts on.

Popular wisdom invites us to verify any topic we want to confirm. Through verification, we can stop assuming or inventing stories. Supposing invites us to invent what does not exist or what exists only in our mind, which can be mere delusions or groundless dreams. Some people suffer daily from their assumptions and the tales they have invented in their minds because they believe them as if they were real.

Finally, it is essential to have clear ideas about yourself, to know yourself well. Other people can and will try to tell you anything to make you feel bad, change you, give you a tough time, lower your self-esteem, or manipulate you. Anyone can say what they want, but only what you think about yourself and how confident you are about yourself will matter. No quality is bad or good. There is no one equal to you; therefore, you have the right to be who you are. Celebrate who you are and how you are because you are unique as a human being. You do not have to compare yourself to others. Be proud of yourself as a person with the bad and the good becauseeverything is yours. Regardless of whether you are skinny, fat, short, tall, light-skinned or dark-skinned, fast, slow, poor, or rich, celebrate everything. You are unique and irreplaceable!

109

Short Curriculum Vitae

Colombia

Hugo Fernando
Valderrama Sánchez

President of High Value Consulting Corporation, with offices in the USA and Colombia

He is currently chairman of the boards of directors of educational, communications, systems, human resources, and security organizations. An active member of the Presidents' Forum and the YPO (Worldwide Organization of Presidents), he is also a member of the ACRIP Editorial Board (Human Resources Federation in Colombia) as a partner at Club El Nogal.

He holds the following degrees: Systems and Computer Engineering, MBA, Specialist in Human Resources, PhD in Business Administration, PADE - INALDE. Harvard President's Class.

He is an entrepreneur, creator, and developer of over 25 organizations, including in information technology and communications, several foundations, consulting companies, educational entities, service providers, manufacturing and sales companies in Colombia, Ecuador, Peru, the United States, and Canada.

An author of nine books on management and senior management (*Guía práctica para la caldiade, Liderazgo 21.2, Ejecutivo Visionario, Gestión Genial, Dirección inteligente, Talento Empresarial, Testimonios de Gestión Humana, Sabiduría Empresarial*, and *Empresario Cerebral*), he has been a guest speaker in over 1,200 conducted conferences throughout the American continent.

He has been a member of over 35 boards of directors, including associations, insurance companies, banks, manufacturing industries in different sectors, universities, and professional service providers.

He worked at IBM Colombia for 15 years, serving as IT manager, sales manager of large accounts in the financial sector, and sales manager in strategic accounts. Subsequently, he worked with NCR Colombia for 15 years as an executive president and chairman of the board of directors. He was also the president of Afina Colombia, Ecuador, and Peru (Afina NOLA Region) for seven years.

Aside from being an entrepreneur and company director, he is an expert in business and sales strategies, change management, and human capital.

Alphabetical Index

ENTREPRENEUR OF LIFE   HUGO VALDERRAMA